E. TREY CLARK

BLACK CONTEMPLATIVE PREACHING

A Hidden History of Prayer, Proclamation, and Prophetic Witness

BAYLOR UNIVERSITY PRESS

© 2024 by Baylor University Press
Waco, Texas 76798

All Rights Reserved. No part of this publication may be reproduced, stored in a retrieval system, or transmitted, in any form or by any means, electronic, mechanical, photocopying, recording, or otherwise, without the prior permission in writing of Baylor University Press.

Cover and book design by Elyxandra Encarnación

Quotations in chapter 3 from "Our God Is Able" by Martin Luther King Jr. reprinted by arrangement with The Heirs to the Estate of Martin Luther King Jr., c/o Writers House as agent for the proprietor, New York. Copyright © 1956 by Dr. Martin Luther King, Jr. Renewed © 1984 by Coretta Scott King.

Library of Congress Cataloging-in-Publication Data

Names: Clark, E. Trey, author.
Title: Black contemplative preaching : a hidden history of prayer, proclamation, and prophetic witness / E. Trey Clark.
Other titles: Contemplation, proclamation, and social transformation
Description: Waco, Texas : Baylor University Press, [2024] | Includes bibliographical references. | Summary: "Explores often-overlooked contemplative dimensions of the Black preaching tradition through the lens of famous Black preachers Howard Thurman, Martin Luther King Jr., and Barbara Harris"-- Provided by publisher.
Identifiers: LCCN 2023051013 (print) | LCCN 2023051014 (ebook) | ISBN 9781481321990 (hardcover) | ISBN 9781481319355 (paperback) | ISBN 9781481319379 (adobe pdf) | ISBN 9781481319362 (epub)
Subjects: LCSH: African American preaching--History--20th century. | Doctrinal preaching--United States--History--20th century. | Spirituality--United States--History--20th century. | Thurman, Howard, 1900-1981. | King, Martin Luther, Jr., 1929-1968. | Harris, Barbara C. (Barbara Clementine)
Classification: LCC BV4208.U6 C63 2024 (print) | LCC BV4208.U6 (ebook) | DDC 251.0089/96073--dc23/eng/20240419
LC record available at https://lccn.loc.gov/2023051013
LC ebook record available at https://lccn.loc.gov/2023051014

To those who prayed for me

Contents

Acknowledgments		ix
Introduction		1
1	Preaching as Prayer *Toward a History of Contemplative Preaching*	13
2	Creating a Friendly World *Howard Thurman as Contemplative Preacher*	37
3	Redeeming the Soul and Society *Martin Luther King Jr. as Contemplative Preacher*	67
4	Embodying Prophetic Contemplation *Barbara Harris as Contemplative Preacher*	95
5	The Endurance of Black Contemplative Preaching	121
Conclusion		149
Appendix A: Definitions		153
Appendix B: Twenty Contemplative Preachers in the Twenty-First Century		159
Bibliography		161
Index		181

Acknowledgments

It takes a village to write a book. In my case, it has taken many villages for this work to come to completion. Unfortunately, space will not permit me to name these many villages and the remarkable people who make them up. Still, I am compelled to mention some. For those whose names do not appear in these pages, please know I cherish you in my heart. Let me first give thanks to the village in which I was born, in Desoto, Texas. I am eternally grateful to God for the persistent support, wisdom, and example of my mother, Algenise Conner Clark, and my father, Edgar Clark II. It is impossible for me to express proper gratitude for the known and unknown sacrifices you have made for the sake of my flourishing over the years. I also am grateful for my siblings, Christa, Duncan, and Taylor, and their spouses, along with my wonderful nieces and nephews. They have provided encouragement, perspective, and joy in weary moments. My grandparents, Dorothy Watson and Geneva Conner, have offered prayer, support, and much-needed moments of laughter. And the life and legacy of my ancestors inspired and affirmed me, particularly Edgar Clark Sr., Alfred Conner, Ruben Conner Sr., Rosa Lee Gipson, and David Medlock Sr.

Outside of biological family, I have been privileged to learn, grow, and serve as part of several church-villages that nurtured my ministry, thinking, and writing. Foremost, I must note Community Bible Church of Dallas, Texas, the Black church in which I first was taught the Christian Scriptures, heard and responded to my call to vocational ministry, and preached some of my first sermons. I am continually humbled by the unending prayers and encouragement this community of remarkable women and men have lavished upon me even years after I left Texas. Special thanks to Pastor Ruben

Conner Jr.! Additionally, I give thanks to God for South Bay Church of God, Second Baptist Church, Metropolitan AME Church, and Restoration Church.

Over the years, I have learned and grown in various academic villages that have comprised a host of mentors, teachers, and friends. For starters, I am grateful for the wonderful teachers I had growing up in the Desoto Independent School District. At Wheaton College, I accrued a further debt to teachers and mentors. I must especially say thank you to Henry Allen, Vincent Bacote, Marilyn Breener, the late Calvin Egler, Tanya Egler, and Rick Richardson. Some of my dear friends at Wheaton have proved to be lifelong companions, supporters, and faithful critics. I particularly give thanks for Rob Eschmann, Michael Fox, Clayton Hall, and Justin West. I owe a significant debt to Justin for introducing me to Howard Thurman. Thank you, brother!

I am also grateful for the village that is Fuller Seminary. Like so many, I have experienced Mark Labberton, the former president of Fuller, as a kind, wise, and encouraging presence in my life in the midst of his full schedule, and our new president, David Emmanuel Goatley, has already proven to be an inspiring and encouraging supporter on "the sacred journey," as he puts it. Likewise, the academic, administrative, and personal support of Amos Yong, Joel Green, Sebastian Kim, Eugen Matei, and Chris Hull has been indispensable. I owe a special expression of gratitude to Amos for introducing me to Baylor University Press. Additionally, Jennifer Ackerman, Clifton Clarke, Erin Dufault-Hunter, Oscar Garcia-Johnson, Todd Johnson, Lisa Lamb, Ahmi Lee, Hak Joon Lee, Doug Nason, Richard Peace, Kara Powell, Dwight Radcliff, Clay Schmit, Love Sechrest, Jaclyn Williams, and others have been critical conversation partners and guides on my academic journey at Fuller. Several friends and colleagues there have provided helpful encouragement and support along the way, such as Phil Allen, Seanita Scott, Daniel Stevenson, Tamisha Tyler, and Anne Zaki. I am indebted to Bill Pannell and Hak Joon Lee for challenging me to include Dr. Martin Luther King Jr. in this book. I also would like to thank my past and present students who have taught me so much and encouraged my work on this book project, especially former students Toni Cooper, Dara Bankole, and Tyler Brewington-Mathis.

I am particularly grateful for my PhD dissertation committee, which laid the foundation for this book: Michael Pasquarello, Frank A. Thomas, and Barbara Holmes. Mike served as my primary mentor and instilled in me a passion for exploring the history and theology of preaching like no one else. Despite relocating to a different academic institution in the midst of my studies, he graciously continued to serve as my doctoral mentor. He has offered constant support and encouragement and been a wonderful reservoir of wisdom. While I never imagined I would write a book on Black proclamation, Frank's life and writings inspired me to partake in what he calls "the ministry of the scribe." It was an honor to have him as my second mentor. I have come to share his passion for preserving the rich history of African American preaching and exploring the wisdom it offers for the present. Even more, Frank has been a model of the kind of human being I would like to become—humble, wise, loving, and full of grace. Barbara Holmes graciously served as an external reviewer of my dissertation. She is a sage. It was a joy to have her wisdom directly inform this project. And, of course, without her pioneering book, *Joy Unspeakable*, this book would not have been written. One more note: while not on my dissertation committee, Kimberly Johnson of Tennessee State University kindly allowed me to complete a directed reading with her that helped me to flesh out the rhetorical dimensions of the book and explore more fully womanist theology and rhetoric.

I first learned about contemplative preaching through the scholarship of the late James Earl Massey. Frank Thomas informed me of his role in writing on contemplative preaching for the anthology *Preaching with Sacred Fire*. Massey's seminal work has informed all of my thought on the subject, and I am forever grateful for his life and witness.

I would be remiss if I did not mention the staff and students of Christian Theological Seminary's PhD program in African American Preaching and Sacred Rhetoric, who graciously welcomed me as a visiting student during my doctoral studies. Their insights, scholarship, questions, and example of pioneering research on Black preaching provided some of the most significant inspiration I needed to not give up in the process of writing this book. I must also mention other academic mentors and supporters who I have been blessed to meet along the way through networking and connecting with professional guilds. Martha

Simmons offered me a timely word of encouragement at the Hampton Minister's Conference and impressed upon me the importance of academic scholarship on Black preaching. David Stark provided an opportunity to lecture and discuss my work in a course at the School of Theology, University of the South. I am grateful for that institution's generosity and the thoughtful engagement and feedback from the students. Moreover, I benefited from conversation with scholars and students at a 2018 Forum for Theological Exploration gathering that provided vital inspiration and encouragement. I am especially grateful for the brilliant insight, wisdom, and coaching of Shanell T. Smith. I also must thank Eboni Marshall Turman for her helpful feedback on my research at a presentation at the 2020 virtual American Academy of Religion gathering. My colleagues in the Academy of Homiletics have been most encouraging. I am especially appreciative of feedback I received after a presentation to the Black Caucus and the Identity, Imagination, and Narrative workgroup in 2021. Additionally, I am thankful for meaningful conversation and support from various scholars, preachers, and spiritual guides who offered insights, feedback, and help with resources for my work in emails and/or conversations, especially Amy Adwalpalker, Darren Adwalpalker, Jared Alcántara, Adam Bond, Gennifer Brooks, Kyle Brooks, Courtney Buggs, Karen Coleman, Wayne Croft, Walter Earl Fluker, Seth Gaiters, Kenyatta R. Gilbert, James Keating, Sheryl A. Kujawa-Holbrook, Willie Jennings, Vincent Lloyd, Donyelle C. McCray, Hyemin J. Na, Maurice J. Nutt, CSsR, Ron Ottenad, Luke A. Powery, Luther Smith, Shively T. J. Smith, Therese Taylor-Stinson, Lisa L. Thompson, Eric Lewis Williams, and Montague Williams. I owe a special thank you to Kelly Brown Douglas and Diane Pound for placing me in contact with the late bishop Barbara Harris. Bishop Harris generously allowed me to interview her on several occasions and made available to me manuscripts of all the sermons she had in her possession. I also give thanks to Ineda Pearl Adesanya, Veronica R. Goines, Luke A. Powery, and Frank A. Thomas for their correspondence amid their busy schedule, as I asked questions about their preaching.

Additionally, my research could not have been completed without the timely assistance and resourcefulness of the library staff at Fuller

Seminary and the Howard Gotlieb Archival Research Center at Boston University. Special thanks to Audrey Chun and Jane Parr!

This is my first book project, and I feel deeply honored to have had the privilege of working with the excellent team at Baylor University Press: David Aycock, Ely Encarnación, Cade Jarrell, Jenny Hunt, Michelle McCaig, and Paul Zetterberg. Dave Nelson, the director of Baylor University Press and my editor, has been a joy to work with. Thank you for your patience, encouragement, and interest in my work. I also am appreciative of the immensely helpful constructive feedback and affirmation that I received from the three anonymous reviewers of my work.

As I sought to finish this book, I benefited immensely from friends and colleagues who volunteered to read it. Thank you, Jane Gulliver, Terry Gulliver, Jon MacDonald, and Steve Porter! I am grateful for your thorough and timely feedback on portions of my work. Special thanks to Joey Baker for his assistance with indexing the book! Of course, none of these individuals, nor the many others mentioned above or below, should be held responsible for what I have written. All views, flaws, and errors are my own.

On a more personal note, I am grateful for the opportunity to acknowledge the tremendous debt of love, support, and grace that I owe to my dear wife, Dominique Monet Clark. I could not have asked for a more gracious human being to share the journey of life with these past fourteen years. Thank you for your patience, forgiveness, and mercy in the midst of my writing, researching, and buying way more books than anyone should ever possess. Not only have you edited almost everything I have written but you have been an invaluable conversation partner and provided indispensable support and love along the way. While I enjoy my work, there is nothing that I enjoy more than sharing life with you. I am excited about the new chapter with our baby girl Khalia. Khalia, you have expanded my capacity to love beyond my imagination. Thank you for being the gift that you are.

Finally, I give honor to the village that is the triune God. God, I am humbled by your grace in my life. Thank you for sustaining me in every season. To you be all the glory now and forever.

Introduction

> Just as it is better to enlighten than merely to shine, so is it better to give to others the fruits of one's contemplation (*contemplata aliis tradere*) than merely to contemplate (*contemplari*).
>
> Thomas Aquinas, *Summa Theologiae*[1]

> The world is the cloister of the contemplative. There is no escape. Always the quest for justice draws one deeply into the heart of God. In this sacred interiority, contemplation becomes the language of prayer and the impetus for prophetic proclamation and action.
>
> Barbara A. Holmes, *Joy Unspeakable: Contemplative Practices of the Black Church*[2]

On January 20, 2021, in the aftermath of the storming of the U.S. Capitol and in the midst of a seemingly unending dual pandemic of ongoing racialized violence and COVID-19, Amanda Gorman delivered a poem at the inauguration of President Joe Biden and Vice President Kamala Harris. Entitled "The Hill We Climb," the poem immediately went viral.[3]

Among other things, Gorman, the youngest inaugural poet in U.S. history, called the deeply divided nation toward a new way of seeing and being. And she did so with profound spiritual sensitivity

---

[1] Thomas Aquinas, *The Summa Theologiae*, trans. Fathers of the English Dominican Province (New York: Benziger Bros, 1947), II-II, Q. 188, A. 6, full text available at the Christian Classics Ethereal Library, https://www.ccel.org/a/aquinas/summa/SS/SS188.html#SSQ188A6THEP1.

[2] Barbara A. Holmes, *Joy Unspeakable: Contemplative Practices of the Black Church*, 2nd ed. (Minneapolis: Fortress, 2017), 110.

[3] Amanda Gorman, "WATCH: Amanda Gorman Reads Inauguration Poem 'The Hill We Climb,'" *PBS NewsHour*, January 20, 2021, YouTube video, 5:52, https://www.youtube.com/watch?v=LZ055illiN4.

and unflinching truth telling. "There is space for grief and horror and hope and unity," Gorman said, reflecting on her poem, "and I also hope that there is a breath of joy in the poem."[4] Not surprisingly, the meditative yet inspiring poem resonated with people across a wide range of backgrounds and beliefs. Gorman courageously shared the fruits of her contemplation in ways that prophetically challenged the nation to confront its past and envision a better future.

While Gorman does not necessarily identify as a preacher, it is hard to argue that the young Black Catholic's poem was not sermonic—a kind of contemplative sermonizing outside the traditional pulpit. In the words of Thomas Merton, hers is a contemplation that seeks not to "escape from the miseries of the world" but rather to engage them with love to foster a world of "unity and peace."[5] We'll briefly return to her poem later in this book. However, for now, I want to suggest that in her own way Gorman reflects a vast tradition of contemplative proclamation in the Black church.[6] This tradition is made up of Spirit-inspired orators, prophets, and preachers who in different ways merge "the mystical" and "the prophetic" to embody a lifegiving, boundary-crossing, contemplative vision that in the midst of the persistence of death, hate, and despair proclaims the possibility of life, love, and hope.[7]

---

[4] Alexandra Alter, "Amanda Gorman Captures the Moment, in Verse," *New York Times*, March 26, 2021, https://www.nytimes.com/2021/01/19/books/amanda-gorman-inauguration-hill-we-climb.html.

[5] Thomas Merton, *New Seeds of Contemplation* (New York: New Directions, 1961), 78.

[6] There is much debate surrounding the term "the Black church." Some scholars question whether there is such a thing as "the Black church." However, following Stacey Floyd-Thomas et al., I use the term Black church to refer to "those churches whose life and cultural sensibilities have reflected, historically and traditionally, a connection to the larger African American community." This includes independent Black churches, churches inside and outside of historically Black denominations and movements, and multiethnic churches whose leadership and cultural identity is African American. For more on this definition see Stacey Floyd-Thomas et al., *Black Church Studies: An Introduction* (Nashville: Abingdon, 2007), xiii–xxiv.

[7] Janet K. Ruffing, introduction to *Mysticism and Social Transformation*, ed. Janet K. Ruffing (Syracuse, N.Y.: Syracuse University Press, 2001), 11.

A More Expansive Spirituality

Unfortunately, the contemplative dimensions of African American or Black spirituality and preaching are often overlooked.[8] This is due, in part, to racist, sexist, and classist stereotypes that perpetuate monolithic images of Black religiosity. For example, Black Protestant preaching is often depicted as loud, extroverted, and ecstatic. Lisa Thompson has called this "the ghostly image" of Black preaching.[9] Just think of the image of the charismatic, energetic Black male preacher with a voice of thunder depicted in classic texts like James Weldon Johnson's *God's Trombones*, novels such as Zora Neale Hurston's *Jonah's Gourd Vine*, or TV shows such as *Blackish*.[10]

As a Black male engaged in various forms of ministry, I have often felt constrained by this singular image of Black preaching. I have always been a rather sensitive, quiet, and reflective person. And, while I do appreciate and sometimes engage in ecstatic worship practices like shouting or even celebratory proclamation, I also am drawn to stillness, meditation, and introspection. In other words, I embrace silence and shouting, reflection and celebration as vital parts of my spirituality and ministry. Deeply shaped by Barbara Holmes' work *Joy Unspeakable*, I hold that contemplation can be experienced in all these realities through the grace of the divine (see appendix A).[11] The thread interwoven throughout

---

[8] In this book, I use the term Black and African American interchangeably to refer to people of African descent living in the United States. Occasionally, the term Black will be employed to reference those people of African descent living in the Africa diaspora more broadly or on the continent of Africa. This will be clear in context.

[9] Lisa L. Thompson, *Ingenuity: Preaching as an Outsider* (Nashville: Abingdon, 2018), 28.

[10] James Weldon Johnson, *God's Trombones: Seven Negro Sermons in Verse* (New York: Penguin Books, [1927] 2008) and Zora Neale Hurston, *Jonah's Gourd Vine: A Novel* (New York: Perennial Library, 1990).

[11] I realize that in employing such a fluid understanding of contemplation I am departing significantly from the understanding of contemplation espoused by various Christian mystics throughout history, such as St. Teresa of Avila and St. John of the Cross. While I affirm that these mystics offer immense insight into the contemplative journey, I do not follow their particular understanding of contemplation in this book, especially their conception of it as a primarily passive experience distinguished from discursive meditation.

diverse manifestations of contemplative practice is "attentiveness to the Spirit of God."[12] In this sense, following Bernard McGinn, I understand mysticism as referring not simply to ecstatic religious experiences but rather to a deep transforming encounter with the presence of God.[13] Such a transformative encounter may happen in the serenity of silence as much as in unrestrained shouting.

Still, I have not always found the freedom to express my more introspective inclinations in certain environments. For example, as a preacher inside and outside of Black church contexts, I notice that there is often an unspoken expectation that my preaching will *always* be ecstatic, celebratory, and extroverted. My conversations with other Black folks in the United States, United Kingdom, Caribbean, and Africa have helped me realize that I am not alone in this experience. Despite the varied spirituality of the Black church, a singular image of proclamation haunts many houses of worship, homiletical classrooms, and the popular imagination.

I should note that in challenging this image I do not seek to undermine the importance of ecstatic, celebratory Black preaching. For one, as a descendant of enslaved folk preachers in East Texas, I realize how, at its best, such preaching has served as a crucial means of worshipping God and sustaining a marginalized people through four hundred years of brutal enslavement, injustice, and oppression. Moreover, it is part of a constellation of ecstatic liturgical practices in the Black church that have helped produce a necessary rupture

---

[12] Holmes, *Joy Unspeakable*, 5.

[13] This is a highly abbreviated version of McGinn's understanding of mysticism. For a more expansive understanding of his evolving heuristic description of mysticism see, Bernard McGinn, *The Foundations of Mysticism: Origins to the Fifth Century* (New York: Crossroad, 1991), xiii–xx; McGinn, ed., *The Essential Writings of Christian Mysticism* (New York: Modern Library, 2006), xiii–xvii; and McGinn, *Modern Mystics: An Introduction* (New York: Crossroad, 2023), 10–15. McGinn's most recent iteration of his heuristic description identifies the six aspects of mysticism in the following manner. He states that mysticism is (1) an element of religious traditions and (2) a process enfolded within the life of the mystic, which (3) involves transformation of consciousness that is (4) in some manner immediate as a result of (5) contact with the presence of God (6) and must be written or expressed in some way.

within "the normative, violent world of western thought and material condition."¹⁴ For instance, celebratory proclamation challenges the repression of emotion and the expectation of silent worship that Gennifer Benjamin Brooks notes is part of the legacy of "the white supremacist culture of missionary preachers" in the British colonies of the Caribbean.¹⁵ In a society that has attempted to silence Black folks (especially Black women), among other things, the ecstasy of Black folk preaching has signaled a refusal to be defined, dehumanized, and controlled by Eurocentric norms of respectability. Third, as mentioned, Black celebratory preaching is a rich folk heritage that I sometimes reflect in my own preaching.

Nevertheless, the dominance of an essentialist image of Black preaching all too often eclipses other valid and valuable streams in the broader river of Black proclamation. It seems, as literary scholar Kevin Quashie notes, that Black culture is perpetually characterized as "expressive, dramatic, or loud."¹⁶ There is no serious attention given to its "quiet" or contemplative dimensions beyond a frame of resistance.¹⁷ As a result, the breadth and depth of Black humanity is circumscribed by a racialized vision of proper Black performance. Many would-be Black religious leaders experience immense pressure to suppress their unique voices to conform to popular expectations. And congregations of all backgrounds miss out on the depth and nuance that come from learning from a wider spectrum of approaches to Black preaching. Clearly, there is a need to affirm a more diverse array of Black preaching practices.

---

[14] Ashon T. Crawley, *Blackpentecostal Breath: The Aesthetics of Possibility* (New York: Fordham University Press, 2017), 5.

[15] Gennifer Benjamin Brooks, "The Missionary Connection: White Preaching in the British Colonies of the Caribbean," in *Unmasking White Preaching: Racial Hegemony, Resistance, and Possibilities in Preaching*, ed. Lis Valle-Ruiz and Andrew Wymer (Lanham, Md.: Lexington, 2022), 24.

[16] Kevin Quashie, *The Sovereignty of Quiet: Beyond Resistance in Black Culture* (New Brunswick, N.J.: Rutgers University Press, 2012), 3.

[17] Quashie, *Sovereignty of Quiet*, 3.

Reclaiming Black Contemplative Preaching

Thus, this book gives special attention to what Martha Simmons and Frank Thomas in their pioneering anthology *Preaching with Sacred Fire* call Black contemplative preaching.[18] While almost all Black preaching has elements that are "well nigh mystical," in this work, I am drawing attention to a particular stream of Black preaching that might be called contemplative—one that stretches back to a broader history of contemplative preachers such as Gregory the Great, Hildegard of Bingen, Meister Eckhart, Jonathan Edwards, Zilpha Elaw, and Sadhu Sundar Singh.[19] Some of the other streams of Black preaching include the womanist, queer, priestly, prophetic, and sage or wisdom streams—to name just a handful.[20] Various expressions of Black contemplative preaching intersect with these streams. However, I focus specifically on the contemplative stream. Unfortunately, though key aspects of Black contemplative preaching can be seen in the life and speech of notable modern Black preachers, such as Gardner C. Taylor and Pauli Murray, it remains one of the most overlooked streams of preaching inside and outside of Black church contexts. This lack of awareness and acknowledgment seems to suggest that it is a mode of proclamation that, like other contemplative practices in the Black church, is "hidden in plain sight."[21]

I aim to render this largely invisible stream of Black preaching more visible. I do so by demonstrating that Black contemplative preaching is an important type of homiletical theology observable

---

[18] Martha Simmons and Frank Thomas, eds., *Preaching with Sacred Fire: An Anthology of African American Sermons, 1750 to the Present* (New York: W. W. Norton, 2010), 491–92. The actual term used by Simmons and Thomas is contemplative preaching, but I qualify their phrase with "Black" given they are focused on how such preaching manifests among ministers shaped by African American cultural contexts.

[19] William Clair Turner Jr., *Preaching That Makes the Word Plain: Doing Theology in the Crucible of Life* (Eugene, Ore.: Cascade, 2008), xiv.

[20] See Kimberly P. Johnson, *The Womanist Preacher: Proclaiming Womanist Rhetoric from the Pulpit* (Lanham, Md.: Lexington, 2017); Nicole Danielle McDonald, "Black Queer Preaching: A Close Reading of Bishop Yvette A. Flunder's Sermon, 'Silent No More,'" *Homiletic* 48, no. 1 (2023): 32–47; and Kenyatta R. Gilbert, *The Journey and Promise of African American Preaching* (Minneapolis: Fortress, 2011). To be clear, these authors do not explicitly use the term "stream" when exploring expressions of Black preaching.

[21] Holmes, *Joy Unspeakable*, 75.

among Black preachers in the past and present. The term homiletical theology refers to theology enfleshed in the preaching life and practices of preachers.[22] Specifically, I show how the distinctives of Black contemplative preaching's homiletical theology can be seen in different ways in three twentieth-century Black preachers: Howard Thurman, Martin Luther King Jr., and Barbara Harris. To be clear, I do not propose that the church should simply be "doing what was done in the past" by contemplative preachers.[23] Rather, while respecting and appreciating the wisdom of various preaching traditions, I suggest that there is theological wisdom to be gleaned from the habits, practices, and embodied witness of Black contemplative preachers. In their own way, theirs is a prophetic witness. I understand their prophetic sermonizing as part of the tradition of the Hebrew prophets and Jesus Christ. It is prophetic speech that critically assesses the status quo in light of the known will of God, communicates a compelling alternative vision of the way things should be, and calls individuals and/or communities to take concrete steps toward establishing a new future through the empowerment of God's Spirit.[24] To be sure, some contemplative preachers do not foreground calling for people to engage in concrete public acts of justice. However, they do call for the kind of deep interior work that inspires and sustains such action as part of love of God, self, neighbor, and creation. Thus, in all its

---

[22] Here I am building on Michael Pasquarello III's insightful work on homiletical theology (or homiletic theology, as he often puts it). See, for example, his *Dietrich: Bonhoeffer and the Theology of a Preaching Life* (Waco: Baylor University Press, 2017), v. Pasquarello is part of the practical theology stream of homiletic theology as delineated in David Schnasa Jacobsen, ed., *Homiletical Theology: Preaching as Doing Theology* (Eugene, Ore.: Wipf & Stock, 2015). For an important critique of homiletical theology that draws heavily on postmodern philosophy, see Jacob D. Myers, *Preaching Must Die! Troubling Homiletical Theology* (Minneapolis: Fortress, 2017).

[23] Stanley Hauerwas, *Dispatches from the Front: Theological Engagements with the Secular* (Durham: Duke University Press, 1994), 188, quoted in Michael Pasquarello III, *Sacred Rhetoric: Preaching as a Theological and Pastoral Practice of the Church* (Eugene, Ore.: Wipf & Stock, 2005), 12.

[24] My understanding of prophetic preaching has been shaped by the work of various scholars. See, for example, Marvin A. McMickle, *Where Have All the Prophets Gone? Reclaiming Prophetic Preaching in America* (Cleveland: Pilgrim, 2006), Walter Brueggemann, *The Practice of Prophetic Imagination: Preaching an Emancipating Word* (Minneapolis: Fortress, 2012), and Kenyatta R. Gilbert, *A Pursued Justice: Black Preaching from the Great Migration to Civil Rights* (Waco: Baylor University Press, 2016).

diversity, Black contemplative preaching offers wisdom that can be enacted in faithful ways in the particular time and place in which we find ourselves today.

This study is particularly crucial amid the series of global crises we are currently experiencing. Religious and racial conflicts, the rise of global warming, an onslaught of natural disasters, profound political polarization and dehumanization of the other, and other crises have all contributed to profound social fragmentation, existential fear, and psychological and spiritual fatigue. Amid these many challenges, there is a need for deeply formed, resilient preachers who embody the way of Jesus with love, joy, patience, and bold humility. Such preachers move beyond homiletical gimmicks, tricks, and techniques. They are not obsessed with gaining a larger following or promoting their own personal agenda. Instead, they seek to be prayerful, faithful, and courageous preachers who advance the common good for the glory of God. While this is not a panacea for the pervasive challenges of our late modern world, there are some important things we can learn from Black contemplative preachers in the past and present.[25] In the midst of our divided and divisive world, Black contemplative preachers call for a more holistic way of being in relationship with God, one another, and all creation. In the midst of profound fear and uncertainty, Black contemplative preachers invite us to be grounded in the One who holds all things in all seasons. And in the midst of fatigue stemming from the pace and demands of late modern society, they challenge us to cultivate rhythms of rest to sustain our varied vocations.

Scope of Study

This book is not the first or the last word on contemplative preaching. I have benefited immensely from the scholarship of others, and I am happy to report that additional studies are forthcoming on various aspects, exemplars, and expressions of contemplative preaching. In other words, while this is the first book-length study of contemplative preaching that I am aware of, it is by no means comprehensive. For instance, the preaching ministries of contemporary leaders such

---

[25] When I use the pronoun "we" in this book, unless specified otherwise, I am referring to the church at large in the United States.

as Barbara Brown Taylor, Eunjoo Mary Kim, Rich Villodas, Ken Shigematsu, and others demonstrate that contemplative preaching manifests in a diversity of cultural contexts. As important as it is to engage the varied cultural expressions of contemplative preaching, I have not sought to do so in this book. Instead, I purposefully limit my focus to examining *Black* contemplative preaching. Why? It is the tradition that I know the best. Furthermore, along with Cleophus LaRue, I believe "an endless engagement of contrasts and comparisons" between Black preaching and other expressions of proclamation (especially European American preaching) can make it difficult to see and appreciate the internal diversity within Black proclamation.[26] Even so, there are many figures, expressions, and historical and cultural precedents of Black contemplative preaching that I do not examine. A second limitation of this study is that given that I focus primarily on the agency of specific Black contemplative preachers, I do not *extensively* analyze the orality of Black contemplative preaching in communal settings. Third, while I recognize that Black religiosity is by no means confined to the traditional expressions of the Judeo-Christian faith, my study focuses mainly on Black contemplative preaching in certain Protestant contexts. Future studies should explore contemplative preaching in more diverse Black religious and cultural contexts.[27]

Finally, though I hope the historical and contemporary examples of contemplative preaching I provide prove helpful, the focus of the book precludes giving specific attention to practical matters such as Scriptural exegesis, sermon design, and delivery. While I realize these

---

[26] Cleophus J. LaRue, *Rethinking Celebration: From Rhetoric to Praise in African American Preaching* (Louisville: Westminster John Knox, 2016), xiii.

[27] For studies that helpfully demonstrate the diversity of Black religiosity, see Anthony B. Pinn, *Varieties of African American Religious Experience: Toward a Comparative Black Theology*, 20th anniv. ed. (Minneapolis: Fortress, 2017), Joseph L. Tucker, *The Other Black Church: Alternative Christian Movements and the Struggle for Black Freedom* (Minneapolis: Fortress, 2020); Rachel E. Harding, *A Refuge in Thunder: Candomblé and Alternative Spaces of Blackness* (Bloomington: Indiana University Press, 2003), Rosemarie Freeney Harding with Rachel Elizabeth Harding, *Remnants: A Memoir of Spirit, Activism, and Mothering* (Durham: Duke University Press, 2015), Rima Vesely-Flad, *Black Buddhists and the Black Radical Tradition* (New York: New York University Press, 2022), and Leonard Cornell McKinnis II, *The Black Coptic Church: Race and Imagination in a New Religion* (New York: New York University Press, 2023).

limitations prevent me from considering several important dimensions of Black contemplative preaching, I hope future scholarship can address any omissions or distortions that may arise due to the narrow scope of my work.

Let me also offer here a brief word about language in this study. Though I prefer gender-inclusive language and realize its absence is offensive to many, throughout this book, when quoting primary source material I will generally respect authors' use of masculine nouns and pronouns to refer to all of humanity. Thus, with only a couple of exceptions for the sake of clarity, I have chosen to not alter the lack of gender-inclusive language in Howard Thurman, Martin Luther King Jr., and others. I recognize that they employed the conventions of their time and place as we do today.

The Journey Ahead

Black Contemplative Preaching explores Howard Thurman, Martin Luther King Jr., and Bishop Barbara Harris as notable twentieth-century African American Protestant religious leaders who form part of a historic tradition of contemplative preaching that has largely remained hidden in plain sight. I suggest that this tradition continues in contemporary preachers such as Ineda Pearl Adesanya, Veronica R. Goines, Luke A. Powery, and Frank A. Thomas. While recognizing that there are significant epistemological challenges related to understanding another person's spiritual or mystical experience, I draw on autobiographical accounts, personal interviews, and especially published and unpublished sermons to examine contemplative proclamation.[28] In so doing, I seek to challenge monolithic portraits of Black Protestant religious identity and practice, shed light on the creative synthesis of spirituality, social justice, and proclamation in the Black church, and recover a rich history of mystical activism among preachers in Christian history.

Though this book is primarily written for students, practitioners, and teachers of preaching, I hope it also proves to be of interest to those researching, teaching, or writing in the areas of Christian

---

[28] McGinn, *Foundations of Mysticism*, xvii–xviii.

spirituality and Black church studies. Additionally, I seek to appeal to everyday Christians and those of other faith traditions or none who are keen to learn from an often unappreciated and misunderstood aspect of Christian history and African American culture. As I was writing, I was particularly concerned about the emerging generations of Black ministry leaders, students, and congregants who, like me, have struggled to fully identify with the prevailing models of spirituality and ministry in the Black church. Even if one does not self-describe as a "contemplative" or "contemplative preacher" per se, it is my deep conviction that learning about a tradition that departs from the stereotypical norm in the Black church can create an aperture for fresh ways of imagining how to embody one's faith, identity, and vocation. And, of course, the embodied wisdom of Black contemplative preachers is something that can enrich and guide the spiritual lives of ordained and lay church folks alike—regardless of color, culture, or creed.

Ultimately, I gesture toward Black contemplative preaching as an enduring source of theological wisdom that can help us address the political, ecological, and spiritual challenges of our times. However, before exploring the contemporary significance of Black contemplative preaching, we must begin with examining its roots. This will help us better appreciate the abiding wisdom that contemplative preaching offers in the present. With this in mind, let us explore the story of its beginnings.

1
Preaching as Prayer
Toward a History of Contemplative Preaching

Let [the preacher] be a pray-er before being a speaker.

Augustine, *De Doctrina Christiana*[1]

Introduction

The story of contemplative preaching has biblical roots. In the Book of Exodus, we encounter Moses trembling near a bush enflamed with the presence of God before being sent to proclaim freedom for his enslaved sisters and brothers in Egypt. In so doing, Moses embodies "the mystic-prophetic dimension and the political dimension of faith and contemplation."[2] This continues in various ways in the ministry of Hebrew prophets such as Isaiah. The record of the prophet's mystical encounter with the Holy One reflects a confrontation with what Rudolf Otto famously termed the *mysterium tremendum et fascinas*, that is, the fearful yet alluring mystery of God.[3] Isaiah is commissioned as a prophet to speak God's love, truth, and justice only after having encountered the mystery of the divine. If

---

[1] Augustine, *Teaching Christianity (De Doctrina Christiana)*, in *The Works of Augustine: A Translation for the Twenty-First Century*, ed. Edmund Hill, trans. John E. Rotelle, (Hyde Park, N.Y.: New City Press, 1996), 4.15.32.

[2] Segundo Galilea, "Liberation as an Encounter with Politics and Contemplation," in *The Mystical and Political Dimension of the Christian Faith*, ed. Claude Geffré and Gustavo Gutiérrez, trans. J. P. Donnelly (New York: Herder and Herder, 1974), 33.

[3] Rudolf Otto, *The Idea of the Holy: An Inquiry into the Non-rational Factor in the Idea of the Divine and Its Relation to the Rational*, trans. John W. Harvey (New York: Oxford University Press, 1950).

we move into the New Testament, the Gospel of Luke shows us young Mary pondering God's shocking word of birth and new life to her virgin womb through the angel Gabriel. Empowered by the Spirit, she is soon announcing the subversive saving acts of God in what we know as the Magnificat.[4] And, in all the Synoptic Gospels, we find Jesus, fully God and fully human, spending forty days in the wilderness fasting and meditating on the Torah before launching into his ministry of bearing witness to the reign of God in word and deed. These figures and others testify to the fact that there is a profound precedent in the biblical witness for liberating proclamation fueled by contemplation. In this chapter, we encounter the story of some of the early women and men of African descent who continued the tradition of Spirit-empowered contemplative proclamation seen in Moses, Isaiah, Mary, and Jesus himself. Given the social and political challenges of our time, it is more important than ever to learn from their witness. They offer a profound model of proclamation that engages difficult social realities with spiritual depth and wisdom.

Unfortunately, this history has been eclipsed, in part because contemplation is often equated with silence, solitude, and disengagement from social realities. As such, contemplative preaching can sound like an oxymoron. However, in Black church traditions, contemplation may or may not include silence and stillness. It simply requires "attentiveness to the Spirit of God."[5] Moreover, as is the case in much of Christian tradition, "there is no contradiction between contemplation and action" in Black spirituality.[6] With this understanding in mind, a close relationship between "contemplation and proclamation" as well as a concern for liberation can be found not only in the biblical figures mentioned above but in the lives of many women and men throughout

---

[4] For an important study on what Mary can teach preachers about preaching, see Jerusha Matsen Neal, *The Overshadowed Preacher: Mary, the Spirit, and the Labor of Proclamation* (Grand Rapids: Eerdmans, 2020).

[5] Barbara A. Holmes, *Joy Unspeakable: Contemplative Practices of the Black Church*, 2nd ed. (Minneapolis: Fortress, 2017), 5.

[6] James A. Noel, "Contemplation and Social Action in African-American Spirituality," *Church and Society* 83, no. 2 (November–December 1992): 62.

history.⁷ The overlooked contemplative witness of these pioneers led to the development of Black contemplative preaching, a meditative mode of preaching that weds mystical and theological insights to promote social and spiritual transformation.⁸ This chapter tells this story.

Early African and European Mystic Preachers

Black contemplative preaching did not emerge in a vacuum. Important factors and figures preceded its development. For example, it is deeply shaped by a rich and diverse African heritage in which "religion permeates all the departments of life."⁹ More specifically, Black contemplative preaching is part of a holistic, communal spirituality, manifests a vibrant orality, and reflects the tradition of the African griot, or storyteller. Furthermore, it stems from a heritage of Africana contemplation that can be traced back to African desert mothers and fathers. These African cultural retentions and indeed an Africana "mode of orienting and perceiving reality" continued beyond the brutality of the Middle Passage (or Maafa), as people of African descent were forcibly brought to live in what would become known as North America.¹⁰ In other words, the various Africana roots of

---

⁷ Jose Varickasseril, "Contemplation and Proclamation: New Testament Perspectives," *Third Millennium* 21, no. 1 (2018): 5–26.

⁸ I offer a more detailed definition near the end of the chapter.

⁹ John Mbiti, *African Religions and Philosophy*, 2nd ed. (Portsmouth, N.H.: Heinemann, 1990), 1.

¹⁰ Charles H. Long, *Significations: Signs, Symbols, and Images in the Interpretation of Religion* (Aurora, Colo.: The Davies Group, 1995), 189. The issue of African cultural retentions was contested in the classic debate of sociologist E. Franklin Frazier and anthropologist Melville Herskovits. See E. Franklin Frazier and C. Eric Lincoln's *The Negro Church in America/The Black Church since Frazier* (New York: Schocken, 1974), especially chap. 1 and Melville J. Herskovits' *The Myth of the Negro Past* (Boston: Beacon, 1990). As Albert Raboteau asserts in his classic *Slave Religion: The "Invisible Institution" in the Antebellum South*, updated ed. (New York: Oxford University Press, 2004), both were right about some things. For example, Frazier was right to note that the continuity of African culture did not persist in a pure form, nor was it the same in all places. Herskovits rightly insisted that African beliefs, values, and patterns of behavior were not eradicated due to slavery even if he did overstate his argument at times. Subsequent scholarship has drawn great attention to how culture perseveres and adapts over generations. Drawing on the work of Gayraud Wilmore, Kenyatta Gilbert helpfully states: "Black culture is transferred from one generation to another and is continuously transforming, taking on new forms, which means the substance of cultural meaning seldom dies." See Kenyatta R. Gilbert, *The Journey and Promise of African American Preaching* (Minneapolis: Fortress,

Black contemplative preaching were not eradicated by the brutality of enslavement. Unfortunately, space does not permit an extensive study of some of these historical and cultural roots. However, I have examined them elsewhere.[11] Here I would like to simply focus on some of the African and European Christian mystics who precede the emergence of Black contemplative preaching. I do not claim that there is a clear, direct link between each of these mystics and Black contemplative preaching. On the contrary, I suggest that there is a contemplative or mystical orientation present in these figures that resonates with parts of Black contemplative preaching. While there are countless examples of mystic preachers from the Eastern and Western church that could be mentioned as preceding Black contemplative preaching, I limit myself to discussing five: Augustine of Hippo, Francis of Assisi, Meister Eckhart, George Fox, and Kimpa Vita.

We begin with the North African bishop Augustine (354–430 C.E.). Along with his contemporaries, such as Basil the Great (330–379 C.E.) and John Chrysostom (347–407 C.E.), Augustine embodied a profound commitment to the contemplative life. Indeed, he has been described by Bernard McGinn as "the founding father" of Christian mysticism.[12] Augustine's mystical thought is visible in his commentaries, autobiography, sermons, and many theological treatises. Among the many things that could be said about Augustine as a contemplative preacher, I draw brief attention to his *De Doctrina Christiana* or *Teaching Christianity*, a preaching manual he wrote for "use in training the clergy to teach and preach" in North Africa.[13] *Teaching Christianity* provides a glimpse into the kind of theological practices that

---

2011), 34. Charles H. Long moves us beyond these debates by drawing our attention to the existence of Africa as a historical reality and religious image or symbol. See Long, *Significations*, chapter 11.

[11] See E. Trey Clark, "Contemplation, Proclamation, and Social Transformation: Reclaiming the Homiletical Theology of Black Contemplative Preaching" (PhD diss., Fuller Theological Seminary, 2021), 33–43.

[12] Bernard McGinn, *The Foundations of Mysticism: Origins to the Fifth Century* (New York: Crossroad, 1991), 228, 231.

[13] Edmund Hill, "Translator's Note," in Augustine, *Teaching Christianity (De Doctrina Christiana)*, 96. Hill argues that *Teaching Christianity* was written to train clergy in preaching at the request of the bishop of Carthage, Aurelius.

orient contemplative proclamation. The book is divided into four parts. Books 1 to 3 focus on discovering God's speech through interpreting the signs of Scripture. Though Augustine affirms learning from a range of sources, for him, preaching primarily emerges from reflecting, meditating, and ruminating on God's speech as revealed in Scripture. To put it differently, contemplative preaching does not begin with us. It begins with the gift of the triune God's self-disclosure. Only in book 4 does Augustine turn to communication of Scripture. Even so, reframing the ancient orator Cicero's purposes of oration for Christian ends, Augustine contends that rhetoric cannot be dependent solely on the skills or knowledge of the preacher. Instead, he insists on reliance on the power of God's Spirit, through becoming "a pray-er more than a speaker."[14] While he certainly emphasizes the importance of praying before one preaches, he ultimately stresses the importance of a kind of lived or embodied prayer as the preacher becomes "an eloquent sermon."[15] In short, Augustine understands preaching as a Spirit-empowered theological practice that emerges from "reverent attention" to God's speech through careful study, prayer, and spiritual devotion.[16]

Following Augustine, several notable mystic preachers emerged, such as Gregory the Great (590–604 C.E.), Bernard of Clairvaux (1090–1153), Hildegard of Bingen (1098–1179), and others. For our purposes, one of the most influential Italian medieval preachers to precede Black contemplative preaching is Francis of Assisi (1181–1226). While St. Francis is primarily known for his commitment to a life of poverty for the sake of the gospel, he was also a preaching friar who founded the Franciscan mendicant order. Along with the Dominican preaching order, the Franciscans made significant contributions to the recovery of preaching among the masses of common people in the medieval period. Francis is the kind of preacher whose life of prayer, discipline, and love led him to be deeply engaged with the world. Regis J. Armstrong and Ignatius Brady, scholars of Franciscan spirituality,

[14] Augustine, *Teaching Christianity*, 4.15.32.
[15] Augustine, *Teaching Christianity*, 4.29.62.
[16] Michael Pasquarello III, *Sacred Rhetoric: Preaching as a Theological and Pastoral Practice of the Church* (Eugene, Ore.: Wipf & Stock, 2005), 21.

write that Francis "was a mystic whose faith had so transformed his vision that he perceived that the entire world was redolent with the power, wisdom, and goodness of the Creator."[17] While legends exist about Francis preaching to birds, one of the clearest and most reliable witnesses to Francis' contemplative proclamation is seen in his famous "Canticle of Brother Sun."[18] In the hymn, Francis articulates a mystical vision that bears witness to the intimate relationship of the triune God with all creation. Francis proclaims the praise of the "Most High, all-powerful, good Lord" who has created "Brother Sun," "Sister Moon," "Brother Wind," "Sister Water," "Brother Fire," "Mother Earth," and "Sister Bodily Death."[19] The expansive vision of the canticle demonstrates that Francis "becomes so intimate and familiar with the wonders of creation that he embraces them as 'brother' and 'sister,' that is, members of one family."[20] In brief, among other things, Francis was a mystic preacher whose homiletical vision reflected a deep love and commitment to the poor and the more-than-human creation.

Shortly after the Franciscan order emerged, the Dominican order was founded by St. Dominic of Guzman (1170–1221). Although it was a mendicant order like the Franciscans, the Dominican order was "founded initially precisely for the sake of preaching and the salvation of souls."[21] Hence, the Dominicans were committed to prayer, study, and preaching as a way of life. The great Dominican theologian and master preacher Thomas Aquinas (1225–1274) famously wrote that "just as it is better to enlighten than merely to shine, so is it better to give to others the fruits of one's contemplation (*contemplata aliis tradere*) than merely to contemplate (*contemplari*)."[22] In other words,

---

[17] Regis J. Armstrong and Ignatius C. Brady, eds. and trans., *The Writings of St. Francis and Clare: The Complete Works* (New York: Paulist Press, 1982), 3.

[18] Francis of Assisi, "The Canticle of Brother Sun," in Armstrong and Brady, *Writings of St. Francis and Clare*, 38–39.

[19] Francis of Assisi, "The Canticle of Brother Sun," 38.

[20] Armstrong and Brady, *Writings of St. Francis and Clare*, 38.

[21] "The Early Dominican Constitutions," in *Early Dominicans: Selected Writings*, ed. Simon Tugwell (New York: Paulist Press, 1982), 457.

[22] Thomas Aquinas, *The Summa Theologiae*, trans. Fathers of the English Dominican Province (New York: Benziger Bros, 1947), II-II, Q. 188, A. 6, full text available at the Christian Classics Ethereal Library, https://www.ccel.org/a/aquinas/summa/SS/SS188.html#SSQ188A6THEP1. See also the same work, III, Q. 40, A. 1, Ad 2.

one's contemplation is meant to overflow for the good of others. This contemplative orientation toward preaching is present in several notable Dominicans, including Humbert of Romans (1200–1277) and Catherine of Siena (1347–1380). Particularly noteworthy, however, is the German theologian, philosopher, priest, and mystic Meister Eckhart (1260–1328), known for rich, mystical theological insights that emerged from his contemplation and scriptural exegesis as both a teacher and preacher. His commitment to mystical proclamation is clearly stated in his own words:

> When I preach, I am accustomed to speak about detachment, and that man should be free of himself and of all things; second, that a man should be formed again into that simple good which is God; third, that he should reflect on the great nobility with which God has endowed his soul, so that in this way he may come again to wonder at God; fourth, about the purity of the divine nature, for the brightness of the divine nature is beyond words. God is a word, a word unspoken.[23]

Eckhart's dense words defy simple summation. However, the four themes he names—detachment, God as the telos of formation, the contemplation of God in the soul, and the purity and mystery of the divine nature—are clearly present throughout his corpus of sermons, even if they are not present in every sermon he preached. Along with other themes, they represent some of the many important theological convictions that informed his practice of contemplative proclamation.

Another Christian mystic who antedates Black contemplative preaching emerged in Europe a few centuries after Eckhart. Following the dawn of the Reformation, some religious groups, such as the Puritans, sought to reform the church and recover a spirituality that, among other things, emphasized personal piety. It was a time of great social and religious instability and violence. During this period, a disillusioned and spiritually hungry young man by the name of George Fox (1624–1691) began to search for enlightenment beyond the established religious authorities and religious dissenters that surrounded him. One day Fox came to experience such enlightenment through

---

[23] Meister Eckhart, "Selected Sermons," in *Meister Eckhart: The Essential Sermons, Commentaries, Treatises, and Defense*, trans. Edmund Colledge and Bernard McGinn (New York: Paulist Press, 1981), 203.

God's gracious inner revelation when he "heard a voice which said: 'There is one, even Christ Jesus, that can speak to thy condition.'"[24] This inner revelation or "opening" by the Spirit brought him great joy and led him to preach a message calling for people to turn to the inner light of Christ rather than external religion.[25] His efforts at preaching and organizing led to the founding of the Society of Friends, or Quakers—a movement that would eventually find its way to North America. The Quakers' commitment to "preaching good news to the poor and denouncing" religious, social, and political forms of oppression eventually led to an embrace of the equality of women and people of African descent.[26] While the Quakers are often noted for their practice of silent worship, Quaker scholar Michael Graves has suggested that a tradition of impromptu preaching can be traced to the movement's earliest beginnings.[27] Rather than relying on intentional preparation, this early preaching emerged through careful listening and attentiveness to what the Spirit might say in any given moment. Of course, this was possible, as Graves argues, because those who preached studied Scripture carefully, lived in a religious subculture that was permeated by spiritual discourse, were trained in a catechetical process that involved regular dialogue and discussion around questions, and practiced speaking around metaphors central to the movement that could become the basis of any talk.[28] George Fox was part of this subculture and thus his own mystical preaching was at least in part shaped by it. His radical impromptu preaching reflected a deep contemplative orientation that also challenged social, political, and religious understandings of his time.

While George Fox was preaching in England in the mid-seventeenth century, a group of Italian Franciscan priests known as the Capuchins arrived in the Kongo, a West African kingdom with

---

[24] George Fox, *The Journal of George Fox*, ed. Rufus Jones (Richmond, Ind.: Friends United, 1976), 82.

[25] Fox, *Journal of George Fox*, 82.

[26] Carole Dale Spencer, "Quaker Spirituality," in *Dictionary of Christian Spirituality*, ed. Glen G. Scorgie (Grand Rapids: Zondervan, 2011), 705.

[27] Michael P. Graves, *Preaching the Inward Light: Early Quaker Rhetoric* (Waco: Baylor University Press, 2009), 1–2.

[28] Graves, *Preaching the Inward Light*, 309–10.

a growing Portuguese presence. Eventually, the Portuguese started a rebellion that led to the collapse of the federation that held the Kongo together. A civil war broke out and the capital of the Kongo, São Salvador, was destroyed. It was within this context of civil and social unrest that the final mystic preacher that I want to highlight emerged: Kimpa Vita (1684–1706). Almost everything that we know about Kimpa Vita (or Dona Beatriz Kimpa Vita, as the Portuguese called her) comes through various journals and records of Capuchin priests who served in the Kongo.[29] Despite the absence of records from Kimpa Vita herself or significant known literary contributions from Kongolese people, her testimony as recorded by the Capuchin priests witnesses to her bold, even if unusual to modern ears, mystical and prophetic proclamation. Recognized at an early age as possessing spiritual gifts, one day Kimpa Vita fell into a spiritual trance and became possessed by St. Anthony, the patron saint of the Portuguese. She was told, "I am Saint Anthony, firstborn son of the Faith and of Saint Francis. . . . I have been sent from God to your head to preach to the people."[30] Obedient to the revered mystic, Kimpa Vita allowed St. Anthony to preach through her Black female body. Three themes in her messages are particularly salient.[31] First, she called for the restoration of the capital city of São Salvador. Second, she rebuked many of the Capuchin priests for their addiction to alcohol, manipulation of political affairs to their advantage, and participation in the growing slave trade in the region. Third, contrary to the Eurocentric teaching of the priests, she proclaimed that Jesus, Mary, and St. Francis were in fact Black and that the church found its roots in the Kongo—not outside of it. Though Kimpa Vita developed a following as she preached in various villages, shortly after giving birth as an unmarried woman she was tragically imprisoned, tried, and burned at the stake. Still, the movement she started was not easily

---

[29] For a brief overview of the primary documents available on Kimpa Vita, see John K. Thornton, *The Kongolese Saint Anthony: Dona Beatriz Kimpa Vita and the Antonian Movement, 1684–1706* (New York: Cambridge University Press, 1998), 2–5.

[30] Thornton, *Kongolese Saint Anthony*, 10.

[31] Here I summarize from the work of Dale T. Irvin and Scott W. Sunquist, *History of the World Christian Movement*, vol. 2, *Modern Christianity from 1454–1800* (Maryknoll, N.Y.: Orbis, 2012), 215–16.

stopped. Along with being a pioneer of indigenous African Christian faith, Kimpa Vita bears witness to a profound inner encounter with the divine that energized the external pursuit of social and political transformation in the midst of colonial power. Her example of prophetic mystical proclamation would continue in various ways in the Americas through Black contemplative preaching in the context of slavery, oppression, and dehumanization.

The Emergence of Black Preaching

There is much that could be said about the beginnings of Black preaching. As Kenyatta Gilbert has shown, a full overview of Black preaching would involve exploring more fully its Africana roots and various historical phases of its development, including colonial North America, the Revival Period, Reconstruction, Great Migration, the civil rights movement, and the post–civil rights era.[32] I do not attempt to offer a complete history of Black preaching in this book.[33] Instead, I offer an abbreviated treatment of its beginnings in North America before turning to explore several African American forerunners of Black contemplative preaching who were shaped by this history.

Black preaching was created by enslaved Africans, mostly from West Africa, who were brutally taken to the British colonies in what would become America. The horror of the Middle Passage and enslavement led to an erosion of some of the particularities of the multiple languages, dialects, and traditions of the enslaved Africans. However, it did not fully eradicate their cultural roots. Africans in America retained a pervasive spiritual outlook, holistic, communal spirituality, and rich oral tradition despite the oppression they faced. Albert Raboteau notes that though there was "widely held justification of slavery as a means of spreading the gospel . . . the process of

---

[32] Gilbert, *Journey and Promise*, 37.

[33] For a concise history of Black preaching, see Gilbert, *Journey and Promise*, 37–56; Gerald Lamont Thomas, *African American Preaching: The Contribution of Dr. Gardner C. Taylor* (New York: Peter Lang, 2009), 7–79; and Henry H. Mitchell, *Black Preaching: The Recovery of a Powerful Art* (Nashville: Abingdon, 1990), 23–55. To my knowledge, the most comprehensive history of Black preaching is Martha Simmons and Frank Thomas, eds., *Preaching with Sacred Fire: An Anthology of African American Sermons, 1750 to the Present* (New York: W. W. Norton, 2010).

slave conversion was blocked by major obstacles."[34] Some of these included the colonists' prioritization of economic profit over Christianization, the belief that Africans were incapable of learning, the fear of Christianization leading to revolt, and the bold resistance of some Africans to the religion of their oppressors. However, over time enslaved Blacks began to convert in larger numbers, principally through the influence of planters, missionaries, and other enslaved persons. Though independent Baptist and Methodist groups connected best with the enslaved Africans brought to America, conversion to the Christian faith was not significant among Africans until the start of the so-called Second Great Awakening around 1790. Among other things, the emotionally charged preaching of ministers and the stress on personal conversion appealed to the enslaved. Some of the revivalist expressions of faith were perceived as similar to expressive West African rituals of dance, shout, oratory, initiation, conjuring, and spirit possession. For our purposes, it is especially vital to note the emotional and energetic revivalist preaching of George Whitefield (1714–1770), Shubal Stearns (1706–1771), Daniel Marshall (1706–1784), and others. Their spiritually evocative preaching resonated with the Africans in North America. As a result, as Henry Mitchell states, the example of these early European American preachers served as a catalyst for Africans to affirm the value of their natural gifts and tendencies as "wholly acceptable to God."[35] Some of the earliest known Black preachers are Rebecca Protten (1718–1780), David George (1742–1810), Harry Hosier or "Black Harry" (1750–1806), George Liele (1750–1828), and others we will explore below in relation to Black contemplative preaching.

As more significant conversions among the enslaved took place in the eighteenth and nineteenth centuries, distinct liturgical practices were developed that formed the Invisible Institution—the secretive Black church of the slavery era. While some interracial worship took place at this time and some Blacks—such as John Jasper (1812–1901)

---

[34] Raboteau, *Slave Religion*, 98.
[35] Henry Mitchell, "African American Preaching," in *Concise Encyclopedia of Preaching*, ed. William H. Willimon and Richard Lischer (Louisville: Westminster John Knox, 1995), 5.

and others—preached to White audiences, Black liturgical involvement was significantly circumscribed by the realities of racism. Indeed, at times, some European Americans "restricted the ability of blacks to preach."[36] The emergence of the Black church was a direct reaction against the White supremacist ideology and practice of European American churches that denied the full humanity and participation of Blacks in the liturgy. As Blacks worshipped in the Invisible Institution, they merged their traditions with that of the Christianity they were exposed to, and the Christian faith was transformed. As Gayraud Wilmore writes in his landmark book on African American religion, "Blacks have used Christianity not so much as it was delivered to them by racist white churches, but as its truth was authenticated to them in the experience of suffering and struggle, to reinforce an enculturated religious orientation and to produce an indigenous faith that emphasized dignity, freedom, and human welfare."[37] Wilmore reminds us of the indigenous nature of Black Christianity in general and Black preaching in particular. Forged in the furnace of slavery, Black preaching is an early testament to the creativity, strength, and genius of Black people as they synthesized their African traditions with revivalist expressions to create an altogether new form of proclamation. Of course, the end of slavery did not signal the end of Black proclamation. It would only continue to evolve during Reconstruction, the period following the end of the Civil War in 1865.

Though oppressive and racist restrictions in many ways intensified for Black people during Reconstruction (1865–1877), Black preachers nevertheless received unprecedented educational opportunities. Of course, African American preachers often displayed profound wisdom, knowledge, and insight through self-education efforts, informal study opportunities, and some rare training at colleges even before Reconstruction. Still, the proliferation of resources for study, the emergence of Black colleges, and the rise in Black instructors significantly increased the accessibility of education. However, it is important to note that, according to Evelyn Higginbotham, "higher

---

[36] Scott Haldeman, *Towards Liturgies That Reconcile: Race and Ritual among African-American and European-American Protestants* (New York: Routledge, 2007), 107.
[37] Gayraud Wilmore, *Black Religion and Black Radicalism: An Interpretation of the Religious History of African Americans*, 3rd ed. (Maryknoll, N.Y.: Orbis, 1998), 25.

education tended to widen the division of labor between black professional men and women," with men predominantly being trained as preachers and women as teachers.[38] That being said, there were more educational opportunities for both men and women than before, which contributed to more Blacks entering the middle class. As a result, during this time, a clearer distinction emerged between the folk and educated stream of Black preaching, two streams that had existed since the beginnings of Black preaching. While these streams of preaching are best understood as "not mutually exclusive or polar opposite categories" but rather as "the extreme positions on a spectrum," it will be helpful to comment on their unique characteristics in some detail.[39] This is especially the case given their enduring influence on Black preaching in general and Black contemplative preaching in particular.

One scholar has defined the Black folk sermon as a "Sunday verbal performance of the black folk preacher who is not seminary-trained but called to the ministry by some visionary experience and whose congregation consists principally of black working-class worshipers."[40] Some early examples of folk preachers include Brother Carper, the Gullah Negro preacher Brudder Coteney, and Sojourner Truth.[41] These preachers often employed Black vernacular English, nondeductive organizational structure, and whooping, or a celebratory close reflective of what W. E. B. DuBois called "the frenzy" or the uninhibited ecstasy of Black worship.[42] While it is important to recognize not all folk preachers are able to whoop, whooping may be one of the most characteristic distinctives of Black folk preaching. Frank Thomas offers the following definition: "Whooping is the rhetorical practice, traditionally at the end of the sermon, in which

---

[38] Evelyn Brooks Higginbotham, *Righteous Discontent: The Women's Movement in the Black Baptist Church, 1880–1920* (Cambridge, Mass.: Harvard University Press, 1993), 41.

[39] O. C. Edwards, *A History of Preaching* (Nashville: Abingdon, 2004), 531.

[40] Walter Pitts, "West African Poetics in the Black Preaching Style," *American Speech* 64, no. 2 (Summer 1989): 137.

[41] Frank A. Thomas, *Introduction to the Practice of African American Preaching* (Nashville: Abingdon, 2016), 14.

[42] W. E. B. DuBois, *The Souls of Black Folk*, in *W. E. B. DuBois: Writings: The Suppression of the African Slave Trade/The Souls of Black Folk/Dusk of Dawn/Essays*, ed. Nathan Huggins (New York: Library of America, 1987), 494.

the preacher sings or chants in rhythmic cadence in the vernacular of call and response that raises the emotional intensity and impact of the sermon."[43] The key feature, according to Martha Simmons, is "tonality."[44] Unfortunately, all too often Black folk preaching that employs whooping and other elements of folk preaching is characterized as lacking in intelligence, wisdom, and structure. However, nothing could be further from the truth for many Black folk preachers of the past and present. At its best, Black folk proclamation has been a tremendous sign of indigenous wisdom, creativity, and insight being used to bring glory to God and sustain a marginalized people through centuries of brutal enslavement and injustice. While this stream was dominant during the early years of Black preaching, it began to diminish somewhat with the rise of the intellectual preaching stream.

This latter emerged mostly from people in the North. Its practitioners often were free by birth or purchase and had some type of educational training. Intellectual preaching tended to employ deductive reasoning, formal language, and a didactic tone. Some early examples include John Chavis, Absalom Jones, and Hosea Easton. While many intellectual preachers saw the dramatic displays of folk preaching as "undignified, emotional, illiterate, buffoonery, and embarrassing," some skillfully employed characteristics of folk preaching in what has been called a "mixed-type sermon," that is, a sermon that merged the folk and intellectual styles to engage a broader audience.[45] Thus, as mentioned above, it is best not to see the two streams as fully independent. Over time they have progressively informed each other in subtle and not so subtle ways. Indeed, some of the most noted Black preachers have been those who integrate from both streams, such as Rev. Dr. Charles G. Adams (known as "the Harvard whooper"), Rev. Dr. Gina M. Stewart, Rev. Jennifer L. Carner, and Rev. Reginald W. Sharpe Jr. In short, the intellectual and folk streams are two important and interrelated aspects of Black preaching from which Black contemplative preaching emerges. Much more could be said about the beginnings of

---

[43] Thomas, *Introduction to the Practice*, 15.

[44] Martha Simmons, "Whooping: The Musicality of African American Preaching Past and Present," in Simmons and Thomas, *Preaching with Sacred Fire*, 864.

[45] Thomas, *Introduction to the Practice*, 14; Wallace D. Best, *Passionately Human, No Less Divine: Religion and Culture in Black Chicago, 1915–1952* (Princeton: Princeton University Press, 2005), 94–100.

Black preaching, but this provides sufficient context to begin to explore some of the forerunners of Black contemplative preaching.

African American Forerunners of Black Contemplative Preaching

From the earliest beginnings of Black preaching, African American preachers have reflected a contemplative orientation in at least some of their life, thought, and/or proclamation. These preachers were shaped both by the various historical and cultural roots and the particular ethos of early African American Christian preaching in North America. In this section, we encounter five early Black preachers who evince a mystical or contemplative dimension in their life and preaching: Lemuel Haynes, Richard Allen, Jarena Lee, Rebecca Cox Jackson, and Mordecai Wyatt Johnson. They anticipate many of the distinctives I will delineate as constitutive of Black contemplative preaching in the final section of this chapter.

The biracial Congregationalist minister Lemuel Haynes (1753–1833) was born to an African American father and a European American mother. Undesired by either of his parents, he was raised by a White family in Massachusetts, where he was an indentured servant until he turned twenty-one. Despite his difficult beginnings, Haynes became a prominent leader in early North America. Among other things, Haynes was a veteran of the American Revolution, an early advocate for human liberty, and one of the first Black pastors of a White church in the United States. While Haynes studied privately for ministry, he was recognized as an erudite minister and was bestowed an honorary master of arts degree by Middlebury College. Simmons and Thomas identify Haynes as "an exemplar of the little-written-about black contemplative preacher."[46]

Haynes' contemplative proclamation is apparent in a meditative sermon he preached entitled "The Presence of God," based on Genesis 4:16, the story of Cain being sent "away from the presence of the LORD" to settle in the land of Nod after killing his brother Abel.[47] As he was an educated preacher, Haynes' sermon utilizes deductive

---

[46] Simmons and Thomas, *Preaching with Sacred Fire*, 56.
[47] Scripture reference from *The New Oxford Annotated Bible: New Revised Standard Version* (New York: Oxford University Press, 2010). See Lemuel Haynes, "The Presence of the

reasoning, formal language, and a didactic tone. Distinguishing between the "essential presence" of God and the "sensible presence" of God, Haynes suggests that the essential presence of God is the inescapable ubiquity of the divine nearness, but the sensible presence of God is sensitivity to God's nearness in particular places where God chooses to be made known (e.g., the story of Jacob in Genesis 28).[48] In the words of Robert Smith Jr., Haynes is "doing *contemplative theology* as a preacher."[49] Reflecting the inclusive worldview of his African ancestors, Haynes' contemplative sermon is a stirring call to live awake to the reality of God's pervasive presence. His deep spirituality, intellectual orientation, and meditative proclamation all signify him as an early Black contemplative preacher.

A second forerunner of Black contemplative preaching is Richard Allen (1760–1831). Born to enslaved parents in Philadelphia, Allen converted to the Christian faith as a teenager and soon after began preaching as part of the Methodist preaching circuit. However, eventually, Allen left the Methodist church due to its recalcitrant racist liturgical practices. For a time, he was part of a Quaker community as he founded the Free African Society, a social organization that provided support to Blacks and advocated for abolition. In time, Allen left the Quaker community and, with others, started the African Methodist Episcopal (AME) church, the first historically Black Protestant denomination.

Teresa Fry Brown, the historiographer of the AME church and Bandy Professor of Preaching at Candler School of Theology, has described Allen as a representative of the Black church's overlooked contemplative preaching tradition.[50] While we have few records of Allen's contemplative preaching, the excerpts of his speeches that we

---

Lord," in *Black Preacher to White America: The Collected Writings of Lemuel Haynes, 1774–1833*, ed. Richard Newman (Brooklyn: Carlson, 1990), 143–47.

[48] Haynes, "Presence of the Lord," 143.

[49] Robert Smith Jr., "Preaching as a Contemplative Theological Task," in *Our Sufficiency Is of God: Essays on Preaching in Honor of Gardner C. Taylor*, ed. Timothy George, James Earl Massey, and Robert Smith Jr. (Macon, Ga.: Mercer University Press, 2010), 151, author's italics.

[50] I heard Rev. Dr. Teresa Fry Brown make this comment at a 2019 address to the Academy of Homiletics in Denver, Colorado.

do have witness to a rather didactic approach to preaching somewhat similar to Haynes. However, the case for Allen as a progenitor of contemplative preaching is perhaps best made by considering his spiritual disposition and mystical orientation as manifested in his proclamatory prayers, particularly the prayers on the theological virtues of faith, hope, and love included in his autobiography.[51] The prayers reflect what mystical theologian Andrew Prevot calls "doxological contemplation," that is, prayer oriented toward the glory of God while simultaneously affirming God's concern for the struggles of the oppressed.[52] For example, in his prayer focused on hope, Allen proclaims,

> O, my God! in all my dangers temporal and spiritual I will hope in thee who art Almighty power, and therefore able to relieve me; who art infinite goodness, and therefore ready and willing to assist me. O precious blood of my dear Redeemer! O gaping wounds of my crucified Saviour! Who can contemplate the sufferings of God incarnate, and not raise his hope, and not put his trust in him. What though my body be crumbled into dust, and that dust blown over the face of the earth, yet I undoubtedly know my Redeemer lives, and shall raise me up at the last day; whether I am comforted or left desolate; whether I enjoy peace or am afflicted with temptations, whether I am healthful or sickly, succoured or abandoned by the good things of this life, I will always hope in thee, O my chiefest, infinite good.[53]

Among other things, Allen's moving prayer testifies to his practice of contemplating God as the ultimate source of hope, a practice that no doubt sustained his activism and preaching in the AME church. In the tradition of Augustine, Allen understood that the preacher must be a pray-er above all else. As such, he is a model of one of the key themes that will emerge among later Black contemplative preachers.

One of the first women to be authorized to preach in the AME church received (belated) approval to do so from Richard Allen. Her name was Jarena Lee (1783–1850). Likely born a free woman in Cape May, New Jersey, Lee was influenced in her early life by

---

[51] Richard Allen, *The Life, Experience, and Gospel Labors of the Rt. Rev. Richard Allen* (Philadelphia: F. Ford & M.A. Riply, 1880), 29–32.
[52] Andrew Prevot, *Thinking Prayer: Theology and Spirituality amid the Crises of Modernity* (Notre Dame, Ind.: University of Notre Dame Press, 2015), 286.
[53] Allen, *Life, Experience, and Gospel Labors*, 31.

Roman Catholics, Presbyterians, and Methodists before being drawn to the ministry of the AME church. Though Lee lived in an era when women preachers were highly unusual and persecuted, somewhat like her African ancestor Kimpa Vita she received a vision in 1807 and sensed a call to preach. Following the call, she withdrew to a "secret place" to pray and had a profound mystical encounter with God that clearly and visually confirmed her call to preach.[54] Even before receiving approval from Allen, she became an itinerant preacher, confident that her gender should not be a barrier to her participation in the work of gospel ministry. Indeed, Joy Bostic in her seminal work *African American Female Mysticism* claims that "Jarena Lee may serve as a paradigmatic figure for black female mystical activism."[55]

Throughout her life, Lee traveled thousands of miles preaching the gospel, driven by her emancipatory and empowering mystical experiences. As Eunjoo Mary Kim notes, it was the Holy Spirit that offered Lee "critical insights and penetrating intuition to interpret the Bible and deepen her theological understanding of the Christian gospel."[56] In her autobiography, having reflected at length on her call to ministry and extensive preaching experience, Lee concludes with words that bear witness to her dependence on the Spirit of God in her Scriptural interpretation and proclamation:

> So it may be with such as [I] am, who has never had more than three months schooling; and wishing to know much of the way and law of God, have therefore watched the more closely the operations of the Spirit, and have in consequence been led thereby. But let it be remarked that [I] have never found that Spirit to lead me contrary to the Scriptures of truth, as I understand them. "For as many as are led by the Spirit of God are the sons of God."– Rom. viii. 14. I have now only to say, May the blessing of the Father, and of the

---

[54] Jarena Lee, "The Life and Religious Experience of Jarena Lee," in *Sisters of the Spirit: Three Black Women's Autobiographies of the Nineteenth Century*, ed. William L. Andrews (Bloomington: Indiana University Press, 1986), 35.

[55] Joy R. Bostic, *African American Female Mysticism: Nineteenth-Century Religious Activism* (New York: Palgrave Macmillan, 2013), 49.

[56] Eunjoo Mary Kim, *Women Preaching: Theology and Practice through the Ages* (Eugene, Ore.: Wipf & Stock, 2004), 102.

Son, and of the Holy Ghost, accompany the reading of this poor effort to speak well of his name, wherever it may be read. AMEN.[57]

Lee claims that her extraordinary preaching ministry has been possible because she learned to follow closely the operations of the Spirit. Her deep sensitivity to the work of the Spirit and practice of retreating to a secret place for prayer and contemplation was critical to her public life of bearing witness to the liberating gospel of Jesus, especially given the persecution she faced as a woman. As such, she is a remarkable forerunner of Black contemplative preaching.

Another important female forerunner of Black contemplative preaching is Rebecca Cox Jackson (1795–1871). Born as a free woman near Philadelphia, in her early life Jackson was affiliated with the AME church where her older brother was a preacher, but later in life she was drawn to the Shaker community, a millenarian spiritualist group. An offshoot of the Quakers, the Shakers valued direct spiritual encounters with the divine alongside celibacy, egalitarian leadership, and charismatic worship. The Shakers were quick to recognize Jackson's spiritual authority and gifting as a preacher. She evinced what Donyelle McCray has called a "mystical homiletic" in that she sought to foster "divine consciousness" as she preached inside and outside of traditional pulpit spaces as a Shaker healer, visionary, and minister.[58]

Unfortunately, to my knowledge, we have no records of her sermons. However, Jean McMahon Humez writes that Jackson's "skills as a public preacher were recognized by the leadership as very unusual. With the exception of eldresses, Shaker sisters did not ordinarily preach—although they did act as spirit instruments, or mouthpieces of the divine, in great numbers. But Rebecca Jackson preached frequently in the Sabbath Shaker meetings that were open to the non-Shaker 'world.'"[59] One early record after a Shaker meeting states, "Sister Rebecca Jackson rose up and spoke beautifully of

---

[57] Lee, "Life and Religious Experience of Jarena Lee," 48.
[58] Donyelle C. McCray, *The Censored Pulpit: Julian of Norwich as Preacher* (Minneapolis: Fortress Academic, 2019), 101.
[59] Jean McMahon Humez, Introduction to *Gifts of Power: The Writings of Rebecca Jackson, Black Visionary, Shaker Eldress*, by Rebecca Cox Jackson, ed. Jean McMahon Humez (Boston: University of Massachusetts Press, 1981), 28.

the good way of God."[60] Jackson appreciated the Shaker community, but she ultimately felt an obligation to engage more directly with the Black community. As part of her contemplative ministry, she started a Black Shaker community in Philadelphia. During this time, she apparently developed a relationship with her contemporary Jarena Lee, who encouraged Jackson in her proclamation of the gospel. In her autobiography, Jackson tells of a visit that she received from Lee around January 1, 1857, in which the two shared a time of prayer and encouragement:

> Sister Jarena Lee called to see me, under the influence of a very kind and friendly spirit. . . . When she got up to go, she said, "I do not know as I would do my duty if I should go away without a word of prayer. Sister, is thee willing?" "Well," I said, "it is our order to pray always." . . . So she sung a few verses and kneeled, and prayed a feeling prayer—and, I believe, a very sincere one. She prayed that the Lord might open the door for me to preach the Gospel, and also prayed for a blessing on my household. To my great surprise, when she was done I felt a gift to pray. . . . Thus have I commenced my New Year. And I pray that it may continue until there shall not be one enemy left, that will not desire that the Gospel of true salvation may be preached to all the world.[61]

While the context of Jackson's words seems to imply that there was some previous tension in her relationship with Lee, here we find a rare picture of two early Black female mystics reconciling, engaging in prayer, and committing themselves to the proclamation of the gospel. It is no wonder that James Earl Massey mentioned Jackson as part of the early tradition of Black contemplative preachers.[62]

The final preacher I consider as a forerunner of Black contemplative preaching is Mordecai Wyatt Johnson (1890–1976). The son of a former slave and Baptist pastor, Johnson was an influential early leader among African Americans in the twentieth century. He received his education at Atlanta Baptist College (now Morehouse College), the University of Chicago, Rochester Theological Seminary, and Harvard University. He went on to serve as the first Black president of the historic Howard University, where he was influential in developing its

---

[60] Humez, "Introduction," 28.
[61] Jackson, *Gifts of Power*, 262–63.
[62] James Earl Massey, "Contemplative Preaching," unpublished manuscript, 10.

national reputation as a leading Black college. Throughout this time, he was known as a respected orator.

Most importantly, for our purposes, Simmons and Thomas describe him as "a contemplative African American preacher."[63] His contemplative proclamation is visible in his sermon "Work, Business, and Religion," preached on August 10, 1924.[64] Drawing on 1 Corinthians 6:19 and Psalm 90:17, Johnson uses a kind of mystical hermeneutic or interpretive lens to make two primary arguments. The first is that "there cannot be any separation between business and work and religion" because the same Spirit-filled human body is engaged in each of the different arenas.[65] The second argument he makes is that "wherever the spirit of God is expressed in a man's work, that work is holy and is itself a religious act wherein a man is in direct touch with the living God."[66] In essence, reflecting the holistic spirituality of his African ancestors, Johnson argues for the unity of all of life and work under God's care. Reflecting on Johnson's sermon, Simmons and Thomas write that it demonstrates Johnson's "controlled and creative tone, his devotional demeanor, accented logic, and grand vision of a healthy relationship between religion and society."[67] Johnson would go on to be one of the significant mentors in the life of a young man by the name of Howard Thurman—the preacher we will explore in the next chapter. However, before turning to his life, I would like to offer a working definition of Black contemplative preaching and its distinctives.

Defining Black Contemplative Preaching

As a way of bringing together the threads of the unrecognized tradition I explore in this chapter, I propose the following definition of Black contemplative preaching: *Black contemplative preaching is proclamation that (1) emerges from a habitus or disposition of prayer, (2) employs a mystical hermeneutical lens, and (3) embodies a meditative homiletical style in order to*

---

[63] Simmons and Thomas, *Preaching with Sacred Fire*, 418.
[64] Mordecai Wyatt Johnson, "Work, Business, and Religion," in Simmons and Thomas, *Preaching with Sacred Fire*, 418–23.
[65] Johnson, "Work, Business, and Religion," 418–19.
[66] Johnson, "Work, Business, and Religion," 418.
[67] Johnson, "Work, Business, and Religion," 418.

lead listeners into a divine encounter that contributes to the flourishing of African Americans and all creation. While there are other potential features of Black contemplative proclamation depending on a host of factors related to the speaker and context of proclamation, my definition highlights three distinctives. First, I propose that Black contemplative preaching emerges from a disposition or habitus of prayer.[68] The term *habitus* has its roots in the word *hexis*, which appears in Aristotle's *Nicomachean Ethics*.[69] For Aristotle, *hexis* (later translated into Latin as *habitus* by Aquinas) refers to "an acquired yet entrenched state of moral character that orients our feelings and desires, and thence our conduct."[70] I use the term *habitus of prayer* to refer to the cultivation of a contemplative way of being and seeing that is attentive to God and God's world. Almost all Black preaching emerges from prayer, but Black contemplative preaching flows from a contemplative way of life cultivated through stillness, introspection, and various forms of meditation alongside more expressive Africana embodied spiritual practices. Ideally, this leads the sermon to being less of a "product" or "performance" and more of a prayer.[71] However, given that the habitus of prayer is integrally connected to the contemplative life of the preacher, it is not always easily discernible in the sermon itself. Nevertheless, it can be glimpsed. As rhetorical scholar Edwin Black notes, there are "tokens of the author" that can be observed in a speech or sermon.[72] This is to say that glimpses of the character of the preacher can be revealed through close analysis of a sermon. Something of the person of the preacher is unavoidably manifested in the sermon itself. As such, a preacher's habitus of prayer can be glimpsed in an opening

---

[68] I draw this illuminating phrase from James Keating, "Contemplative Homiletics: Being Carried into Reality," *Nova et Vetera* 17, no. 1 (2019): 5. Unfortunately, Keating does not offer a robust definition of the term.

[69] Aristotle, *Aristotle's Nicomachean Ethics*, trans. Robert C. Bartlett and Susan D. Collins (Chicago: University of Chicago Press, 2011).

[70] Loïc Wacquant, "A Concise Genealogy and Anatomy of Habitus," in *The Oxford Handbook of Pierre Bourdieu*, ed. Thomas Medvetz and Jeffrey J. Sallaz (New York: Oxford University Press, 2019), 528.

[71] Lisa Cressman, *Backstory Preaching: Integrating Life, Spirituality, and Craft* (Collegeville, Minn.: Liturgical, 2018), 9.

[72] Edwin Black, "The Second Persona," in *Contemporary Rhetorical Theory: A Reader*, 2nd ed., ed. Mark J. Porrovecchio and Celeste Michelle Condit (New York: Guilford Press, 2016), 296.

or closing sermonic prayer, a personal story or illustration, or in sermonic content related to prayer or spirituality in general.

Second, Black contemplative preaching employs a mystical hermeneutical lens. At its most basic level, a mystical hermeneutic is not about the venerable tradition of seeking the *sensus plenior* (or fuller meaning) of texts;[73] nor is it simply about ecstatic mystical experiences. Rather it refers to reading and interpreting Scripture and other texts with a bias toward an emancipatory encounter with God. In other words, a liberating, "direct experience of God" is the ultimate aim.[74] Of course, all Black preaching is committed to seeking to encounter the living God in Scripture. However, the mystical hermeneutic of Black contemplative preaching is further characterized by three things that set it apart: a focus on certain biblical texts and/or themes related to divine encounter (especially in the Psalms and Gospels); incorporation of varied sources of spiritual wisdom and guidance to nurture interiority (such as ancestral wisdom, philosophy, poetry, hymns); and an inclusive, nondualistic vision for cultivating a lifegiving and liberating relationship with God, self, neighbor, and creation.[75]

Third and finally, the most obvious distinctive of Black contemplative preaching is its meditative homiletical style. It almost never involves whooping. In this sense, Black contemplative preaching often appears to lack what has been called the most characteristic feature of

---

[73] Origen (184–253 CE) was one of the first Christian theologians to propose a systematic way to read Scripture for its multiple senses with his three-fold allegorical method. See Origen, *On First Principles: A Reader's Edition*, trans. John Behr (New York: Oxford University Press, 2020).

[74] Celia Kourie, "Reading Scripture through a Mystical Lens," *Acta Theologica* 31, no. 15 (2011): 141. Kourie states: "A mystical hermeneutic of scripture is one in which a direct experience of God, or Ultimate Reality, or the One is the end result." Future research should relate the mystical hermeneutic of Black contemplative preachers to Barbara Holmes's intriguing notion of "griosh," a contemplative reading of Scripture informed by the tradition of the African storyteller or griot and the practice of Jewish midrash. See Holmes, *Joy Unspeakable*, 95.

[75] I realize the term nondual is used in multiple ways, as noted by Cynthia Bourgeault in *The Heart of Centering Prayer: Nondual Christianity in Theory and Practice* (Boulder: Shambhala, 2016), 43–52. Here I use the term as it is often employed by Richard Rohr. Rohr suggests that a nondualistic or contemplative way of seeing can move us beyond "the dualistic thinking" that is "the foundation of almost all the discontent and violence in the world." See Richard Rohr, *The Naked Now: Learning to See as the Mystics See* (New York: Crossroad, 2009), 29.

Black preaching—a celebratory, uplifting sermon close. However, it may be that Black contemplative preaching does not completely lack a celebratory dimension; rather, it simply transposes celebration into a different modality than is commonly expected. Noted homiletician Cleophus LaRue reminds us that there are many forms of celebration in Black preaching, including meditative, contemplative expressions.[76]

One final note: the distinctives of Black contemplative preaching correlate broadly with Aristotle's three means of persuasion.[77] Thus, the habitus of prayer reflects the ethos (or the character) of the preacher, the mystical hermeneutic reflects the logos (or the logical arguments) of the preacher, and the meditative homiletical style reflects the pathos (or the emotional appeal) of the preacher. This will be demonstrated later as I explore the theo-rhetorical dimensions through close readings of contemplative sermons.

To be sure, the definition of Black contemplative preaching that I have articulated is fluid—not least because I am speaking of something as slippery as contemplation. Contemplative proclamation manifests in a multiplicity of ways. In fact, some exemplars of it may reflect features that I have not articulated. And, of course, all labels have their limits. Nevertheless, I argue that a habitus of prayer, a mystical hermeneutic, and a meditative homiletical style are three distinctives that most often manifest in contemplative preaching. While they also partially appear in other expressions of Black preaching, together they reflect the unique Black contemplative preaching stream.

With this definition in mind, we now turn to explore the story of Black contemplative preaching in the twentieth century. We begin with Howard Thurman.

---

[76] Cleophus J. LaRue, *Rethinking Celebration: From Rhetoric to Praise in African American Preaching* (Louisville: Westminster John Knox, 2016), 52.

[77] Aristotle, *On Rhetoric: A Theory of Civic Discourse*, trans. and ed. George A. Kennedy (New York: Oxford University Press, 1991), I.2, 1355b26–27.

2
Creating a Friendly World
Howard Thurman as Contemplative Preacher

> The core of my preaching has always concerned itself with the development of the inner resources needed for the creation of a friendly world of friendly men.
>
> Howard Thurman, *With Head and Heart*[1]

Introduction

Over thirty years before the celebration of the first Earth Day and the establishment of the Environmental Protection Agency in the United States, a young Howard Thurman delivered a lecture entitled "Man and the World of Nature" to religious leaders at the National Assembly of Student Christian Associations at Miami University in Oxford, Ohio.[2] The group was composed of 1,350 delegates and other personnel representing over 300 higher education institutions from forty-three states as well as countries outside the United States. Among other things, echoing the humanitarian Albert Schweitzer, Thurman challenged the leaders in attendance to cultivate "a kind of reverence for all expressions of life" as part of an ethic that would contribute towards creation's flourishing.[3] While such eco-conscious religious proclamation or "creation-crisis preaching" is slowly becoming less of an anomaly amid the fierce challenges facing our fragile planet in the early twenty-first century, this was not the case

---

[1] Howard Thurman, *With Head and Heart: The Autobiography of Howard Thurman* (New York: Harcourt Brace, 1979), 160.
[2] Howard Thurman, "Man and the World of Nature," in *The Papers of Howard Washington Thurman*, vol. 2, *Christian, Who Calls Me Christian? April 1936–August 1943*, ed. Walter Earl Fluker (Columbia: University of South Carolina Press, 2012).
[3] Thurman, "Man and the World of Nature," 105.

in Thurman's time.⁴ Thurman was an outlier. It was not common to address ecological issues from a faith perspective, especially among Black religious leaders. However, as leading Thurman scholar Walter Earl Fluker asserts, throughout Thurman's life, without the "sentimentalizing of nature," he demonstrated a profound attention to and concern for the natural world.⁵ Though he didn't articulate a full-blown systematic ecotheology, Thurman's contemplative disposition and vision led him to affirm the interrelatedness of all life and to teach and preach in ways that promoted wholeness for all people and creation. Given our current climate emergency and profound polarization and division, Thurman's contemplative proclamation is an important source of wisdom for us to learn from. But who was Howard Thurman? And on what basis might we claim he was a contemplative preacher?

Howard Washington Thurman (1899–1981) was a trailblazing African American mystic, philosopher, and pastor who lived during tumultuous times of war, racism, and intransigent segregation.⁶ In the midst of the various personal and social crises he faced, he founded one of the first interracial churches in the United States—the Church for the Fellowship of All Peoples, worked as the dean of Chapel at Boston University and Howard University, and served as the director of religious life at Morehouse College and Spelman College. In *Preaching with Sacred Fire*, Martha Simmons and Frank Thomas describe Thurman as one of the most notable exemplars of the understudied Black contemplative preaching stream.⁷ I wholeheartedly agree. This complements the work of Luther Smith, whose groundbreaking work, *Howard Thurman: The Mystic as Prophet*, argued that Thurman's "primary identity was that

---

⁴ Leah Schade, *Creation-Crisis Preaching: Ecology, Theology, and the Pulpit* (St. Louis, Mo.: Chalice, 2015).

⁵ Walter Earl Fluker, introduction to Howard Thurman, "Man and the World of Nature," 102.

⁶ This chapter is an expansion of my article "Hidden in Plain Sight: Reclaiming the Witness and Wisdom of Black Contemplative Preachers," *Homiletic* 47, no. 2 (2022): 3–14.

⁷ Martha Simmons and Frank Thomas, eds., *Preaching with Sacred Fire: An Anthology of African American Sermons, 1750 to the Present* (New York: W. W. Norton, 2010), 492.

of mystic."[8] Of course, it is important to note that Thurman never explicitly described himself as a contemplative preacher. Moreover, he was resistant to labeling his religious experience. He once stated, "I think there's something so wonderful and free about being able to experience life, or reality, or religion without being bothered about how you label it."[9] While I am sympathetic to Thurman's resistance, there is value in using labels as a heuristic device to better understand and appreciate the particularities of a phenomenon—even if the labels have their limits. With this in mind, I argue that Thurman is one of the most significant representatives of the homiletical theology of Black contemplative preaching and that his holistic spirituality offers critical wisdom for our fragmented world today.

Reflecting on the preaching of the interracial Fellowship Church where he pastored in San Francisco, Thurman once wrote, "The preaching deals almost always with the practices of religion and man's encounter with the Spirit of the Living God. Very little of the preaching concerns itself with social issues as they are generally conceived. It is never forgotten that we are a church and not merely some kind of social whip and protest group. We propose to offer experiences of deep moment for the spirit of man during which he can reestablish his sense of direction, lift his sights, renew his commitment and get strength for the struggles of life at the point of his vocation and function."[10] Thurman's preaching ministry addressed the glaring issues of racism and segregation somewhat indirectly. As a mystic, he focused on the liberating possibilities present when one encounters the Spirit of the living God, and, in the words of James Earl Massey,

---

[8] Luther Smith, *Howard Thurman: The Mystic as Prophet*, 3rd ed. (Richmond, Ind.: Friends United, 2007), 15. For a study on the mystical dimensions of Thurman's aesthetic see Amy Elizabeth Steele, "The Mystical Aesthetic: Howard Thurman and the Art of Meaning" (PhD diss., Vanderbilt University, 2012). See also Amy E. Steele's illuminating article "Howard Thurman and the Roots of a Black Mystical Aesthetic," *Spectrum: A Journal on Black Men* 9, nos. 1–2 (Autumn 2021): 183–210.

[9] Howard Thurman, *Mysticism and Social Action: Lawrence Lecture and Discussions with Dr Howard Thurman* (International Association for Religious Freedom, 2015), loc. 358 of 1080, Kindle.

[10] Howard Thurman, "Building a Friendly World," *Growing Edge* (Winter 1950): 13, quoted in Alton Pollard, *Mysticism and Social Change: The Social Witness of Howard Thurman* (New York: Peter Lang, 1992), 75.

attended to "the renewal of the inner life."[11] For Thurman, preaching in the context of worship was a kind of Spirit-animated intervention to unshackle the soul from the fetters of oppression. Or, to put it still another way, his preaching was an attempt to free people internally, so that they might be energized by the Spirit to be agents of freedom externally. Thurman knew that he could not accomplish this on his own. Thus, similar to Lemuel Haynes and Rebecca Jackson, he sought to prayerfully lead people to an emancipatory encounter with God. Or, as Patrick Clayborn puts it, Thurman's "homiletic of spirituality" embraced preaching as "a lively guide for the human spirit and for the formation of community" in God.[12] In doing so, Thurman embodied the three distinctives that I argue make up Black contemplative preaching—a habitus of prayer, mystical hermeneutic, and meditative homiletical style.

Becoming Prayer

Howard Thurman's habitus or disposition of prayer emerged through several experiences and influences during his early life in Daytona Beach, Florida. For one, Thurman was naturally interested in spiritual matters in his community. In his autobiography, *With Head and Heart*, he says, "I prayed to God, I talked to Jesus . . . God was a reality. Jesus was a fact."[13] Reflecting the holistic religious worldview of his African ancestors, for Thurman, all of life was charged with a sense of the sacred.[14] This was seen in the extended time he spent in introspection enjoying "the strength of the quiet and the aliveness of the woods."[15] Thurman especially appreciated a special oak tree that provided him companionship.[16] Indeed, in the words of Donyelle McCray, trees became an essential "part of the landscape of Howard's

---

[11] James Earl Massey, "Thurman's Preaching: Substance and Style," in *God and Human Freedom: A Festschrift in Honor of Howard Thurman*, ed. Henry J. Young (Richmond, Ind.: Friends United, 1983), 114.

[12] Patrick Clayborn, "A Homiletic of Spirituality: An Analysis of Howard Thurman's Theory and Praxis of Preaching" (PhD diss., Drew University, 2009), 204.

[13] Thurman, *With Head and Heart*, 266.

[14] Clayborn, "Homiletic of Spirituality," 108.

[15] Thurman, *With Head and Heart*, 7.

[16] Thurman, *With Head and Heart*, 7.

prayer life."[17] He found spirituality, nature, and prayer crucial for survival. However, Thurman did not approach prayer as a tool through which humans find God. Rather, as he later wrote, he believed that "fundamental to the total fact of prayer in the Christian religion is the persuasive affirmation that the God of religious experience is a seeking and a beseeching God."[18] In other words, we can only find God because God has first found us. This was good news for young Thurman, as he faced challenges in his youth. Along with experiencing sadness in childhood due to his father's death, Thurman felt his racialized environment "left its scars deep in [his] spirit."[19] He recovered a sense of connection with life through contemplation of the natural world. In other words, God met him in nature. Thinking back upon his childhood, Thurman wrote, "I had the sense that all things—the sand, the sea, the stars, the night, and I—were one lung through which all of life was breathing."[20] To echo Timothy Robinson, Thurman's disposition of prayer led him to not only relate to humans differently but to also "think differently" about his relationship to the more-than-human creation.[21] Much like St. Francis, he saw trees, lakes, bees, dogs, and more as part of a single tapestry of life. Said differently, he developed a disposition of attentiveness not only to God but also to God's creation.

Another important early influence on Thurman's cultivation of a disposition of prayer was his grandmother Nancy Ambrose, who was formerly enslaved. Along with the Baptist church in which Thurman was raised, Ambrose served as a central channel through which the rich holistic, communal spirituality of Thurman's African ancestors

---

[17] Donyelle C. McCray, "Solomon's Son: The Wise Tenderness of Howard Thurman," in *Can I Get a Witness? Thirteen Peacemakers, Community Builders, and Agitators for Faith and Justice*, ed. Charles Marsh, Shea Tuttle, and Daniel P. Rhodes (Grand Rapids: Eerdmans, 2019), 51.

[18] Howard Thurman, *The Creative Encounter: An Interpretation of Religion and the Social Witness* (Richmond, Ind.: Friends United, [1954] 1972), 38.

[19] Howard Thurman, *The Luminous Darkness: A Personal Interpretation of the Anatomy of Segregation and the Ground of Hope* (Richmond, Ind.: Friends United, 1965), x.

[20] Thurman, *Mysticism and Social Action*, loc. 132 of 1080, Kindle.

[21] Timothy Robinson, "He Talked to Trees! 'Thinking Differently' about Nature with Howard Thurman," *Spiritus* 21, no. 1 (Spring 2021): 12. Robinson draws the phrase "thinking differently" from the ecofeminist philosopher Val Plumwood.

flowed. Long before Thurman would formally study mystical spirituality with Quaker scholar Rufus Jones, Ambrose was introducing him to a lifegiving Christian spirituality "forged in the fiery furnace of slavery."[22] One story Thurman's grandmother often told him was of a slave preacher who would always end his sermons declaring to the enslaved, "You are not slaves, you are not niggers—you are God's children."[23] This instilled in Thurman that despite there being no successful "revolution" to dismantle structures of oppression, he could still have a strong sense of dignity, worth, and value.[24] In other words, Ambrose was an example of one who had cultivated a habitus of prayer that could sustain her against the vicissitudes of life. Another key way that Ambrose shaped Thurman was by introducing him to Psalm 139. This was Ambrose's favorite Scripture, and it was through her that Thurman came to count it as his favorite passage. Indeed, Thurman once said that if the whole Bible was destroyed and only one portion could be preserved, he would choose Psalm 139.[25] Its vision of a life lived enveloped by the caring and universal presence of the Spirit of God became the mode in which Thurman lived.

These early influences and experiences, among others, shaped how Thurman came to understand the value of the preacher's habitus of prayer as an ordained Baptist minister. In the words of Kenyatta Gilbert, for Thurman, preaching was a "form of prayer as well as its fruit."[26] Indeed, he observed that "when a man prays he is not merely performing an act, he is *being* something."[27] In other words, prayer is cultivating a way of being. For Thurman, this kind of attentiveness to God and God's world is the foundation out of which a preaching

---

[22] Diana Hayes, *Forged in the Fiery Furnace: African American Spirituality* (Maryknoll, N.Y.: Orbis, 2012), 2.

[23] Thurman, *With Head and Heart*, 21.

[24] Mary E. Goodwin, "Racial Roots and Religion: An Interview with Howard Thurman," *Christian Century* 90, no. 19, May 9, 1973, 533.

[25] Landrum Bolling, "Landrum Bolling Interviews Howard Thurman," January 17, 2013, YouTube video, 2:02:08, https://www.youtube.com/watch?v=CGX4-Wv9UD0&t=6259s.

[26] Kenyatta R. Gilbert, *The Journey and Promise of African American Preaching* (Minneapolis: Fortress, 2011), 138.

[27] Howard Thurman, *The Centering Moment* (Richmond, Ind.: Friends United, 1969), 11, author's italics.

ministry should emerge. Thus, later in life, while addressing ministry leaders on the discipline of prayer, Thurman once stated, "Sometimes, during each day, everything should stop, and the sheer art of becoming still be practiced. For some temperaments, this will not be easy, because the entire nervous system and organism have been geared over the years to activity, to overt intense functioning. Nevertheless, the art of being still must be practiced until development and habit are sure."[28] Thurman's description makes clear that, in the words of Lerita Coleman Brown, he "was practicing contemplative spirituality before we started calling it contemplative spirituality."[29] Or, at least, before it was popular to do so. Similar to spiritual writers like Thomas Keating, Thurman suggests that silence and stillness are important to developing a disposition of prayer in all of life, such that one has a deep "reservoir of interior silence" throughout ordinary activities.[30] Though he struggled with overwork and burnout throughout this life, he never gave up on trying to maintain rhythms of renewal through silence and meditation.[31] For Thurman, the practice of meditation should include attending to the body. As a Black person in the Jim Crow South in the early twentieth century, he was aware of how racial trauma "always happens *in the body*" and leaves scars in the soul.[32] Before his time, Thurman knew that in the midst of the stresses and strains of a racist society "the body keeps the score."[33] While recognizing that stillness and other contemplative practices

[28] Howard Thurman, "Dilemmas of the Religious Professional," Hester Lectures III, side A (Golden Gate Baptist Theological Seminary, Mill Valley, Calif., February 11, 1971), transcript from the Howard Thurman Digital Archive, Pitts Theology Library at Emory University, Atlanta, 2020, https://thurman.pitts.emory.edu/items/show/258.

[29] Lerita Coleman Brown, quoted in *Backs against the Wall: The Howard Thurman Story*, directed by Martin Doblemeier, American Public Television, 2019, https://www.pbs.org/video/backs-against-the-wall-the-howard-thurman-story-cgv9gi/.

[30] Thomas Keating, *Open Mind, Open Heart: The Contemplative Dimension of the Gospel* (New York: Continuum, 1997), 123.

[31] For some of the occasions of Thurman's overwork and burnout, see Peter Eisenstadt, *Against the Hounds of Hell: A Life of Howard Thurman* (Charlottesville: University of Virginia Press, 2021), 146, 159–60, 239, 363.

[32] Resmaa Menakem, *My Grandmother's Hands: Racialized Trauma and the Pathway to Mending Our Hearts and Bodies* (Las Vegas: Central Recovery, 2017), 7, author's italics.

[33] Bessel A. Van Der Kolk, *The Body Keeps the Score: Brain, Mind, and Body in the Healing of Trauma* (New York: Penguin, 2014).

might be difficult given the realities of modern society, he insists that they are essential, helping us to become more alive to ourselves, God, and God's world. And these practices are particularly crucial for the preacher, since preaching flows from a life of contemplation: "The sermon is the distillation of the thinking, reading, observation, brooding, and meditation of the preacher."[34]

Thurman's sermons often called others to develop the kind of disposition of prayer that he himself sought. For example, he typically offered readings of meditations and prayers before his sermons. "Their primary purpose," Thurman said, "is to aid the listeners in bringing their minds into focus upon some searching insight and to make available the centered spirits."[35] Sometimes these meditations were excerpts from books, poems, and prayers that Thurman found valuable in his personal and ministerial life. At other times, they came from Thurman's own private musings before the presence of God. In other words, Thurman's Spirit-guided life of prayer and formation in private was critical to his ability to nourish the spirits of his listeners in public. In the words of Luke Powery, we might say Thurman understood that "prayer is more than a utilitarian magic trick for a 'home run' sermon. It is an integrated part of a preacher's life that implies the essential movement of God within a preacher, whether preaching or not. It provides an interior space where the Spirit may work on us before she works on others in the congregation. . . . Prayer is more than an act we do just for the purpose of preaching; it is not a means to an end. It is a way of life that forms everything about a preacher."[36] Indeed, throughout his long ministry, Thurman embraced prayer as a way of life that shaped all he did in public.

Thurman's sermon's also focused on encouraging attentiveness to God and God's world. In the sermon entitled "The Mood to Linger,"

---

[34] Howard Thurman, "Worship and Word: A View of the Liberal Congregation and Its Sermons," in *The Papers of Howard Washington Thurman*, vol. 4, *The Soundless Passion of a Single Mind, June 1949–December 1962*, ed. Walter Earl Fluker (Columbia.: University of South Carolina Press, 2017), 331.

[35] Howard Thurman, *The Growing Edge* (Richmond, Ind.: Friends United, 1956), ix.

[36] Sally A. Brown and Luke A. Powery, *Ways of the Word: Learning to Preach for Your Time and Place* (Minneapolis: Fortress, 2016), 59.

reflecting on his experience of becoming alert to previous unknown sounds while walking at night, Thurman states, "There are things of which you cannot become aware, things you cannot sense until at last all of the surface of confusion and chaos and noise of your life is somehow quieted. And it is then that your ears pick up sounds that come from the deeper regions of your life."[37] Here we see Thurman inviting his listeners into a healing stillness. His words resonated: people were deeply impacted through hearing him preach. As one student reportedly said, "Some men talk about God, which is of value if it inspires devotion to him. But, when Howard Thurman speaks, you somehow experience God. He seems to take God with him; or rather, he seems propelled by God."[38] In essence, as a Spirit-guided preacher, Thurman was one who did not just say prayers: he lived prayer.

Seeking Common Ground

The second distinctive of Black contemplative preaching in Thurman is a mystical hermeneutic. As already suggested, his grandmother Nancy Ambrose shaped Thurman's penchant for reading from Scriptures that focused on divine encounter. For example, Ambrose loved hearing the Bible read and would often ask Thurman to read to her since she had been barred from learning to read as a former slave. She had Thurman read "the more devotional Psalms, some of Isaiah, [and] the Gospels again and again."[39] Through reading and reflecting on the Gospels with his grandmother, Thurman came to meditate deeply on Jesus' life and person. Thurman states, "I learned more, for instance, about the genius of the religion of Jesus from my grandmother than from all the men who taught me. . . . Because she moved inside the experience and lived out of that kind of center."[40] However, Ambrose also developed in Thurman a hermeneutic of suspicion that led him to think critically about the social performance of certain passages of Scripture. With the exception of 1 Corinthians 13, she would

---

[37] Howard Thurman, *Sermons on the Parables*, ed. David B. Gowler and Kipton E. Jensen (Maryknoll, N.Y.: Orbis, 2018), 122.
[38] Mary Jenness, *Twelve Negro Americans* (New York: Friendship Press, 1936), 153.
[39] Howard Thurman, *Jesus and the Disinherited* (Boston: Beacon, [1949] 1996), 30.
[40] Howard Thurman, interview by Roberta Byrd Barr, Seattle, Wash., January 1969, quoted in Smith, *Mystic as Prophet*, 39.

never let Thurman read from Paul, due to the way the slave masters used the apostle's writings to reinforce subservience.[41] In other words, long before Thurman would formally study hermeneutics or read liberal theology, he was introduced to the need to read Scripture in ways that spoke a lifegiving word to people with their "backs against the wall."[42]

Of course, Thurman would go on to receive formal instruction in theology at Rochester Theological Seminary (RTS) in New York. At Rochester, he studied with two notable liberal theologians, George Cross and Henry B. Robins, and was exposed to historical and critical Bible scholarship. Space does not permit a full study of how RTS shaped Thurman's theology, but let me note a few ways his experience seems to have affected his mystical hermeneutic. For one, though Thurman was skeptical of external religious authority before RTS, this tendency deepened in the course of his studies and shaped his reading of Scripture. Reflecting the religious subjectivity of Schleiermacher as filtered through Cross and Robins, Thurman came to focus "on philosophical and religious aspects of a text or of some experience in correspondence to biblical truths."[43] For Thurman, this was based on the assumption that nothing can supplant the importance of "the conscious and direct exposure of the individual to God."[44] Second, while at RTS, Thurman would have learned about historical and critical tools for understanding the biblical text. As a preacher and contributor to the *Interpreter's Bible Commentary*, Thurman demonstrated that he was "well-aware of the results of historical-critical methodology in biblical analysis."[45] However, given his early formation with his grandmother, he saw historical scholarship as complementing, not supplanting, his tendency to consider how scriptural texts spoke to the inner religious experience.[46] Third, at RTS, Thurman seems to have come to stress the priority of Jesus' exemplary

---

[41] Thurman, *Jesus and the Disinherited*, 30–31.
[42] Thurman, *Jesus and the Disinherited*, 15.
[43] Simmons and Thomas, *Preaching with Sacred Fire*, 576.
[44] Thurman, *Creative Encounter*, 20.
[45] Howard Thurman, "Exposition to the Book of Habakkuk" and "Exposition to the Book of Zephaniah," in *The Interpreter's Bible*, vol. 6, ed. George A. Buttrick et al. (Nashville: Abingdon, 1956); Robert A. Bennett, "Howard Thurman and the Bible," in Young, *God and Human Freedom*, 138.
[46] Bennett, "Howard Thurman and the Bible," 138.

religious experience over referencing Jesus as God incarnate. Indeed, Peter Eisenstadt notes that it was likely at RTS that Thurman referred to Jesus as "the Son of God" for the last time.[47] Space does not permit an analysis of Thurman's Christology.[48] I simply note that for Thurman Jesus was a poor, oppressed Jewish man who is worthy of emulation because of his unique experience of the divine. In other words, Jesus is to be followed as a guide for religious experience.

Thurman's mystical hermeneutic continued to develop over time. For example, it was in seminary that Thurman came across the writings of the South African feminist and author Olive Schreiner. Among other things, her work served as a catalyst to Thurman emphasizing "the unity of all of life" in his preaching.[49] As Thurman later wrote in an anthology he completed of her writings, *A Track to the Water's Edge: The Olive Schreiner Reader*, "[Olive Schreiner] possessed what comes through to me as an innate, instinctual sense of the unity of all life. It was this emphasis in her writing that was the first external confirmation of what had always been an active ingredient in my own awareness of life."[50] Later Thurman would continue his studies as a special student at Haverford College under the Quaker mystic Rufus Jones, who at the time was "the foremost American scholar of mysticism."[51] Under Jones, along with being exposed to Quaker thought and practice, Thurman was introduced to the formal study of mysticism, writing papers on mystics such as Madame Guyon, the seventeenth-century French mystic, and St. Francis of Assisi. He also took part in a seminar on Meister Eckhart. As Timothy Robinson notes, Thurman would learn to adapt the work of mystics such as Eckhart and St. Francis for prophetic ends.[52]

---

[47] Eisenstadt, *Against the Hounds of Hell*, 89.
[48] For an overview of Thurman's Christology, see Thurman, *Jesus and the Disinherited*, 11–35; Alonso Johnson, *Good News for the Disinherited: Howard Thurman on Jesus of Nazareth and Human Liberation* (Lanham, Md.: University Press of America, 1997); Smith, *Mystic as Prophet*, 62–72; and Clayborn, "Homiletic of Spirituality," 95–104.
[49] Thurman, *With Head and Heart*, 225.
[50] Thurman, *With Head and Heart*, 225. See Olive Schreiner, *A Track to the Water's Edge: The Olive Schreiner Reader*, ed. Howard Thurman (New York: Harper & Row, 1973).
[51] Eisenstadt, *Against the Hounds of Hell*, 112.
[52] Timothy Robinson, "'Resisting Whatever Separates One from the Ground of Being': Howard Thurman's Prophetic Appropriation of the Christian Mystical

Indeed, Thurman says this period of study was "a crucial experience, a watershed from which flowed much of the thought and endeavor to which I was to commit the rest of my working life."[53]

One of the obvious ways Thurman's time with Jones shaped his hermeneutic is seen in his openness to sources of spiritual wisdom and guidance outside the Scriptures. Some of his sermons encouraged the contemplation of spiritual exemplars in history, for example the sermon series entitled "Men Who've Walked with God," which explored the spiritual wisdom of figures such as Buddha, St. Francis, and Meister Eckhart.[54] Given Thurman's wide learning, his sermons were also populated with references from literature, philosophy, personal stories, poetry, and poignant observations from everyday life and nature.[55] Of course, at times, Thurman specifically addressed matters of prayer and contemplation. This is seen, for example, in his sermons "Prayer and Silence," "Prayer and Pressure," and others.[56] However, to cite Mozella Mitchell, even when Thurman is not explicitly speaking of prayer, he is almost always seeking to encourage "closer communion with God and with all of life."[57]

Thurman's commitment to pursuing communion with all creation led to a mystical hermeneutic that combined spirituality and social engagement. Indeed, Thurman's lifelong pursuit was "the search for common ground," that is, the search for community.[58] For example, due to a formative experience in India where he was one of the first African Americans to meet Gandhi, Thurman came to be an influential exponent of nonviolence to address the evils of racism and colonialism. He argued that these evils corroded the "spirit" or "soul" of

---

Tradition," in *Mysticism and Contemporary Life: Essays in Honor of Bernard McGinn*, ed. John J. Markey and J. August Higgins (New York: Herder & Herder, 2019), 127–44.

[53] Thurman, *With Head and Heart*, 77.

[54] Howard Thurman, *The Way of the Mystics*, ed. Peter Eisenstadt and Walter Earl Fluker (Maryknoll, N.Y.: Orbis, 2021).

[55] Massey, "Thurman's Preaching," 112.

[56] See, for instance, Thurman, *Growing Edge*, 29–53, and Thurman, *Sermons on the Parables*, 116–23.

[57] Mozella G. Mitchell, *Spiritual Dynamics of Howard Thurman's Theology* (Bristol, Ind.: Wyndham Hall, 1985), 90. Mitchell's words emerge in the context of her intriguing exploration of Thurman as a shaman, particularly in relationship to his view of conversion.

[58] Howard Thurman, *The Search for Common Ground: An Inquiry into the Basis of Man's Experience of Community* (Richmond, Ind.: Friends United, 1971).

both the oppressed and the oppressor.⁵⁹ As narrated in his important work *Jesus and the Disinherited*, he believed that the religion of Jesus offered a love ethic that challenges the fear, deception, and hatred that can dominate the lives of those with their backs against the wall.⁶⁰ This "liberating spirituality," or love ethic, was made visible in Thurman's sermons.⁶¹ As Gary Dorrien writes, Thurman's "sermons expounded a mystical vision of spiritual unity and an ethical-spiritual commitment to nonviolence, urging that all forms of violence, oppression, and prejudice offend against the divine good."⁶² For instance, after the gruesome murder of young Emmett Till at the hands of White supremacists in 1955, Thurman delivered a provocative series of sermons that, among other things, called for nonviolence in the Black community and warned against redefining our enemies "out of the human race."⁶³ Indeed, in the midst of the great pain Blacks experienced due to the horror of Till's murder, Thurman says to his enemies, "I must cultivate the inner spiritual resources of my life to such a point that I can bring you to my sanctuary, before His Presence, until, at last, I do not know you from myself."⁶⁴ Thurman's mystical hermeneutic also led him to address the more-than-human creation. For instance, a few months after the celebration of the first Earth Day in April 1970, Thurman preached a sermon at Colonial Church of Edina, Minnesota (now known as Meetinghouse Church), entitled "Jesus and the Natural Order."⁶⁵ His words are worth quoting at length:

> In our power over nature, and in our radical unremembering of the fact that we are a part of nature, we feel that we can abuse nature. We can poison the streams as we hear much about now. We can

---

⁵⁹ Thurman, *Luminous Darkness*, 26.

⁶⁰ Thurman, *Jesus and the Disinherited*, 89. Thurman notes that fear, deception, and hatred are the survival tactics of the oppressed. However, he believes that they ultimately prevent one from fully flourishing as children of God.

⁶¹ Vincent Harding, foreword to Thurman, *Jesus and the Disinherited*.

⁶² Gary Dorrien, *Breaking White Supremacy: Martin Luther King Jr. and the Black Social Gospel* (New Haven: Yale University Press, 2018), 169.

⁶³ Thurman, *Growing Edge*, 16.

⁶⁴ Thurman, *Growing Edge*, 28.

⁶⁵ Howard Thurman, "What Shall I Do with My Life? The Natural Order," Howard Thurman Virtual Listening Room, Howard Gotlieb Archival Research Center, Boston University, accessed July 15, 2020, http://archives.bu.edu/web/howard-thurman/virtual-listening-room/detail?id=358566. Thurman introduces the sermon's title as "Jesus and the Natural Order or The Great Delusion."

pollute the atmosphere. We can ravage and denude the hills. And do this with impunity because the error is that we regard ourselves as not being a part of the world of nature. But in truth we are of the essence of the ebb and flow of the heartbeat of nature, so that we cannot do violence to nature without there being an echo of agony moving through all the corridors of the spirit, of the mind, of the psyche that makes for derangement of all kinds which will increase as the ravaging continues.[66]

Here we see Thurman call for a new way of relating to a creation groaning in travail, in a recognition of the one Creator who binds all of life together. In this sense, though it is not fully developed, Thurman provides a glimpse of what Douglas Christie calls "contemplative ecology."[67] By this he means "an understanding of spiritual practice that places the well-being of the natural world at the center of its concerns, and an approach to ecology that understands the work of cultivating awareness as critical and necessary to its full meaning."[68] Thurman sought to model and preach the kind of contemplative vision that would transform his listeners' relationship with all of life. Thurman's mystical hermeneutic, then, was not one that was disengaged from the world. It was profoundly engaged in the world. For, as Thurman clearly stated, "The core of my preaching has always concerned itself with the development of the inner resources needed for the creation of a friendly world of friendly men."[69] His contemplation of Scripture and other sources was a means of nourishing the spirits of listeners that they might foster a lifegiving and liberating relationship with God, self, others, and all creation.

Sharing Silence

The final distinctive of Black contemplative preaching that I consider in Thurman is his meditative homiletical style. In his childhood, Thurman was exposed to educated or otherwise intellectual preachers who were more meditative than ecstatic in style. Reflecting

---

[66] Thurman, "What Shall I Do with My Life?"
[67] Douglas Christie, *The Blue Sapphire of the Mind: Notes for a Contemplative Ecology* (New York: Oxford University Press, 2013), xi.
[68] Christie, *Blue Sapphire*, xi.
[69] Thurman, *With Head and Heart*, 160.

on his upbringing, he notes, "The preachers in my church were not 'whoopers'. . . . At the core of their preaching was solid religious instruction and guidance which augmented rather than diminished the emotional intensity of their words."[70] This example of preaching that combined head and heart marked him deeply. Others would further deepen this commitment, such as Mordecai Wyatt Johnson, the first Black president of Howard University and a forerunner of Black contemplative preaching. Upon first hearing Johnson preach at a YMCA gathering, the teenaged Thurman perceived him as "a living inspiration" and was eager to have him as a mentor.[71] James Earl Massey writes that Thurman was impressed by Johnson's "controlled and creative speaking style, his devotional demeanor, his accented logic, and grand religious vision."[72]

Thurman's meditative homiletical style would continue to be shaped during his time at Morehouse College, a prestigious historically Black college known for developing young Black men into confident, respectable, dignified "Morehouse men" with, in Thurman's words, a "dramatic sense of self."[73] At Morehouse, among many other things, Thurman participated on the debate team and delivered required orations before the student body without any notes—an experience that may have contributed to his habit of preaching without notes.[74] However, like other fine institutions, Morehouse was not without its challenges. As Eboni Marshall Turman has contended in *Toward a Womanist Ethic of Incarnation*, there is a moral problem embedded in the making of the Morehouse man.[75] To oversimplify, for her, this process—a legacy of the social gospel and U.S. liberalism—produces

---

[70] Thurman, *With Head and Heart*, 17.
[71] Howard Thurman, "To Mordecai Wyatt Johnson, 18 June 1918," in *The Papers of Howard Washington Thurman*, vol. 1, *My People Need Me, June 1918–March 1936*, ed. Walter Earl Fluker (Columbia: University of South Carolina Press, 2010), 1.
[72] James Earl Massey, "Contemplative Preaching," unpublished manuscript, 13.
[73] Thurman, *With Head and Heart*, 36.
[74] Thurman, *With Head and Heart*, 34, 37.
[75] Eboni Marshall Turman, *Toward a Womanist Ethic of Incarnation: Black Bodies, the Black Church, and the Council of Chalcedon* (New York: Palgrave Macmillan, 2013), especially chap. 4. Turman bases her conclusions on interviews she conducted with Morehouse alumni. For a recent sociological examination of the formation of Black masculinity at Morehouse, see Saida Grundy, *Respectable: Politics and Paradox in Making the Morehouse Man* (Oakland: University of California Press, 2022).

Black males who believe they are "divinely authorized to value/or devalue other bodies that defy their normativity."[76] Among other things, the inflated sense of self-importance of *some* Morehouse men could lead to minimizing or marginalizing the role of Black women in the church, particularly in the pulpit. As one shaped by his time and place, Thurman was not immune to this tendency. He was a confident Black male preacher who believed he was divinely destined to make a difference in the Black community. In his autobiography, he writes, "I was profoundly affected by the sense of mission the college inculcated in us. We understood that our job was to learn so that we could go back into our communities and teach others."[77] Thurman's training may have predisposed him to overvalue male voices. However, his early examples of strong Black women—particularly Nancy Ambrose and Mary McLeod Bethune—and his later genuine partnerships with women (especially his second wife, Sue Bailey Thurman) seemed to temper the kind of male chauvinism that Turman argues Morehouse often instills in its students.[78] He was a confident yet humble meditative preacher.

After Morehouse, Thurman's homiletical formation continued at RTS. From one of his homiletic professors, Thurman came to believe "the preacher is never under obligation to preach a great sermon but he is always under obligation to wrestle with a great idea."[79] In other words, for Thurman, the sermon was an opportunity to contemplate a glorious insight or idea like a diamond from a variety of angles. The sermon was a Spirit-guided searching experience with words. Indeed, Thurman expressed that his favorite medium for communication was the spoken word.[80]

Reflecting perhaps unconsciously the power of nommo or "the sacred power of the spoken word to create and generate reality," Thurman's meditative musings sometimes led to a mystical connection that was difficult to understand.[81] One such experience occurred in

---

[76] Turman, *Toward a Womanist Ethic of Incarnation*, 131.
[77] Thurman, *With Head and Heart*, 35.
[78] Thurman, *With Head and Heart*, 36–37.
[79] Thurman, *Growing Edge*, x.
[80] Thurman, *With Head and Heart*, 227.
[81] Gilbert, *Journey and Promise*, 34.

a gathering with the Federation of Indian Chiefs of Saskatchewan, Canada, in 1962 in which he spoke without a translator to a group that had little or no exposure at all to the English language. Thurman says that though the talk began with puzzlement, "as if by some kind of magic, the wall vanished and I had the experience of sensing an organic flow of meaning passing between them and me."[82] Thurman's meditative preaching was graced by God with an aura that seemed to lead people across boundaries of race to experience the community at the very heart of the message he proclaimed. Indeed, for Thurman, the very experience of contemplation in preaching could be a mystical moment that evidenced the common ground of all life. In the midst of pervasive social fragmentation, he witnessed to the unity of life in God. Thus, Thurman did not aim primarily to inspire, motivate, or even teach his listeners; rather, his preaching was "almost entirely devoted to the meaning of the experience of man's common quest and journey" toward God.[83]

Thurman's meditative approach to preaching was further shaped through his experience of regularly attending Quaker worship while studying with Jones at Haverford.[84] Through this experience, he "acquired a Quaker sensibility and a deeper appreciation of the importance of silence, meditation, and spiritual spontaneity."[85] For example, he was exposed to the Quaker practice of sitting in silence to listen for the promptings of the Spirit or "inner light" that might lead a person to offer a word to those gathered.[86] This would shape Thurman's understanding of the Spirit's presence and action through the sermon in relationship to worship as a whole. Reflecting on the place of the sermon in the context of worship, Thurman once shared, "For me the sermon is an act of worship in which the preacher exposes his spirit and mind as they seek to reveal the working of the spirit of the living God upon them. It is a searching moment! The atmosphere is one charged with the dynamics of worship and the surrender and

---

[82] Thurman, *With Head and Heart*, 246.
[83] Thurman, *With Head and Heart*, 73.
[84] Eisenstadt, *Against the Hounds of Hell*, 113.
[85] Eisenstadt, *Against the Hounds of Hell*, 113.
[86] Howard Thurman, *Disciplines of the Spirit* (Richmond, Ind.: Friends United, 1963), 97.

commitment which worship inspires."[87] In essence, Thurman's meditative preaching emerged from the context of attending to the Spirit in the collective worship experience. He would develop this focus in his ministry at the Fellowship Church and later Boston University.

One of the most characteristic dimensions of Thurman's meditative homiletical style at Fellowship Church, Boston, and other venues was his incorporation of silence. Homiletician Evans Crawford argues that Thurman was a master of using "the sermon pause" to cultivate a shared silence.[88] For Thurman, this was not a technique or trick. Rather, it was an act of *phronesis*, or practical wisdom, that flowed from the prayerful disposition that Thurman had cultivated over time.[89] As such, silence was used in the right way and at the right time and for the right end, namely, to attend to God's gracious presence in community. Or, in the words of Martin Laird, it was a way for Thurman to surrender control to the divine in hopes of encounter.[90] For, as Thurman once stated, "God speaks loudest in silence."[91] Communication is not confined to "spoken words."[92] To be sure, some did not share Thurman's love for silence. Some listeners reportedly fell asleep or complained because it took him so long to say what he wanted to say.[93] Still, as Shively T. J. Smith notes, Thurman's "aesthetic playfulness" often helped forge meaningful bridges that created an experience of "authentic common ground" for listeners.[94]

---

[87] Thurman, *Growing Edge*, x.
[88] Evans Crawford with Thomas Troeger, *The Hum: Call and Response in African American Preaching* (Nashville: Abingdon, 1995), 25–35.
[89] The term *phronesis* (translated as practical wisdom, practical reasoning, or prudence) can be traced back to the corpus of Aristotle. Essentially, Aristotle understands *phronesis* as the cultivation of character that enables one to act in the right way, at the right time, and for the right end. See *Aristotle's Nicomachean Ethics*, trans. Robert C. Bartlett and Susan D. Collins (Chicago: University of Chicago Press, 2011), 115–34.
[90] Martin Laird, *Into the Silent Land: A Guide to the Christian Practice of Contemplation* (New York: Oxford University Press, 2006), 3.
[91] Thurman, "Dilemmas of the Religious Professional," side A.
[92] Patrick Clayborn, "Preaching as an Act of Spirit: The Homiletical Theory of Howard Thurman," *Homiletic* 35, no. 1 (2010): 9.
[93] Thurman, *Growing Edge*, 35.
[94] Shively T. J. Smith, "'I Can See It. Now, How to Say It?' Hearing the Aesthetic Dimension of Howard Thurman, the Interpreter," in *The Unfinished Search for Common Ground: Reimagining Howard Thurman*, ed. Walter Earl Fluker (Maryknoll, N.Y.: Orbis, 2023), 32–33.

Along with his penchant for silence, Thurman was known for his exaggerated gestures, energy, and animation. His proclamation was one of controlled passion whether he was before Black, White, or multiethnic audiences.[95] It was through this that he prayerfully offered his sermon in hopes that it might lead to an encounter with the living God. In one of the rare publicly available videos we have of Thurman preaching, he offers a dynamic meditation that shows his unique meditative preaching style. He proclaims, "Every living thing, including man, belongs to every other living thing. And I can never be what I want to be until the last living manifestation of life is what it ought to be. For better or for worse, I am tied into the idiom of everything that lives. And if I forget this, [long pause] I profane God's creation. If I remember it, [short pause] I come to myself in you, and you come to yourself in me."[96] Thurman's provocative words display his mystical vision, including a hint of a nonanthropocentric understanding of nature. However, even more than his words, Thurman's meditative homiletical style facilitates an experience of the words' meaning. He speaks about the oneness of all creation, but he ultimately hopes his listeners encounter that oneness in worship. In other words, Thurman leads his listeners to a lifegiving and liberating relationship with God, self, neighbor, and all creation. It is perhaps best to end this section with the testimony of Francis Hall, a noted Quaker author, reflecting back on the impact of Thurman's preaching on his life in his younger years at a conference:

> He had held me entranced each day by his deeply meditative style of speaking. You felt the creative spirit at work; indeed it was the Spirit of Christ that was speaking through him. I hung on every word as it was given birth and waited eagerly for the full sentence and the total message. Thurman did not speak from an obvious outline, in a systematic way, and in this next-to-the-last message of the conference he began to weave the call of Jesus in and out of his elaborations. I do not recall those elaborations but know that the call of Jesus was beginning to echo in my heart. Toward the

---

[95] Dorrien makes the case that Thurman was consistent in his preaching style. See Dorrien, *Breaking White Supremacy*, 162.

[96] Howard Thurman, "Howard Thurman," Museum of the African Diaspora, November 27, 2018, YouTube video, 14:50, https://www.youtube.com/watch?v=xg2mlTu25qs&t=104s.

end of his sharing he once more spoke the call, and suddenly the words were no longer transmitted by Howard Thurman. They were the living words of Christ and they sank deep into my being, where they exploded and infused me and gripped me. In that depth of my being was a glad response, 'I come!' Tears rose in my eyes; a tingling ran up and down my back; I seemed to be lifted out of myself.[97]

Ultimately, Thurman's contemplative preaching was not about Thurman. Howard Thurman was a channel through whom the Spirit worked in a particular way to bear witness to the living God. God freed people internally through the ministry of Thurman to engage in pursuing freedom externally. Thurman's habitus of prayer, mystical hermeneutic, and meditative homiletical style all reflect his insistence on leading people to an inner encounter with the divine so that they might be transformed and contribute to the outward flourishing of African Americans and all creation. He offers an inspiring example to learn from in the context of our ongoing social challenges.

"Teach Us to Pray": A Close Reading

In this final section, we closely examine one of Thurman's sermons to further illuminate how he embodied the homiletical theology of Black contemplative preaching. To recall, I argue that the distinctives of Black contemplative preaching correlate broadly with Aristotle's three means of persuasion. Thus, the habitus of prayer reflects the ethos of the preacher, the mystical hermeneutic reflects the logos of the preacher, and the meditative homiletical style reflects the pathos of the preacher. While my research examined several sermons that demonstrate the characteristics of Black contemplative preaching, space will only permit a close analysis of one of Thurman's sermons. This is fitting because I am not seeking to give a comprehensive study of Thurman's preaching. Instead, I wish only to suggest how the distinctives of Black contemplative preaching are seen in Thurman's homiletical practice.

My analysis will focus on a sermon entitled "Teach Us to Pray," which appears in a published collection of his sermons called *The*

---

[97] Francis B. Hall, *Practical Spirituality: Selected Writings of Francis B. Hall*, ed. Howard Alexander, Wilmer Cooper, and James Newby (Dublin, Ind.: Prinit, 1984), 13.

Growing Edge.[98] The occasion and audience of the sermon is not listed in that volume. Thurman simply states that all the sermons in the book were given in various worship settings. Despite this lack of information, it seems the sermon we will examine was likely preached during the 1950s as were some of the other sermons in the volume. Though "Teach Us to Pray" does not directly reference the experience of racism and segregation, this was the reality of the culture in which Thurman lived, moved, and had his being. Therefore, it should be assumed as part of the cultural backdrop of the sermon. Moreover, the oration was clearly conceived as one part of a larger worship experience.[99] It is preceded by meditative readings and a prayer to help ready the listeners' spirits to encounter God.

In the sermon, Thurman draws on a habitus of prayer (ethos), a mystical hermeneutic (logos), and a meditative homiletical style (pathos) in order to invite his audience to embrace their dependence on God through the practice of prayer. The sermon can be arranged into four movements. In the first, Thurman introduces Jesus as an exemplary model of prayer. He does so by exploring the words of the disciples to Jesus in the Gospel of Luke 11:1: "Lord, teach us to pray."[100] This is the core scriptural text for Thurman's mystical hermeneutic here. However, in this case, Thurman does not place the text in its historical and cultural context. He does not provide commentary on the larger literary features of the pericope. Instead, he simply invites his listeners to contemplate Jesus' example. Thurman surmises that the reason the disciples ask Jesus to teach them to pray is because he exuded the life of one who had a unique "experience with God."[101] They come to recognize with "unerring insight" that Jesus' life of prayer is the "key to the meaning of his life."[102] And, so, they ask Jesus to help them cultivate a praying life. Like the disciples, Thurman invites his listeners to attend to the wisdom of Jesus to learn what it means to pray.

---

[98] Thurman, *Growing Edge*, 29–36.
[99] Thurman, *Growing Edge*, ix.
[100] Thurman, *Growing Edge*, 32.
[101] Thurman, *Growing Edge*, 32.
[102] Thurman, *Growing Edge*, 32–33.

In the second movement, Thurman begins to delve into why his listeners, like the disciples, need prayer. He states his point plainly: "We wish never to be left, literally, to our own resources."[103] The term *resource*—which appears a total of twelve times in the sermon—is critical in Thurman's development of the idea that humans are meant to rely on a power or source beyond themselves. It is important to state that by using this term Thurman is not reducing the spiritual life to a matter of technique. Nothing could be further from the truth. The term, for him, simply speaks of being supplied energy, power, and life beyond ourselves. Thurman modeled his own commitment to not living on his own resources by beginning the sermon with meditative readings and prayer. As a minister, he knows that he lives dependent on resources outside himself. He now explores with his listeners the limits of their own resources. Like his African ancestors, he argues that as humans "we are not self-contained" but rather "utterly dependent" on people before us.[104] This echoes the concept of Ubuntu, that is, that our life cannot be understood apart from the larger community.[105] For Thurman, "all life is one."[106]

Employing a meditative homiletical style to establish his emotional appeal, Thurman uses rhetorical questions to move his audience to contemplate their contingency as creatures.[107] First, he invites them to consider their dependence on other human beings through something as basic as the alphabet. He stresses that we do not have words on our own; instead we inherit them from our ancestors. Based on this, he presses the question: "And the words we use?"[108] He states that if our alphabet is based on the legacy of others, the words themselves

---

[103] Thurman, *Growing Edge*, 33.

[104] Thurman, *Growing Edge*, 33.

[105] Peter Paris, *The Spirituality of African Peoples: The Search for a Common Moral Discourse* (Minneapolis: Fortress, 1995), 51; Hak Joon Lee, *We Will Get to the Promised Land: Martin Luther King, Jr.'s Communal-Political Spirituality* (Cleveland: Pilgrim, 2006), 28–29; Michael Battle, *Reconciliation: The Ubuntu Theology of Desmond Tutu* (Cleveland: Pilgrim, 1999); and Diana L. Hayes, "A Great Cloud of Witnesses: Martin Luther King Jr.'s Roots in the African American Religious and Spiritual Traditions," in *Revives My Soul Again: The Spirituality of Martin Luther King Jr.*, ed. Lewis V. Baldwin and Victor Anderson (Minneapolis: Fortress, 2018), 45.

[106] Howard Thurman, *Meditations of the Heart* (Boston: Beacon, 1981), 117–18.

[107] Thurman, *Growing Edge*, 33.

[108] Thurman, *Growing Edge*, 33.

speak "about the involvement of hundreds of thousands of minds and spirits, in successes and failures, in heartaches and trepidations, before at last, language, the miracle of communication, became possible."[109] For Thurman, the language that we speak itself witnesses to the foolishness of seeking to live based on our resources alone.

Thurman uses a second rhetorical question to draw attention to our dependence on God. Humans, he says, often neglect to "apply our sense of dependence to our personal relationships to God."[110] And yet there is a dependence upon the divine that is almost inescapable. He invites the audience to reflect with him: "What is the most dramatic utterance that we make when pressure bears down upon us?"[111] The answer: "We cry out Something to Somebody."[112] Like Ann Ulanov and Barry Ulanov, Thurman recognizes that "everybody prays."[113] It is our "primary speech."[114] It manifest itself in ways that at times are "conventional" and at times "not quite conventional."[115] Regardless, we as creatures are dependent on our Creator, no matter how "powerful we may seem to be at other times."[116] Thurman is inviting his listeners to consider the primal experience of being human. Like Jesus himself, they are to embody a lived dependence upon God. The question becomes, of course, how is this possible. This leads to the third movement of the sermon.

Thurman argues that prayer is the ideal way of accessing "resources that are beyond ourselves."[117] Again, it is important to note that Thurman established his credibility early on as one who practices prayer. However, his habitus of prayer is further revealed in that he is speaking from experience. Thurman has no intention of drawing attention to himself, but he can speak about prayer with a certain bold humility as one who has experienced it as a reliable

---

[109] Thurman, *Growing Edge*, 33.
[110] Thurman, *Growing Edge*, 33.
[111] Thurman, *Growing Edge*, 33.
[112] Thurman, *Growing Edge*, 33.
[113] Ann Ulanov and Barry Ulanov, *Primary Speech: A Psychology of Prayer* (Atlanta: John Knox, 1983), 1.
[114] Ulanov and Ulanov, *Primary Speech*, 1.
[115] Thurman, *Growing Edge*, 33.
[116] Thurman, *Growing Edge*, 34.
[117] Thurman, *Growing Edge*, 34.

resource for reaching out to the God who has graciously first reached out to us.[118] However, Thurman realizes that some resistance often prevents us from embracing prayer as a resource. He addresses two areas of resistance. The first is that people are more prone to pray for their loved ones rather than for the renewal and revitalization of their own life. He notes that this is especially the case when a "loved one is threatened."[119] However, he seems to suggest that we fail to see that our own life can also be threatened when we fail to care for our inner life with God through prayer.

Thurman elaborates at length on the second area of resistance. He speaks of the ways in which we question if it is possible to access "resources beyond ourselves" at all.[120] In other words, we ask, does prayer truly lead us to a power external to the self? Thurman responds to this inquiry drawing on three sources that further reveal how his mystical hermeneutic helps establish his logical arguments. First, he turns to Scripture again. Thurman recounts the story told in the Gospel of Mark of the desperate father who approaches Jesus. The father's child is tormented by a spirit that leaves him convulsing and harming himself.[121] Jesus tells the father that it is possible to heal his son if the father has faith. The father replies, "I have faith, help thou my lack of faith."[122] Reflecting on the father's reply, Thurman states, "It is as part of the awareness of faith itself that the sense of the lack of faith arises."[123] In short, Thurman contends that the father's desire for faith is evidence of faith. Or, said differently, he witnesses to the fact that we can access resources beyond ourselves in prayer because the desire to do so comes from a source beyond ourselves. God is always before us.

Thurman continues to elaborate on this theme through turning to a second source that shapes his mystical hermeneutic. He recalls a book of philosophy entitled *Richard Kane Looks at Life*.[124] The book

---

[118] Thurman, *Creative Encounter*, 38.
[119] Thurman, *Growing Edge*, 34.
[120] Thurman, *Growing Edge*, 34.
[121] See Mark 9:14–29.
[122] Thurman, *Growing Edge*, 34.
[123] Thurman, *Growing Edge*, 34.
[124] Irwin Edman, *Richard Kane Looks at Life: A Philosophy Book for Youth* (Boston: Houghton Mifflin, 1926).

contains various letters exchanged between a philosophy professor and a thoughtful student. The student writes of his struggle to find the meaning of life, and yet he insists that he cannot give up on the quest in spite of having "not been able to find what he sought."[125] The student begins to wonder if God was what he was seeking on his quest all along. According to Thurman, the professor responded that perhaps "the hunger itself was God."[126] Thurman invites his audience to consider not only that the desire to pray is evidence of a desire for God but that the desire itself is God.

Thurman concludes the third movement of the sermon by mentioning a final source as he advances his logical argument. He suggests that contact with God is clearly possible because the one whom we seek to contact is already within. He turns to the ancient philosopher Plotinus for support, suggesting that "the beyond is within."[127] For Plotinus, the beyond refers to the three hypostases—the One, the Intellect, and the Soul—that constitute the unseen reality.[128] For Thurman, the beyond is the God of the Christian Scriptures. This transcendent yet immanent God is the reason that his listeners can be sure that it is possible to access resources beyond themselves in prayer. Despite the contradictions of life around them, this God is in them. However, this still begs the question of how one is able to learn to concretely connect with this God in prayer.

In the final movement, Thurman addresses this issue by speaking of how "some preparation" is essential to "tap the resources that are beyond ourselves."[129] It is vital to state yet again that Thurman is speaking from experience: he began his sermon by preparing the listeners through meditation and prayer. Preparation is particularly important, Thurman says, because "we are all in a hurry."[130] With a

---

[125] Thurman, *Growing Edge*, 34.
[126] Thurman, *Growing Edge*, 34.
[127] Thurman, *Growing Edge*, 34.
[128] Plotinus, *The Enneads*, ed. Lloyd P. Gerson, trans. George Boys-Stones et al. (New York: Cambridge University Press, 2018), vol. 1, 10.5–9. The phrase "the beyond is within" was often used by Rufus Jones, too. However, as Lloyd Gerson helpfully pointed out to me, the notion is found in Plotinus' work, though translations differ in how they render it.
[129] Thurman, *Growing Edge*, 34–35.
[130] Thurman, *Growing Edge*, 35.

sympathetic and understanding tone, Thurman states that in such a frenzied state of life it is difficult to "ready our spirits" for the kind of centered living Jesus himself experienced with God.[131] There is a need for external quiet to experience internal quiet. To illustrate, Thurman tells a story from his personal experience.

He recounts visiting the house of a woman who was a member of the first church he pastored during a time when her husband was ill. The woman was known for falling asleep each Sunday morning during worship services. As Thurman was leaving her house, the woman told him she sleeps each week in service due both to the slow pace of his speech and to the chronic fatigue she suffers from due to caring for her ill husband. Thurman responded, "Now that I have visited your home and seen the kind of turmoil in which you live six and a half or seven days a week, I feel that the greatest contribution the church can make to you is to provide a quiet place, once a week, in which you can sit down and go to sleep in peace."[132]

Through offering this story Thurman does at least three things. For one, he removes any impression that he is seeking to make the audience feel guilty about their busyness. He does this by increasing his identification with them through engaging in what Kenneth Burke called "the simplest case of persuasion," that is, identifying with his audience through showing he can speak their language.[133] Thurman makes clear that he recognizes his audience's unique struggles. Everyone has a particular story. Second, he elevates a woman as an example of what it means to practice dependence upon God. While Thurman's first church was notable for crossing racial barriers, it is possible that the woman he mentions is African American. If this is the case, Thurman demonstrates that the woman is engaging in what later womanist scholars such as Delores Williams would call a life-affirming survival strategy of self-care.[134] Reflecting a womanist impulse, Thurman praises her practice of "redemptive self-love"

---

[131] Thurman, *Growing Edge*, 35.

[132] Thurman, *Growing Edge*, 35

[133] Kenneth Burke, *A Rhetoric of Motives* (Berkeley: University of California Press, 1969), 55.

[134] Delores Williams, *Sisters in the Wilderness: The Challenge of Womanist God-Talk*, anniv. ed. (Maryknoll, N.Y.: Orbis, 2013), 209.

through sleeping.[135] This reflects his mystical hermeneutic concerned with developing a lifegiving relationship with self and God. Third, related to this, Thurman's story shows that he understands that there are a wide range of ways through which one might need to connect with God in the busyness of modern life. He says, "We cannot prescribe the rules by which spiritual power is available to us."[136] He does not promote a one-size-fits-all spirituality. Instead, Thurman aims to help his audience develop an inner life that can sustain them in the work of their outer life through advocating a range of spiritual practices—even sleeping in the context of worship.

As Thurman draws the sermon toward an end, he does not engage in a typical Black sermonic ending through celebration. On the contrary, he moves the audience emotionally through inviting them into additional reflection with his meditative homiletical style. To do so, he raises a rhetorical question that includes anaphora: "Who are we, with our little conceits, with our little arrogances, with our little madnesses, to lay down the conditions upon which we will accept the resources of life that sustain and confirm the integrity of our being?"[137] Thurman asks his audience to contemplate the folly of seeking to "prescribe the rules" through which God's power can come to us.[138] Instead, he advocates for the "discipline" of leaning into appropriate and particular rhythms of quiet that fit our life stage, age, and season. Amid the pain, trauma, and challenges of life, Thurman invites his audience to find spiritual rhythms that can bring healing to their body. As part of his spiritual counsel, he asserts, "We must find, each of us for himself, the kind of rhythmic pattern which will control our stubborn and

---

[135] In *Deeper Shades of Purple: Womanism in Religion and Society* (New York: New York University Press, 2006), Stacey Floyd-Thomas articulates four conceptual terms to correspond to Alice Walker's classic four-part definition of womanism: radical subjectivity, traditional communalism, redemptive self-love, and critical engagement. Redemptive self-love is a commitment to love and care for oneself regardless of what one may face. To be clear, I am not suggesting that Thurman should be understood as womanist in his orientation. I am rather hinting at a womanist impulse present in his preaching. For a treatment of the "redemptive self-love" attribute of womanist preaching, see Kimberly P. Johnson, *The Womanist Preacher: Proclaiming Womanist Rhetoric from the Pulpit* (Lanham, Md.: Lexington, 2017), especially chap. 4.

[136] Thurman, *Growing Edge*, 35.
[137] Thurman, *Growing Edge*, 35.
[138] Thurman, *Growing Edge*, 35.

unyielding and recalcitrant nervous systems, and nourish our spiritual concerns and our growth in grace."[139] He calls for us to turn to God with all of our bodies that we might learn how to pray in ways that fit our particularities.

Reflecting again a disposition of prayer, Thurman concludes the sermon with a brief supplication. Like the disciples who approached Jesus, he desires to learn how to pray. "Teach me to pray, O God, my Father," he says, "that I may find the rhythmic pattern of my own spirit, which will lead me to the source of all life, lest my soul perish."[140] Here we see Thurman's ultimate goal: to be brought to "the source of all life," namely God.[141]

Conclusion

Many people encounter contemplative preaching in the Black church for the first time through the books, meditations, and sermons of Howard Thurman. Though he passed over forty years ago, his wisdom continues to inspire people of diverse backgrounds as we face the challenges and opportunities of the twenty-first century. For Thurman, preaching was a Spirit-inspired attempt to liberate people internally so that they might become active participants in creating a more friendly world. His practice of Black contemplative preaching reveals a strong commitment to divine encounter as a personal experience with the potential to transform one's life with God, others, self, and even creation. Throughout his journey, Thurman affected the life and ministry of many preachers through his writings, mentorship, and preaching. One of the best-known of these preachers was Martin Luther King Jr.

Though Thurman did not interact extensively with King, he did have some involvement in his life and was on good terms with his family.[142] King became acquainted with Thurman while a student at Boston University, where Thurman was dean of chapel. King "always

---

[139] Thurman, *Growing Edge*, 35–36.
[140] Thurman, *Growing Edge*, 36.
[141] Thurman, *Growing Edge*, 36.
[142] Thurman, *With Head and Heart*, 254–55.

listened carefully when Thurman was speaking" in chapel.[143] Eventually, King echoed his thought in some of his own sermons. Later in life, as Walter Fluker has demonstrated, the two would exchange letters periodically.[144] At one crucial moment, as recorded in his autobiography, Thurman provided counsel that enriched King's spiritual life during the civil rights movement.[145] It has also been widely circulated that King carried Thurman's *Jesus and the Disinherited* as he marched for justice.[146] In brief, though quite different from Thurman in various ways, King was clearly impacted by Thurman's writing, mentorship, and preaching. We now turn to consider King's unique embodiment of the homiletical theology of Black contemplative preaching. He, too, offers wisdom for us to learn from today.

---

[143] This comment is made by Philip Lenud, a former student at Boston University and King's friend, who was interviewed by Lewis Baldwin. See Lewis V. Baldwin, *There Is a Balm in Gilead: The Cultural Roots of Martin Luther King, Jr.* (Minneapolis: Fortress, 1991), 300–301.

[144] See, for example, the letters in *The Papers of Howard Washington Thurman*, vol. 44, 153, 222, 231, 251–53.

[145] Thurman, *With Head and Heart*, 255.

[146] Thurman's influence on King is mentioned by civil rights activists Jesse Jackson, John Lewis, and others in the documentary *Backs against the Wall*. Thurman himself apparently was told that his book was influential in King's life. However, he made it clear that he did not hear this directly from King. For a helpful discussion on Thurman's influence on King, see Walter E. Fluker, *They Looked for a City: A Comparative Analysis of the Ideal of Community in the Thought of Howard Thurman and Martin Luther King, Jr.* (Lanham, Md.: University Press of America, 1989), 197–99. For an even stronger brief proposal of how Thurman influenced King, see Dorrien, *Breaking White Supremacy*, 171. After my own study of Thurman and King, I find Dorrien's case convincing.

3
Redeeming the Soul and Society
Martin Luther King Jr. as Contemplative Preacher

Above all, I see the preaching ministry as a dual process. On the one hand I must attempt to change the soul of individuals so that their societies may be changed. On the other hand I must attempt to change the societies so that the individual soul will have a change.

Martin Luther King Jr., "Preaching Ministry"[1]

Introduction

It is one of the best-known addresses in U.S. history: the "I Have a Dream" speech delivered by Rev. Dr. Martin Luther King Jr. at the March on Washington for Jobs and Freedom in Washington, D.C., on August 28, 1963.[2] The speech was one part of a gathering, organized by Bayard Rustin and A. Philip Randolph, that drew a quarter of a million people from across racial and economic backgrounds. While certain dimensions of King's prophetic speech are often overlooked, such as his critique of capitalism, no one can deny the speech has received significant attention. For example, countless scholars and theorists have commented on the rhetoric, theology, and political dimensions of King's memorable address. And much of its language and imagery has become part of North American

---

[1] Martin Luther King Jr., "Preaching Ministry," in *The Papers of Martin Luther King, Jr.*, vol. 6, *Advocate of the Social Gospel, September 1948–March 1963*, ed. Clayborne Carson (Berkeley: University of California Press, 2007), 72. Hereafter, I refer to this volume as *TPMLK*, vol. 6.

[2] While King delivered the "I Have a Dream" speech, the address was initially drafted with the assistance of Stanley Levison and Clarence B. Jones. For an account of the speech's development and influence, see Clarence B. Jones and Stuart Connelly, *Behind the Dream: The Making of a Speech that Transformed a Nation* (New York: St. Martin's, 2011).

culture. Of course, in discussing King's speech, it is important to not perpetuate what Erica Edwards calls "the fiction" of "a single charismatic leader" who enacts social change.[3] In the past and present, King has been elevated in ways that eclipse the voices of others in the civil rights movement, especially women.[4] Still, at its best, King's speech is emblematic of the ways in which he "used his voice to amplify the voices of the voiceless."[5] Indeed, the "I Have a Dream" speech is memorialized as one of the most important catalysts in advancing the fight for freedom and economic justice for Black people in the United States during the civil rights movement.

And, yet, despite all the attention that King's "I Have a Dream" speech/sermon has received, rarely is it seen as a contemplative moment. However, if we reexamine the occasion carefully, some things come into view that have tended to remain hidden in plain sight. For example, as historian Henry Louis Gates notes, the most memorable refrain of the speech and its subsequent title ("I Have a Dream") emerged from a prayer from Rev. Dr. Prathia Hall—a line that King had previously borrowed in his speeches and included in the Washington, D.C., speech at the urging of the noted gospel singer Mahalia Jackson, who was present in the audience.[6] King's receptivity to the prompting of Jackson to "Tell them about the dream" hints at a kind of contemplative attunement to the moment that proved to be profoundly impactful.[7] Moreover, the

---

[3] Erica R. Edwards, *Charisma and the Fictions of Black Leadership* (Minneapolis: University of Minnesota Press, 2012), xv.

[4] For a classic study that honors the contributions of ordinary people in the civil rights movement, see Charles M. Payne, *I've Got the Light of Freedom: The Organizing Tradition and the Mississippi Freedom Struggle*, 2nd ed. (Berkeley: University of California Press, 2007).

[5] Barbara A. Holmes, *Joy Unspeakable: Contemplative Practices of the Black Church*, 2nd ed. (Minneapolis: Fortress, 2017), 130. Later in this chapter, I will briefly suggest King's preaching voice is more shaped by women than is often recognized.

[6] Henry Louis Gates Jr., *The Black Church: This Is Our Story, This Is Our Song* (New York: Penguin, 2021), 138–39.

[7] Gates, *Black Church*, 139. Though most people affirm Jackson's influence on King's speech, it is important to note that some have contested whether or not she actually said these words to King given they are not discernible in the recordings that are publicly available of the speech. However, Clarence B. Jones, who was present for the speech, attests to hearing Jackson's words to King. For a helpful discussion of this issue, see Maurice O. Wallace, *King's Vibrato: Modernism, Blackness, and the Sonic Life of Martin Luther King Jr.* (Durham: Duke University Press, 2022), 109, nn. 318–19.

speech rejects binary thinking. Instead, it evinces "a nondualistic way of seeing" characteristic of contemplatives as King unites White and Black, Jew and Gentile, rich and poor in a compelling vision of justice for all.[8] In fact, it may be that the holistic, mystical vision of the speech contributed to its lasting impact across race, class, religious, and geographic boundaries. And, most practically, even though King's speech reflects many traditional characteristics of Black sermonizing (e.g., call-and-response, a celebratory close), the address has a rather slow, meditative pace and does not include the whooping often associated with Black folk preaching. The rhythm of the speech facilitated deep reflection and a challenging call to enact embodied justice. Much more could and should be said about the contemplative and mystical dimensions of King's speech in Washington. However, I hope my point is clear: there may be more to King and his speeches than is often recognized. In the face of ongoing racial oppression, economic injustice, and violence in the twenty-first century, there is a need to learn from King's contemplative proclamation as we forge diverse alliances to address the most pressing issues of our time to create a better future.

Unfortunately, while Martin Luther King Jr. (1929–1986) has been heralded as a "prophet of the [civil rights] movement," a preacher of God's "cosmic reconciliation," a "pessimistic prophet," and more, few have examined him as a contemplative preacher.[9] And yet he embodied a profound contemplative orientation throughout his life. As Beverly J. Lanzetta says, "Martin Luther King Jr. was a prophetic mystic-contemplative who brought the virtues of the interior life into the public sphere, in service of the dignity of all beings and the alleviation of racism, poverty, and war."[10] Far from taming or domesticating

---

[8] Richard Rohr, *The Naked Now: Learning to See as the Mystics See* (New York: Crossroad, 2009), 12.

[9] Kenyatta R. Gilbert, *A Pursued Justice: Black Preaching from the Great Migration to Civil Rights* (Waco: Baylor University Press, 2016), 110; Sunggu Yang, *King's Speech: Preaching Reconciliation in a World of Violence and Chasm* (Eugene, Ore.: Cascade, 2019), 2; Andre E. Johnson and Anthony J. Stone, "'The Most Dangerous Negro in America': Rhetoric, Race, and the Prophetic Pessimism of Martin Luther King Jr.," *Journal of Communication and Religion* 21, no. 1 (2018): 10.

[10] Beverly J. Lanzetta, "The Heart of a World Citizen: Martin Luther King Jr. as Social Mystic," in *Revives My Soul Again: The Spirituality of Martin Luther King Jr.*, ed. Lewis V. Baldwin and Victor Anderson (Minneapolis: Fortress, 2018), 239.

King's ministry, the contemplative orientation empowered and deepened him—giving him the courage and clarity to take stands that would lead many to turn against him inside and outside the Black community. Surprisingly, while there is a growing number of invaluable studies on King's spirituality, I am not aware of research that explicitly looks at the contemplative dimensions of King's preaching.[11] This chapter seeks to address this lacuna in the literature. Drawing on select published and unpublished works, we will discover how the homiletical theology of Black contemplative preaching is visible in the life, thought, and preaching of arguably the best-known preacher of the twentieth century.[12] He embodies wisdom that can enrich the life and leadership of people seeking to unite deep spirituality with social concern today for the sake of the gospel and the good of the world.

Contemplation in Action

The spiritual formation of Martin Luther King Jr.'s disposition of prayer began long before King's birth. In fact, it started with his forebears. As Hak Joon Lee, Diana Hayes, and others note, King grew up deeply shaped by the holistic, communal spirituality of his African ancestors.[13]

---

[11] Of course, there are some studies that consider King's prayer life and preaching. See, particularly, Lewis V. Baldwin, *Never to Leave Us Alone: The Prayer Life of Martin Luther King Jr.* (Minneapolis: Fortress, 2010), especially chapter 3. Also, Mervyn A. Warren's chapter "To Tell the Truth: Martin Luther King Jr.'s Preaching and Spirituality," in Baldwin and Anderson, *Revives My Soul Again*, 169–84, makes a valuable contribution to our understanding of King's spirituality and preaching. Holmes's *Joy Unspeakable* considers King as representative of the Black contemplative spiritual tradition, 129–32.

[12] While scholars James Cone and David Garrow have argued for the unreliability of King's published works due to his use of ghostwriters, following Lewis Baldwin I believe that in general there are "no important discrepancies between what appears in King's edited and sometimes ghostwritten works and what is included in his extemporaneous, unpublished texts." Lewis V. Baldwin, *There Is a Balm in Gilead: The Cultural Roots of Martin Luther King, Jr.* (Minneapolis: Fortress, 1991), 13. See also David J. Garrow, "The Intellectual Development of Martin Luther King, Jr.: Influences and Commentaries," *Union Seminary Quarterly Review* 40, no. 4 (January 1986): 5–6 and James H. Cone, "The Theology of Martin Luther King, Jr.," *Union Seminary Quarterly Review* 40, no. 4 (January 1986): 39, n. 30. For a helpful discussion of the revisionist nature of Garrow and Cone's scholarship, see Baldwin, *There Is a Balm in Gilead*, 11–14.

[13] Hak Joon Lee, *We Will Get to the Promised Land: Martin Luther King, Jr.'s Communal-Political Spirituality* (Cleveland: Pilgrim, 2006), especially 15–108, and Diana L. Hayes, "A Great Cloud of Witnesses: Martin Luther King Jr.'s Roots in the African American

This spirituality, which embraced the African understanding of Ubuntu or the conviction that our life cannot be understood apart from community, pervaded the cultural, familial, and liturgical traditions of his upbringing in Georgia.[14] His spiritual roots, along with his comfortable, safe, and stable home environment, made it easy for him to relate to God as a personal being through prayer. In a religious autobiography composed in seminary, King shared, "It is quite easy for me to think of a God of love mainly because I grew up in a family where love was central and where lovely relationships were ever present."[15] Though Thurman also grew up experiencing loving relationships, King was enveloped with more stability and safety—even as he lived in the segregated South. In this context, King nurtured a life of prayer. According to Lewis Baldwin, a leading King scholar, alongside regularly attending worship services, he learned the value of personal and corporate prayer in family, church, and even school.[16]

As a seminary student, King enjoyed experiencing God in the quiet beauty of nature. Reflecting on his time as a student, he recalled, "I can remember very vividly how in my recent seminary days, I was able to strengthen my spiritual life through communing with nature . . . Every day I would sit on the edge of the campus by the side of the river and watch the beauties of nature. My friend, in this experience, I saw God."[17] Like Thurman, he had a contemplative posture toward nature reflective of his African ancestors, who saw God's presence pervasive in creation. King's spiritual practice would be developed in other ways as he was in ministry. According to records of his schedule, during at least part of his life, King kept "one

---

Religious and Spiritual Traditions," in Baldwin and Anderson, *Revives My Soul Again*, 41–42.

[14] Peter Paris, *The Spirituality of African Peoples: The Search for a Common Moral Discourse* (Minneapolis: Fortress, 1995), 51; Lee, *We Will Get to the Promised Land*, 28–29; Michael Battle, *Reconciliation: The Ubuntu Theology of Desmond Tutu* (Cleveland: Pilgrim, 1999); and Hayes, "A Great Cloud of Witnesses," 45.

[15] Martin Luther King Jr., "An Autobiography of Religious Development," in *The Papers of Martin Luther King, Jr.*, vol. 1, *Called to Serve, January 1929–June 1951*, ed. Clayborne Carson (Berkeley: University of California Press, 1992), 360.

[16] Lewis V. Baldwin, "The Attuning of the Spirit: Martin Luther King Jr. and the Circle of Prayer," in Baldwin and Anderson, *Revives My Soul Again*, 137–41.

[17] Martin Luther King Jr., "'O That I Knew Where I Might Find Him,'" in *TPMLK*, vol. 6, 594.

to two (and sometimes three) days each week" for "Silence and Meditation."[18] Moreover, Wyatt Tee Walker, a long-time associate of King, has described what was called King's "self-imposed 'Day of Silence'" in which he turned down the volume on all the distractions of life.[19] In the words of Meister Eckhart, King understood that "the outward work will never be puny if the inward work is great."[20] While King struggled to preserve space for renewal, his days of silence allowed him to enrich his inner life and gain the clarity needed to plan effective outer engagement for the struggle for freedom. King's disposition of prayer was powerfully manifest in his preaching as he depended on God's Spirit. His preaching was preceded by prayer and punctuated by prayer. Some of the many brief prayers present in King's sermons include "Lord teach me to unselfishly serve humanity," "God remove all bitterness from my heart and give me the strength and courage to face any disaster that comes my way," and "God grant that the day will come when we all can live in this society as brothers and children of a common father on a non-segregated basis."[21] In a word, prayer pervaded King's life and preaching. Indeed, Lewis Baldwin argues that "prayer for King was more than simply an indispensable part of preaching; his prayers became sermons and his sermons, to some extent, prayers."[22] To put it differently, prayer was the foundation of King's sermons, and King's sermons were a form of prayer. As one who developed a habitus of prayer, he offered his sermons as prayers of radical dependence on the Spirit of God in hopes of seeing personal and social change.

However, it is important to note that for King a disposition of prayer must be *explicitly* connected to social action—merging the *vita contemplativa* with the *vita activa*. Like Richard Allen, Sojourner Truth, and other African American mystic-activists, he contended that prayer is not a substitute for action; rather, prayer must energize

---

[18] Mervyn A. Warren, *King Came Preaching: The Pulpit Power of Dr. Martin Luther King Jr.* (Downers Grove, Ill.: InterVarsity, 2001), 136.
[19] Wyatt Tee Walker, foreword to Baldwin, *Never to Leave Us Alone*, vii.
[20] I have been unable to find the original source of this quote.
[21] Martin Luther King Jr., *"Thou, Dear God": Prayers That Open Hearts and Spirits*, ed. Lewis V. Baldwin (Boston: Beacon, 2012), 15, 97, 155.
[22] Baldwin, *Never to Leave Us Alone*, 44–45.

action. It is worth quoting King at length on this point. In one of his sermons, entitled "The Answer to a Perplexing Question," he states:

> The idea that man expects God to do everything leads inevitably to a callous misuse of prayer. For if God does everything, man then asks him for anything, and God becomes little more than a "cosmic bellhop" who is summoned for every trivial need. Or God is considered so omnipotent and man so powerless that prayer is a substitute for work and intelligence. . . . I am certain we need to pray for God's help and guidance in this integration struggle, but we are gravely misled if we think the struggle will be won only by prayer. . . . Prayer is a marvelous and necessary supplement of our feeble efforts, but it is a dangerous substitute.[23]

In short, King argues that while a commitment to prayer is essential, it cannot replace concrete action. He developed a lifestyle of regular meditation, reflection, and introspection that was not severed from his lifestyle of advocating for the poor, the oppressed, and the marginalized. In the words of Charlotte Radler, like other mystics in the Christian tradition, King sought to embody a way of life "that is both grounded in God's mystical presence and open to authentic engagement with the world."[24] As a result, we might say that King's sermons emerged from a life of prayer that was both spoken and lived.

Before ending my discussion of King's habitus of prayer, it is interesting to note that "the most decisive speech" he gave as a young leader was fully dependent on his having cultivated a disposition of prayer.[25] On December 5, 1955, he was unexpectedly asked to come speak to the Montgomery Improvement Association at Holt Street Baptist Church, and he only had "twenty minutes" to prepare.[26] While initially nervous and anxious, he turned to God in prayer as was his habit. Twenty minutes later, without notes of any kind, King

---

[23] Martin Luther King Jr., *Strength to Love* (Minneapolis: Fortress, 2010), 138. See also Martin Luther King Jr., "The Misuse of Prayer," in *TPMLK*, vol. 6, 590–91.

[24] Charlotte Radler, "*Actio et Contemplatio*/Action and Contemplation," in *The Cambridge Companion to Christian Mysticism*, ed. Amy Hollywood and Patricia Z. Beckman (New York: Cambridge University Press, 2012), 222.

[25] Martin Luther King Jr. *Stride toward Freedom: The Montgomery Story* (Boston: Beacon, 2010), 47.

[26] King, *Stride toward Freedom*, 47.

gave a speech that "evoked more response than any speech or sermon" he had ever given up to that point—a speech that distinguished him as the spiritual leader of the civil rights movement.[27] It may be tempting to see the speech as an act of overnight success. But this is far from reality. As one spiritual writer notes, "A successful performance at a moment of crisis rests largely and essentially upon the depths of a self wisely and rigorously prepared in the totality of its being—mind and body."[28] This was the case for King. His embrace of prayer as a way of life, disciplined study, and deep immersion into preaching practices within the Black church formed him into the kind of person who could be responsive to the Spirit in a moment of crisis to proclaim a timely message that was fitting, faithful, and fruitful.

Beholding God and the Beloved Community

Unlike King's habitus of prayer, his mystical hermeneutic is not as clearly present in his sermonizing and speeches. Still, much of King's preaching does reveal marks of the mystical hermeneutic. This makes sense given his immersion in a southern Black church culture in which Scripture was constantly preached, taught, sung, and prayed in an immediate, experiential way. As "the son of a Baptist preacher, the grandson of a Baptist preacher, and the great-grandson of a Baptist preacher," King inherited a rich spiritual heritage.[29] Additionally, he was raised in a loving Christian home and surrounded by gifted preachers while growing up. All this and more helped King cultivate a robust scriptural imagination that led him to believe in a good, all-powerful, and benevolent God who could be encountered in a personal way. Of course, King was also raised in an educated household and would go on to graduate from Morehouse College and receive seminary training at Colgate Rochester and his PhD from Boston University in theology. His exposure to liberal theology and historical and critical scholarship in these contexts shaped his theology and preaching (especially moving it away from fundamentalism), but it

---

[27] King, *Stride toward Freedom*, 52.
[28] Dallas Willard, *The Spirit of the Disciplines* (New York: HarperCollins, 1988), 4.
[29] Martin Luther King Jr., "The UnChristian Christian," *Ebony* 20, no. 10 (August 1965): 77.

did not fully supplant the spiritual beliefs, convictions, and practices he inherited from his Black church roots. Indeed, as Baldwin argues, it mainly developed that which had been initially planted in him through the Black church.[30] This would show up in his hermeneutic, which at times combined historical scholarship with a mystical lens. Alongside the prophet Amos, King often quoted the Gospels. Some of his favorite Gospel texts included the Sermon on the Mount and the Parable of the Good Samaritan. He was deeply interested in Jesus' moral wisdom and example. Later in life, he spoke especially about the kingdom of God. However, he also valued the Psalms, and, like Thurman, often referred to Psalm 139. In other words, King's hermeneutic was immersed in Scripture. As Richard Lischer notes, he dwelt in the storied world of Scripture and preached in ways that "enrolled" his listeners in that world.[31] As such, King's scriptural imagination was a means of leading his listeners to encounter the personal God witnessed to in the story of Scripture and to cultivate a moral life that reflected God's character in the world.

Of course, King drew on Scripture alongside additional sources of wisdom. Among the many different sources King quoted in his speeches and sermons were philosophy, poetry, spirituals, history, psychology, and more. As a result of his study of personalism at Boston and, even more, due to his Africana and Black church roots, King was an articulate proponent of what Gary Dorrien and others have called the Black social gospel.[32] While Dorrien recognizes at least four (or five) different streams of this phenomenon, he offers the following definition: "The full-fledged black social gospel combined an emphasis on black dignity and personhood with protest activism for racial justice, a comprehensive social justice agenda, an insistence that authentic Christian faith is incompatible with racial prejudice,

---

[30] Baldwin, *There Is a Balm in Gilead*, 171–72.

[31] Richard Lischer, *The Preacher King: Martin Luther King, Jr. and the Word That Moved America* (New York: Oxford University Press, 1995), 200–201.

[32] Gary Dorrien, *Breaking White Supremacy: Martin Luther King Jr. and the Black Social Gospel* (New Haven: Yale University Press, 2018), 22. Dorrien does not acknowledge the deep Africana roots that shape King and others, but this is noted in Lee's emphasis on the holistic, communal-political spirituality that is present in King. See Lee, *We Will Get to the Promised Land*.

an emphasis on the social ethical teaching of Jesus, and an acceptance of modern scholarship and social consciousness."[33] King's embodiment of the Black social gospel may be seen throughout his ministry efforts. For example, as the slogan of the Southern Christian Leadership Conference made clear, King desired to "redeem the soul of America" through a progressive understanding of Christianity that would use nonviolence to promote justice, equality, and freedom for all.[34] Many of his sermons were shaped by the thought of social gospel proponents, such as Walter Rauschenbusch and others. He also often quoted figures such as Henry David Thoreau, G. W. F. Hegel, and Paul Tillich. At times, similar to Thurman, he invited listeners to contemplate the life and wisdom of spiritual exemplars, including Augustine, St. Francis, and Gandhi.[35] Indeed, on one occasion he preached an entire sermon on Gandhi at Dexter Avenue Baptist Church.[36] For King, the goal in drawing on Scripture and other sources of wisdom was to nurture the interior life of his listeners in order that they might be able to constructively fight against the brutalities of racism and injustice with nonviolent resistance.

As a "theologian of reconciliation," King evinced his mystical hermeneutic in how he proclaimed an inclusive vision to help his listeners cultivate a lifegiving and liberating relationship with God, self, neighbor, and creation.[37] Drawing on Josiah Royce, King termed this vision "the beloved community."[38] He would later speak of "the great world

---

[33] Gary Dorrien, *The New Abolition: W. E. B. and the Black Social Gospel* (New Haven: Yale University Press, 2016), 3.

[34] Adam Fairclough, *To Redeem the Soul of America: The Southern Christian Leadership Conference and Martin Luther King, Jr*, rev. ed. (Athens: University of Georgia Press, 2001).

[35] See Martin Luther King Jr., "Unfulfilled Dreams," in *A Knock at Midnight: Inspiration from the Great Sermons of Reverend Martin Luther King, Jr.*, ed. Clayborne Carson and Peter Holloran (New York: Warner, 1998), 192–93, 196; Martin Luther King Jr. "On Accepting the St. Francis Peace Medal," *Peace* 1 (March 1964): 11–15; and Baldwin, *Never to Leave Us Alone*, 3.

[36] Martin Luther King Jr., *The Radical King*, ed. Cornel West (Boston: Beacon, 2015), 23–38.

[37] Johnny Bernard Hill, *The Theology of Martin Luther King, Jr. and Desmond Mpilo Tutu* (New York: Palgrave Macmillan, 2007), 1.

[38] Walter E. Fluker, *They Looked for a City: A Comparative Analysis of the Ideal of Community in the Thought of Howard Thurman and Martin Luther King, Jr.* (Lanham, Md.: University Press of America, 1989), 81–152.

house," or "the world house."³⁹ Reflecting the holistic, communal-political spirituality of his African roots, this was a vision of freedom, equity, and justice for all peoples and nations. His preaching embodied this inclusive, reconciling vision. Indeed, Dorrien claims that "every sermon that King ever gave was a gloss on the beloved community."⁴⁰ King's understanding of the beloved community challenged people to reorder their lives in ways that reflected the all-encompassing nature of the gospel. For example, in his famous sermon "The Three Dimensions of a Complete Life," he calls for his listeners to live a full or whole life through developing a right relationship with God, self, and neighbor.⁴¹ Later in life, King's inclusive vision became more radical as he took unpopular positions. This is visible in the backlash he experienced for his speech against the Vietnam War, entitled "A Time to Break Silence."⁴² As Hak Joon Lee argues, King moved beyond the boundaries of race, geography, and nationality to affirm the dignity, worth, and value of Vietnamese people even when it cost him significant loss of support within and beyond the Black community.⁴³ Lee challenges James Cone's view of King's radicalism articulated in *Martin & Malcolm & America* by suggesting that while King's prophetic voice intensified in later years given the recalcitrance of White racism, he "never moved outside the bounds of his communal spirituality."⁴⁴ I agree with Lee. However, I would add that this also reflects how King did not depart from a contemplative orientation in his proclamation in later years. Said differently, King's profound contemplative orientation led him to intensify his prophetic voice. This holds true for his radical critique

---

³⁹ Martin Luther King Jr., *Where Do We Go from Here: Chaos or Community* (Boston: Beacon, 2010), 177.

⁴⁰ Dorrien, *Breaking White Supremacy*, 441.

⁴¹ Martin Luther King Jr., "The Three Dimensions of a Complete Life," in Carson and Holloran, *A Knock at Midnight*, 121–49. Many scholars have noted that this sermon is not completely original to King. Lischer does a good job exploring how King's sermon is critically adapted from Phillips Brooks' work. In other words, it is not a wholesale imitation of someone else's sermon. See Lischer, *Preacher King*, 94–98.

⁴² See Martin Luther King Jr., "A Time to Break Silence," in *A Testament of Hope: The Essential Writings and Speeches of Martin Luther King, Jr.*, ed. James M. Washington (New York: HarperSanFrancisco, 1991), 231–45.

⁴³ Lee, *We Will Get to the Promised Land*, 132–34.

⁴⁴ James Cone, *Martin and Malcolm and America: A Dream or a Nightmare*, 20th anniv. ed. (Maryknoll, N.Y.: Orbis, 2012), 235–43; Lee, *We Will Get to the Promised Land*, 99.

of economic injustice and growing frustration with White liberals as his ministry progressed. King's contemplative spiritual impulse engendered a nondualistic, inclusive vision that only expanded to include and challenge more people as he neared the end of his life.

In King's final Sunday sermon before his death, "Remaining Awake through a Great Revolution," he offers a stirring challenge to be alert to the globalized reality of life in the world—what we would today call globalization. Arguing against fragmentation, he echoes Thurman when he states, "For some strange reason I can never be what I ought to be until you are what you ought to be. And you can never be what you ought to be until I am what I ought to be. This is the way God's universe is made; this is the way it is structured."[45] Like Thurman, King was committed to seeing all life as one. However, for King, this meant both leading people to a lifegiving and liberating encounter with God that redeems the soul and proclaiming the need for structural change in systems that dehumanize and scar the soul.[46]

Celebration, Meditation, and Proclamation

Though scholars such as Hortense Spillers, Keith Miller, and Richard Lischer have explored various important stylistic dimensions of King's preaching, I primarily focus here on the third distinctive of Black contemplative preaching: a meditative homiletical style.[47] While many factors contributed to King's style, some of these include his personality, education, and exposure to preachers who modeled a more intellectual orientation in their preaching. Based upon Mervyn Warren's personal study and observation of King, we can say he was not a boisterous person in temperament, but, rather, like his mother, was naturally calm and easygoing.[48] He had a tendency toward introversion—though he technically saw himself as an "ambivert," that is, a person who reflects

---

[45] Martin Luther King Jr., "Remaining Awake through a Great Revolution," in Washington, *A Testament of Hope*, 269.

[46] Lanzetta, "Heart of a World Citizen," 255.

[47] Hortense J. Spillers, "Martin Luther King and the Style of the Black Sermon," *Black Scholar* 3, no. 1 (September 1971): 14–27; Keith D. Miller, *Voice of Deliverance: The Language of Martin Luther King Jr. and Its Sources* (New York: Free Press, 1992); and Lischer, *Preacher King*, 119–41.

[48] Warren, *King Came Preaching*, 21.

qualities of an extrovert and introvert.[49] He encountered the ecstatic preaching style characteristic of most of the southern Black church of his time at an early age. However, the younger King was embarrassed by demonstrative, "excessive" displays of emotion. Reflecting on his views when he was younger, he says, "I had doubts that religion was intellectually respectable. I revolted against the emotionalism of Negro religion, the shouting and the stamping. I didn't understand it and it embarrassed me."[50] This would eventually dissipate somewhat, as King was drawn to merge his Black Baptist roots with his educational training. For him, it was important to merge both head and heart. This was modeled in the preaching of several of his mentors and role models, such as his father, Martin Luther King Sr., Benjamin Mays, Howard Thurman, J. Pius Barbour, Gardner C. Taylor, and others. These preachers provided King with alternative ways to imagine engaging in Black proclamation that better fit his temperament, inclinations, and theological views.

Unfortunately, the influence of women on King's preaching style is often overlooked. To be sure, King's formal preaching mentors were men. King himself articulated his homiletical formation within a patrilineal genealogy.[51] And, as a Black male preacher evincing the male chauvinism that Eboni Marshall Turman suggests is often inculcated in the making of the Morehouse man, King often failed to honor the voices and contributions of women in his ministry.[52] James Cone and others have noted his sexist bias.[53] Still, as Maurice Wallace argues, women such as Alberta King (King's mother), Coretta Scott King, Mahalia Jackson, and Aretha Franklin did shape King's preaching voice.[54] For Wallace, these women make up a "countergenealogy of *musical women*" who influenced the sound of Black religiosity in the mid-twentieth century in general and "the sonic quality of King's remarkable, resonant preaching" voice in particular.[55] Earlier

---

[49] Warren, *King Came Preaching*, 21.
[50] Martin Luther King Jr., "Man of the Year," *Time*, January 3, 1964, 14.
[51] King, "The UnChristian Christian," 77.
[52] See chapter 2 for a brief discussion of Turman's work.
[53] Cone, *Martin and Malcolm and America*, 272–79.
[54] Wallace, *King's Vibrato*, chapter 5.
[55] Wallace, *King's Vibrato*, 139.

in this chapter, we saw how King's contemplative attunement to Jackson's Spirit-inspired nudge during the "I Have a Dream" speech enhanced his proclamation. In this sense, though not articulated by King himself, his meditative style of proclamation was at least indirectly shaped by the voices of Black women.

As a Baptist preacher, King believed in the priority of the sermon, but he also recognized the value of prayer and song in the liturgy of both the church and the civil rights movement. Indeed, his preaching was understood as inseparable from them. Still, preaching was prominent. King's preaching drew on some of the standard stylistic features of African American preaching—parallelism, rhythm, repetition, storytelling, rhetorical questions, and more—and modulated these into a contemplative key through his pacing and use of the sermon pause. For example, as Valentino Lassiter notes, a "powerful silence" is often evident in King's preaching.[56] He was not typically an extroverted preacher. Indeed, Warren claims it was quite unusual for King to display much physical motion during his sermons.[57] He tended to stay in the same spot, used deliberate hand movement, and made masterful eye contact. However, it is important to underline that, unlike Thurman, King tended to preach differently to Black audiences than he did before White ones. Specifically, as Baldwin notes, he whooped at times, especially when he was preaching to responsive Black congregations in the South.[58] Reflecting on the development of King's preaching, Coretta Scott King, King's wife, once stated:

> Martin also altered his style of speaking to relate to his audience. In the sober, intellectual atmosphere of New England he talked quietly, with reasoned argument and little emotion. That was generally his style as a young minister. Later, when he preached in the South to more emotional congregations, he became less inhibited. He responded to their expectations by rousing oratory; and as they were moved, he would react to their excitement, their rising emotions exalting his own. The first thunderous "Amen" from the people would set him off in the old-fashioned preaching

---

[56] Valentino Lassiter, *Martin Luther King in the African American Preaching Tradition* (Eugene, Ore.: Wipf & Stock, 2001), 42.
[57] Warren, *King Came Preaching*, 162.
[58] Baldwin, *There Is a Balm in Gilead*, 290, and Baldwin, *Never to Leave Us Alone*, 125.

style. We called it "whooping." Sometimes, after we were married, I would tease him by saying, "Martin, you were whooping today." He would be a little embarrassed. But it was very exciting, Martin's whooping.[59]

Coretta Scott King's words suggest that King's preaching was ecstatic and demonstrative at times. Reflecting the power of nommo, King's Spirit-inspired, dialogical preaching often moved his audience deeply. However, while King could appreciate the whooping of Caesar Clark and C. L. Franklin, his own whooping was largely confined to his younger years. As King's close associate Ralph D. Abernathy, recalled, "Martin seldom did it, but he could whoop."[60] For all that, King's preaching was more inspirational and celebratory than Thurman's. This makes sense not only due to the expressive Black congregations to whom King preached but also given he regularly decried unjust systems and sought to motivate people toward direct efforts to change them. His more inspirational contemplative style fit his context and goal. It is worth noting that on those occasions when King did engage in a more demonstrative style, it was often tempered by his introverted, pensive, and intellectual orientation. In the words of one contemporary observer, King was "a link between the fervid, old-time shouting religion of the Baptists" before him and "the quiet, deep-thinking, measured philosophy" of modern Baptist preachers in his time.[61] In short, King's preaching was meditative and celebrative, reflective and emotive, intellectual and inspirational.

King's meditative inspirational style is seen in the final speech/sermon he gave before his death, when he was in Memphis, Tennessee fighting for better wages for sanitation workers. The sermon is often entitled "I've Been to the Mountaintop."[62] It was delivered

---

[59] Coretta Scott King, *My Life with Martin Luther King, Jr.* (New York: Avon, 1969), 72–73, 98–99, quoted in Baldwin, *There Is a Balm in Gilead*, 285–86.

[60] Ralph D. Abernathy, interview conducted by Lewis Baldwin, March 17, 1987, quoted in Baldwin, *There Is a Balm in Gilead*, 299.

[61] Alfred Duckett, "New Negro in the South: The Martin Luther King Story," *Sepia*, March 22, 1957, 2.

[62] Martin Luther King Jr., "I See the Promised Land," in Washington, *A Testament of Hope*, 279–86. The speech is often entitled "I've Been to the Mountaintop," but Washington describes it as "I See the Promised Land."

at the Mason Temple, the headquarters of the Church of God in Christ on April 3, 1968. After preliminary remarks, King begins his sermon with meditative musings in which he converses with God about the ideal place and time of his life. With a slow pace, he invites the audience to travel with him through time before ultimately suggesting that he would rather "live just a few years in the second half of the twentieth century" than any other time period.[63] Later in the sermon, reflecting upon the story of the Good Samaritan who helps a man in need in Luke 10:25–37, King uses rhetorical questions to guide his audience to ponder what it means to "develop a kind of dangerous unselfishness."[64] Contemporizing the story, he raises a series of pointed questions, concluding by stating, "If I do not stop to help the sanitation workers, what will happen to them? That's the question."[65] The audience is invited to contemplate their response. Finally, King's meditative homiletical style is seen here in the inspiring concluding vision of the sermon. Like the mystic-prophet Moses, King declares:

> Well, I don't know what will happen now. We've got some difficult days ahead. [pause] But it doesn't matter with me now. Because I've been to the mountaintop. [applause] . . . And I've looked over. And I've seen the promised land. [brief applause] I may not get there with you. [start of heightened speech] But I want you to know tonight, that we, as a people will get to the promised land. [applause] And I'm happy, tonight. I'm not worried about anything. I'm not fearing any man. Mine eyes have seen the glory of the coming of the Lord.[66]

While King's famous words might easily be seen as indicative of Black celebratory preaching at its best, they might better be seen as Black contemplative celebratory preaching at its best. His pacing is slow. His speech is measured. While he raises his voice in a heightened manner at the very end and seems to almost engage in tuning, that is, speaking with a melodious quality of voice in preparation of

---

[63] King, "I See the Promised Land," 280.
[64] King, "I See the Promised Land," 284.
[65] King, "I See the Promised Land," 285.
[66] King, "I See the Promised Land," 286. I have added the insertions to signify the meditative and inspirational nature of King's speech.

whooping, he does not fully begin whooping.[67] The deeply moving exploration he offers of his mountaintop vision requires a meditative inspirational style. As Barbara Holmes observes, King's introduction of the metaphor of a mountain in a place with no mountains is perhaps a "hint about his own contemplative journey" toward complete dependence on God.[68] Having encountered God on the mountaintop and seen the promise of a better future, King has come to the place of fully entrusting himself to God. Of course, though he speaks rather slowly and meditatively, the audience is still deeply moved and responds with verbal affirmations. He is moved to an elevated voice and speaks in an inspiring manner about his personal experience of God. But King's final public words are not about King. They are about God. His eyes had gazed upon the beauty, wonder, and transforming power of God's glory. And this had given him hope. To put it another way, King's final words to the world were a meditative summons to join him in gazing upon God in the journey toward justice.

"Our God Is Able": A Close Reading

In the final section of this chapter, we encounter in more detail how the theo-rhetorical distinctives of Black contemplative preaching appear in King's sermonic practice; we do so through a close reading of one of his sermons. As the reader will recall, the habitus of prayer relates to the ethos of the preacher, the mystical hermeneutic relates to the logos of the preacher, and the meditative homiletical style relates to the pathos of the preacher. The sermon we will focus on for the close reading is entitled "Our God Is Able" and appears in King's published collection of sermons *Strength to Love*.[69]

Before turning to the sermon, it is important to note a few challenges related to offering this close reading. The first is that the sermon is not completely original to King.[70] The text, title, and several

---

[67] Martha Simmons, "Whooping: The Musicality of African American Preaching Past and Present," in Simmons and Thomas, *Preaching with Sacred Fire*, 865.
[68] Holmes, *Joy Unspeakable*, 131.
[69] King, *Strength to Love*, 109–17.
[70] This should not be too much of a surprise. There is a long tradition in the history of preaching of adapting (or even directly using) the sermonic material of others, and King was part of this tradition. For a helpful assessment of King's borrowing

brief lines or references are drawn directly from a European American preacher named Frederick Meek. However, overall, the sermon is clearly King's work. Second, some may object to the selection of "Our God Is Able" for my analysis given scholars suggest the sermons in *Strength to Love* were edited by the publisher in ways that obscured King's voice at certain points. As Clayborne Carson asserts, the editors at times "modified King's words out of a concern that his prose was too hard-hitting or, in some cases, politically too radical."[71] For example, in "Our God Is Able," the editors abbreviated King's criticism of colonialism and removed his reference to people who are silent in the face of injustice.[72] These are noticeable but minor changes that amount to the removal of a couple of brief sentences. Still, the editors preserved King's insistence that colonialism is evil as well as his call for ongoing social change. Indeed, a careful comparison of the original notes of the sermon "Our God Is Able" as delivered at Dexter Avenue and the sermon draft that King submitted to the editor alongside the published version reveals no major changes in the general thought and flow of the sermon.[73] Still, there is a third concern with offering a close reading of this sermon to highlight the distinctives of Black contemplative preaching: a sermon is meant to be heard, not read. Indeed, this was a conviction King shared, as noted in the preface to *Strength to Love*.[74] Nevertheless, he was compelled by others to publish his sermons. As a result, "Our God Is Able" has clearly been edited for a reading audience. Thus, while the sermon cannot capture the orality or eventfulness of King's preaching, I suggest that the text as it is printed in *Strength to Love* is a reliable basis for showing how the distinctives of Black contemplative preaching manifest in King's

---

from various White liberal sources without citing the source, see Lischer, *Preacher King*, 108–13. For a broader discussion of King's academic plagiarism, see David J. Garrow, "King's Plagiarism: Imitation, Insecurity, and Transformation," *Journal of American History* 78, no. 1 (June 1991): 86–92.

[71] Clayborne Carson, "Editorial Note," in *TPMLK*, vol. 6, 457.

[72] See Martin Luther King Jr., "Draft of Chapter XIII, 'Our God Is Able,'" in *TPMLK*, vol. 6, 530–31. It is worth noting that some of the language regarding the evils of colonialism is retained in a different part of the sermon.

[73] Compare King, "Our God Is Able," in *TPMLK*, vol. 6, 243–46; King, "Draft of Chapter XIII" 527–34; and King, *Strength to Love*, 109–17.

[74] King, *Strength to Love*, xiv

sermonic practice. For, as King states, the sermons in the volume seek to "bring the Christian message to bear on the social evils that cloud our day and the personal witness and discipline required."[75] In other words, the sermons are representative of King's commitment as a Black contemplative preacher to seek spiritual and social change in the midst of crisis.

In "Our God Is Able," Martin Luther King Jr. draws on a habitus of prayer (ethos), mystical hermeneutic (logos), and meditative homiletical style (pathos) to strengthen the inner life of his listeners so that they might endure the challenges of their time as they seek personal and social transformation. The sermon is introduced with an epigraph from Jude 24: "Now unto him that is able to keep you from falling."[76] King does not provide any historical, literary, or theological commentary on the passage in relationship to its immediate biblical context. However, the theme of the passage—especially the character of God as one who is able to sustain and strengthen humanity—is central to the sermon. The message has five primary movements that revolve around the text's insistence that God is able.

In the first movement, King's mystical hermeneutic is clearly seen in his decision to ground the sermon in what is essentially a prayer. The Scripture, Jude 24, appears at the end of the letter of Jude as a benediction celebrating God's glorious capacity to "keep" or "sustain" Christians from stumbling amid a time of deception, moral vacuity, and instability.[77] The prayer chosen as the center of the sermon also reflects King's habitus of prayer. He is able to highlight a prayer as the text of the sermon because he has cultivated a life of prayer. He has experienced what he speaks about, as will become clearer later in the sermon. However, as a recognized spiritual and moral leader and advocate for nonviolent action, King does not need to establish his ethos extensively. He begins the sermon simply: "At the center of the Christian faith is the conviction that in the universe there is a God of power who is able to do exceedingly abundant things in nature and

---

[75] King, *Strength to Love*, xiii.
[76] King, *Strength to Love*, 109.
[77] King, *Strength to Love*, 109.

in history."[78] Alluding to Jude 24, King signals with the first sentence of the sermon that he will be contemplating the sufficiency of God. Thus, he introduces the central claim of the sermon: "God is able."[79] This phrase will appear a total of eighteen times throughout the sermon and will be alluded to many other times indirectly, showcasing King's meditative homiletical style. Again and again, he will repeat the phrase like a prayer word used in centering prayer to invite his audience into the reality of the God of whom he speaks.

The remainder of the first movement addresses two factors often put forth to question the conviction that God is able. The first is that "only man is able."[80] King traces the roots of this prevalent belief to the Renaissance, the Age of Reason, and the Industrial Revolution. He contends that during this time span humans began to replace a universe that centered God with one that centered humanity. As a result, people came to believe God was not essential to life. King gives special attention to the scientism that centered humans and decentered God. Describing a series of ways in which humans celebrate the advances of modern science without reference to God, King shows his meditative homiletical style by raising a sarcastic rhetorical question: "Have not these amazing achievements assured us that man is able?"[81] He responds with a resounding "no," as he laments how scientific advancements that were once the hope of humanity became its doom. He concludes that humans are incapable of bringing salvation to themselves.

The second factor that King names challenging "the ableness of God" is the "stark and colossal reality of evil in the world."[82] Showing his mystical hermeneutic, he quotes the poet John Keats' "The Fall of Hyperion: A Dream" to advance his argument.[83] Echoing Keats, he speaks of the enormous pain and agony manifest in natural disasters that destroy lives, congenital mental illnesses, and the pain of war.

---

[78] King, *Strength to Love*, 109.
[79] King, *Strength to Love*, 109.
[80] King, *Strength to Love*, 109.
[81] King, *Strength to Love*, 110.
[82] King, *Strength to Love*, 110.
[83] For Keats' complete poem, see Poetry Foundation, John Keats, "Hyperion," accessed October 26, 2023, https://www.poetryfoundation.org/poems/44473/hyperion.

King raises a rhetorical question to facilitate theological reflection in light of these realities: Why do bad things happen if God is all-powerful? King, of course, is raising what is often termed the problem of evil, or theodicy. How could a good God permit so much suffering in the world? He does not pretend that he can solve what is ultimately a complex mystery, but he does offer a brief response. Essentially, he concludes that this sad state of affairs is a result of the sinfulness of humanity and the distorted use of freedom. He does not say much more than this. For he is convinced that "there is and always will be a penumbra of mystery surrounding God."[84] God's purposes are beyond what limited minds can fully grasp. Still, in the midst of evil and the limits of our understanding, we must not lose sight of God's reliable sufficiency.

Having introduced the core theme that God is able, King begins the second movement of the sermon by considering how God is able to "sustain the vast scope of the physical universe."[85] Like the contemplative David in Psalm 19, King meditates on the wonders of God's creation as evidence of God's power, might, and glory. Drawing on his meditative homiletical style, he seeks to move the audience through rhetorical questions to the realization that human achievements cannot compare to God. He goes on to draw on various scientific facts about creation to advance his logical argument. Here we see his mystical hermeneutic turn to nature to validate the scriptural claim that God is able.

Let me highlight two facts about the expansiveness of the solar system that King raises in order to contemplate God's glorious splendor. First, he draws attention to the speed of the earth. Imagining a race through space, he suggests the fastest jet would be sixty-six thousand miles behind Earth within the first hour of a racing competition around the sun. In other words, we live in a grand and vast universe. Second, King turns to consider the marvels of the sun more directly. Recognizing the sun as the center of the solar system, he speaks of how Earth rotates around it annually while traveling 1.6 million miles per day. The details of King's observations reveal that he is not offering

---

[84] King, *Strength to Love*, 110–11.
[85] King, *Strength to Love*, 110–11.

impromptu observations; rather, he demonstrates his own habitus of prayer. He has spent time thinking, reflecting, and meditating on the wonders of God's creation. In the words of Thomas Aquinas, he is sharing the fruits of his contemplation.[86] Reflecting on God's creation, he concludes, "So when we behold the illimitable expanse of space, in which we are compelled to measure stellar distance in light years and in which heavenly bodies travel at incredible speeds, we are forced to look beyond man and affirm anew that God is able."[87]

The third movement transitions to contemplating how God is able to "subdue all the powers of evil."[88] King affirms that the fact that God can subdue the powers of evil assumes the reality of evil. While not disparaging other spiritual and religious traditions, such as Buddhism, King states that Christianity does not see evil as simply an illusion or a failure of mental perception. On the contrary, he states that evil is a self-defeating reality. Turning to Scripture, King echoes the words of Psalm 37 as part of his mystical hermeneutic. He suggests that history witnesses to how evil forces are ultimately "cut down like the grass and wither as the green herb."[89]

To develop this argument further, King turns to three historical examples to show how God overcomes the powers of evil. Drawing on a reference from Frederick Meek's sermon "Perhaps Your God Is Not Big Enough," King begins by focusing on the Battle of Waterloo as depicted in Victor Hugo's *Les Misérables*.[90] For King, Napoleon's downfall at Waterloo represents every military power that seeks to unjustly carry out violence and crush the human spirit. They cannot win. His second example of how God overcomes evil is colonialism in Africa and Asia. This might seem odd given the reality of colonial and neocolonial powers then and now. However, echoing the British prime minister Harold Macmillan's beliefs concerning African

---

[86] Thomas Aquinas, *The Summa Theologiae*, trans. Fathers of the English Dominican Province (New York: Benziger Bros., 1947), III, Q. 40, A. 1, Ad 2, full text available at the Christian Classics Ethereal Library, https://www.ccel.org/a/aquinas/summa/SS/SS188.html#SSQ188A6THEP1.
[87] King, *Strength to Love*, 112.
[88] King, *Strength to Love*, 112.
[89] King, *Strength to Love*, 112.
[90] King, "Our God Is Able," 246, n. 9.

nations' rise in national consciousness, King believed that "the wind of change" had begun to blow.[91] Thus, he draws attention to the fall of the colonial empires that led to the development of independent nations. He sees this as the liberating work of God, work that involved "releasing more than 1,500,000 people from the crippling manacles of colonialism."[92] Finally, King draws attention to segregation in the United States as his third example of an evil system that has been challenged by the divine. King is unflinching in his condemnation of the way segregation dehumanizes and denies basic God-given rights. Yet King suggests that one thing after another has occurred to "bring a gradual end to the system of segregation."[93] In fact, he declares that it is "dead."[94] For him, the question that looms is "how costly will be the funeral."[95] King uses these three examples of evil—war, colonialism, and segregation—to speak of how systems of injustice have been challenged because at root they are out of alignment with the moral laws of the world, laws that have their origin in God. And so they are evidence of how "God is able to conquer the evils of history."[96] He brings the third movement to a close by quoting one of his favorite poems from the nineteenth-century American Romantic poet James Russell Lowell.[97] For King, God is able to overcome evil and injustice for God's own people. Thus, King is hopeful about God's care over his people in their pursuit of justice.

In the fourth movement of the sermon, King shifts to reflecting on how God is able to "give us interior resources to confront the trials and difficulties of life."[98] Demonstrating once again his mystical hermeneutic, he draws a simile between the natural world and human life to advance his argument, contrasting summer and winter, flooding and drought. He continues to name the existential

---

[91] King, *Strength to Love*, 113. See King, "Draft of Chapter XIII," 531, n. 19.
[92] King, *Strength to Love*, 113.
[93] King, *Strength to Love*, 113.
[94] King, *Strength to Love*, 113.
[95] King, *Strength to Love*, 113.
[96] King, *Strength to Love*, 114.
[97] King, *Strength to Love*, 114. For the full poem by Lowell, see James Russell Lowell, "The Present Crisis," Poets.org, accessed October 26, 2023, https://poets.org/poem/present-crisis.
[98] King, *Strength to Love*, 114.

struggle of life, turning to the noted African American poet Paul Laurence Dunbar's "Life," a poem that speaks of the brutal challenges of maintaining the basic essentials of life in an unjust world.[99] Still, despite the brutality of life, King announces yet again that "God is able."[100] God is able "to provide inner peace amid outer storms."[101] Reflecting on Jesus in the Gospels, he states that this is the primary legacy of Jesus to his disciples. Jesus does not provide a legacy of "material resources nor a magical formula" that removes us from the brutality of life, but he does give us a legacy of peace.[102] "Peace I leave with you," Jesus said.[103] King anticipates that some may conclude that God is not needed. However, he contends that part of the trouble of the world is that people have turned to rely on "gods rather than God."[104] Human history witnesses to our habit of turning to the gods of science, pleasure, and money as the object of our worship. But King argues that these are ultimately fleeting gods that lack the capacity to bring salvation or happiness. For, again, "only God is able."[105]

King draws the fourth movement to a close by calling for his audience to return to this most foundational truth. Drawing on anaphora, repetition, and rhetorical questions, he moves the audience to contemplate God as the source of life amid death, family struggles, and failing health. No matter the personal inner turmoil that one might be experiencing, King is convinced that God is able to sustain and strengthen one to move forward. After contemplating the sufficiency of God through looking at the cosmic realities of the universe, the social realities of history, and the personal realities of life, he brings the sermon to a conclusion by considering the intimate struggles of his own journey.

---

[99] King, *Strength to Love*, 115. For the full poem by Dunbar, see Paul Laurence Dunbar, "Life," Poets.org, accessed October 26, 2023, https://poets.org/poem/life-5.

[100] King, *Strength to Love*, 115.

[101] King, *Strength to Love*, 115. This line seems to have been modified by editors, specifically the later clause. Still, it easily could have been found in other speeches or sermons by King.

[102] King, *Strength to Love*, 115.

[103] King, *Strength to Love*, 115. See John 14:27.

[104] King, *Strength to Love*, 115.

[105] King, *Strength to Love*, 116.

Specifically, King offers a personal testimony of experiencing God's strength in the midst of his own trials and difficulties. This, perhaps more than anything else in the sermon, reveals his habitus of prayer. However, it does so not through showing King's spiritual strength but rather his weakness and dependence upon the divine. In other words, King draws attention to the sufficiency of God in his lowest moment. He starts by speaking of how until the age of twenty-four his life was deeply fulfilling, safe, and comfortable. He had no major problems or burdens. He went through high school, college, seminary, and a doctoral program without any substantial issues. However, King says his life began to change when he entered into leadership in the Montgomery bus protest. As he advocated for justice for African Americans, he faced trials that he had not experienced thus far in life. He began receiving "threatening telephone calls and letters."[106] He grew discouraged, tired, and fearful.

In a profoundly personal and pensive moment, he shares how one day after yet another angry call threatening his life, he felt he had "reached the saturation point."[107] He wanted to give up, quit, and step out of leadership. However, King goes on to tell his audience that, having come to the limits of his own powers, he was led to God in prayer. Sitting at the kitchen table with his head in his hands, he bowed before God and prayed aloud a prayer of surrender: "I am at the end of my powers. I have nothing left. I've come to the point where I can't face it alone."[108] In that moment of honest confession and desperation, he "experienced the presence of the Divine" in an unprecedented way.[109] He did not hear an audible voice. His situation did not supernaturally change. But, in the sanctuary of his kitchen, God graciously came to King and strengthened his inner spirit. "The outer situation remained the same," King says, "but God had given me inner calm."[110] He sensed an inner voice speaking to him: "Stand up for righteousness, stand up for truth. God will be at

---

[106] King, *Strength to Love*, 116.
[107] King, *Strength to Love*, 116. The following widely circulated story is sometimes referred to as King's "kitchen table experience."
[108] King, *Strength to Love*, 117.
[109] King, *Strength to Love*, 117.
[110] King, *Strength to Love*, 117.

your side forever."[111] His fears were removed. He knew God was with him. Three days later his house was bombed. However, King says, "I knew now that God is able to give us the interior resources to face the storms and problems of life."[112]

The message ends with an inspirational yet meditative call to faith. Speaking in the heart of the civil rights movement, King encourages his audience to not give up in their fight for justice amid the personal and social challenges they face. They can press forward because God is able "to make a way out of no way."[113] God is able to "transform dark yesterdays into bright tomorrows."[114] God *is* able.

Conclusion

During his first semester as a seminary student, Martin Luther King Jr. completed a writing assignment for a preaching course that anticipated the shape of his future preaching ministry. "Above all, I see the preaching ministry as a dual process," the young King wrote. "On the one hand I must attempt to change the soul of individuals so that their societies may be changed. On the other hand I must attempt to change the societies so that the individual soul will have a change."[115] As King grew and developed, he would demonstrate this commitment, even as he embraced more explicitly that ultimately it is God who redeems souls and societies through human instruments. Today, in some contexts, preaching is divorced from faithful discipleship in the world. For King, the two could not be separated. Throughout his short but full life, King fought passionately for the establishment of the beloved community inside and outside the pulpit. He was concerned about contemplation and action, the inner life and the outer life, the soul and society.

Many struggled, served, and marched alongside him in his journey for justice. One of these people was Barbara Harris, the first woman to be ordained a bishop in the Anglican communion. Harris

---

[111] King, *Strength to Love*, 117.
[112] King, *Strength to Love*, 117.
[113] King, *Strength to Love*, 117.
[114] King, *Strength to Love*, 117.
[115] King, "Preaching Ministry," 72.

did not know King personally, but, like others, she counted him a role model, example, and inspiration.[116] Indeed, she participated in King's historic march from Selma to Montgomery in 1965. Interestingly, Harris, like King, was also deeply impacted by Howard Thurman.[117] Both Thurman and King, among others, proved to be critical to her life, ministry, and preaching. In her own unique way, she sought to lead people to inner transformation that manifested in outward flourishing for African Americans and all creation. We now turn to consider the timely wisdom Barbara Harris offers today as a twentieth-century representative of Black contemplative preaching.

---

[116] At one point, she apparently counted King as one of the two most important mentors in her life. See Betty Cuniberti, "The Bishop of Controversy: Barbara Harris, Whose New Role Shatters Tradition, Tries a Touch of Diplomacy on Her Divided Church," *Los Angeles Times*, February 15, 1989.

[117] Fredrica Harris Thompsett, ed., *In Conversation: Michael Curry and Barbara Harris* (New York: Church, 2017), 31.

4
Embodying Prophetic Contemplation
Barbara Harris as Contemplative Preacher

> Perhaps, [the] contemplative and prophetic do not have to be mutually exclusive.
>
> Barbara Harris, personal interview[1]

Introduction

Barbara Harris (1930–2020) was a pioneering twentieth-century African American priest and advocate for justice. As a third-generation Episcopalian, she was actively engaged in the civil rights struggle in the 1960s, worked to overcome the Episcopal Church's ban on the ordination of women priests, and eventually was ordained as "the first female bishop in the Anglican communion."[2] As such, Harris was part of a long line of path-breaking Black female preachers.[3] Known for seeking to speak the truth in love, she united spiritual and social

---

[1] Barbara Harris, personal interview with author, February 26, 2019.
[2] Robert W. Prichard, *A History of the Episcopal Church: Complete through the 78th General Convention*, 3rd rev. ed. (New York: Morehouse, 2014), 333.
[3] For historical studies that examine some of these pioneering Black female preachers, see William L. Andrews, ed., *Sisters of the Spirit: Three Black Women's Autobiographies of the Nineteenth Century* (Bloomington: Indiana University Press, 1986); Bettye Collier-Thomas, *Daughters of Thunder: Black Women Preachers and their Sermons, 1850–1979* (San Francisco: Jossey-Bass, 1998); Martha Simmons and Frank Thomas, eds., *Preaching with Sacred Fire: An Anthology of African American Sermons, 1750 to the Present* (New York: W.W. Norton, 2010); Chanta M. Haywood, *Prophesying Daughters: Black Women Preachers and the Word, 1823–1913, Revised Edition* (Columbia: University of Missouri, 2016); and Kate Hanch, *Storied Witness: The Theology of Black Women Preachers in 19th-Century America* (Minneapolis: Fortress, 2022).

concerns in advocating for, in her words, "the least, the lost, and the left out."[4]

As part of my research, I was privileged to speak with Bishop Harris on several occasions over the phone. In 2019, shortly before she passed, she kindly allowed me to visit her home outside of Boston. Though I knew that Martha Simmons and Frank Thomas briefly described Harris as a part of "the contemplative preaching tradition" in their anthology on African American preaching, I wasn't sure whether Bishop Harris herself agreed with this assessment.[5] Clearly, she was not a "typical" contemplative. As the Episcopal News Service correspondent Pat McCaughan put it, she was an "irrepressible, no-holds-barred, gravelly-voiced, cigarette smoking" bishop.[6] This was confirmed when I met her in person. For nearly three hours, she held my attention with her storytelling, wit, and deep wisdom—all while smoking her cigarettes. The more I got to know Bishop Harris the more I realized she was challenging my narrow conceptions of what a contemplative might be like. As it turns out, while she resisted any notion of contemplative proclamation that was socially disengaged and solely intellectual in orientation, she suggested that she might be considered a contemplative preacher if the "contemplative and prophetic do not have to be mutually exclusive."[7] Her description of herself as a kind of prophetic contemplative preacher comports well with Black contemplative preaching as it is understood in this book. Given the persistence of patriarchal oppression alongside other injustices in our world, there is a dire need to learn from the embodied wisdom of Barbara Harris. She reveals to us a holistic spirituality and preaching that can help us in our own place and time as we proclaim the fullness of the gospel in ways that contribute to the flourishing of Black women and all creation.

---

[4] Simmons and Thomas, *Preaching with Sacred Fire*, 696.
[5] Simmons and Thomas, *Preaching with Sacred Fire*, 696.
[6] Pat McCaughan, "Service Celebrates Barbara Harris, Champion of 'the Last, the Least, and the Left Out,'" Episcopal Diocese of Los Angeles (blog), March 17, 2021, https://diocesela.org/news/service-celebrates-barbara-harris/.
[7] Harris, personal interview, February 26, 2019.

Unfortunately, as of now, there is no substantive study of Harris as a Black contemplative preacher. Indeed, I am only aware of a handful of works that reference her theology and preaching.[8] Among other reasons, this is unfortunate because she offers a unique embodiment of contemplative preaching. For instance, though she may or may not fully reflect a womanist homiletic, unlike Thurman and King, at the very least she *clearly* has quasi-womanist elements that appear in her preaching. With this in mind, let me say a word about womanism.

While the term "womanist" was coined by Alice Walker, various theologians, ethicists, biblical scholars, and others have elaborated on its meaning.[9] I use the term here to refer to "a black woman or woman of color who identifies with feminism and is committed to the survival and wholeness of all people [including herself] regardless of race, class, gender, or sexuality."[10] In light of this definition, we can see Harris' womanist orientation in her contemplative proclamation as she leads people to emancipatory encounters with God amid unjust structures while also prophetically advocating for justice for the most marginalized, including African American women. In what follows, this womanist orientation will be apparent as we discover the wisdom embodied in her life, thought, and practice of contemplative preaching—wisdom that continues to speak to the social, spiritual, and political challenges of the contemporary moment.

---

[8] For example, see John B. Clane, "Parting Words—Not Last Words," foreword to *Parting Words: A Farewell Discourse*, by Barbara C. Harris (Cambridge, Mass.: Cowley, 2003); Thelma M. Panton, "Thy Rich Anointing: The Lives and Ministries of Pauli Murray and Barbara Clementine Harris," *Sewanee Theological Review* 51, no. 4 (2008): 387–404; and Fredrica Harris Thompsett, ed., *In Conversation: Michael Curry and Barbara Harris* (New York: Church, 2017).

[9] The term womanist as developed by Alice Walker is a four-part definition. In brief, she states that a womanist is (1) "a black feminist or feminist of color," (2) "a woman who loves other women, sexually and/or nonsexually," (3) one who loves life and herself no matter what, and (4) "is to feminist as purple is to lavender." See Alice Walker, *In Search of Our Mothers; Gardens: Womanist Prose* (Orlando: Harcourt, 1983), xi–xii. In *Deeper Shades of Purple: Womanism in Religion and Society* (New York: New York University Press, 2006), Stacey Floyd-Thomas articulates four conceptual terms to correspond to Walker's four-part definition: radical subjectivity, traditional communalism, redemptive self-love, and critical engagement.

[10] Kimberly P. Johnson, *The Womanist Preacher: Proclaiming Womanist Rhetoric from the Pulpit* (Lanham, Md.: Lexington, 2017), xvii.

Womanist Wisdom on Prayer

Barbara Harris' habitus or disposition of prayer emerged as part of what Kelly Brown Douglas calls her "'womanist' DNA."[11] Growing up, Harris was surrounded by remarkable Black women who passed along "Mother wit" or everyday spiritual wisdom, such as her mother, Beatrice Price Harris, and her maternal great-grandmother, Ida Brauner Sembley (or Mom Sem, as she was affectionately known).[12] Of these women, I draw particular attention to Harris' maternal grandmother, Mary Matile Sembley Price. Price worked daily in the face of racism and sexism. Every Friday, the young Harris would join her in the grueling labor of cleaning a private day school. While walking home late after work, Price would start "singing hymns or breathing out little one-line prayers such as 'Lord, if I just can make it to my Father's house,' or 'Jesus, God from glory, come down here.'"[13] At other points, Price's prayer was simply, "I thank you, Jesus and I thank you, Lord."[14] Like African American female mystics before her, such as Jarena Lee and Sojourner Truth, young Barbara was habituated into a life of prayer in community as a means of resistance and hope in the midst of racist and sexist conditions.[15] Thereby she reflects what Emilie Townes calls a womanist spirituality of social witness.[16] "Womanist spirituality," Townes writes, "stands as a protest against the demeaning and death-dealing status quo. It seeks justice in the midst of evil, peace in the midst of violence, freedom as a counterbalance to oppression, and community rather than injustice."[17] As an African American woman, Harris embodies this spirituality, among other things, in her prayer life. For her, prayer was not simply a matter of offering words to God: it was a matter of offering one's life to God for the sake of survival. This was

---

[11] Barbara C. Harris with Kelly Brown Douglas, *Hallelujah, Anyhow! A Memoir* (New York: Church, 2018), 6.

[12] Teresa Fry Brown, *God Don't Like Ugly: African American Women Handing on Spiritual Values* (Nashville: Abingdon, 2000), 10.

[13] Harris with Douglas, *Hallelujah, Anyhow*, 9.

[14] Harris with Douglas, *Hallelujah, Anyhow*, 9.

[15] Joy R. Bostic, *African American Female Mysticism: Nineteenth-Century Religious Activism* (New York: Palgrave Macmillan, 2013).

[16] Emilie M. Townes, *In a Blaze of Glory: Womanist Spirituality as Social Witness* (Nashville: Abingdon, 1995).

[17] Townes, *In a Blaze of Glory*, 123.

crucial, as she faced tremendous racism and sexism throughout her life, such as discrimination in her high school, the brutal violation of rape, bigotry in the workplace, and fierce criticism and even death threats as she was considered for the position of bishop.[18] Her deep faith in God and life of prayer sustained her inner spirit as she persevered in calling for justice in word and deed despite these challenges. In short, Harris learned from her grandmother that prayer is a way of living attentive to God as a source of hope, life, and renewal amid the fiercest opposition and oppression.

A second early influence that shaped Harris' disposition of prayer was the ubiquitous presence of hymns in the Episcopal Church and in her home. She begins her memoir stating, "Hymns permeate my life. They are for me a form of prayer or an entry into prayer. From my earliest days in Sunday school the hymns were the best part of church for me."[19] If to sing is to pray twice, as Augustine reportedly said, then Harris' life of prayer was constantly being formed through her practice of singing.[20] Indeed, her memoir is named after one of her favorite hymns, "Hallelujah, Anyhow."[21] Harris writes, "Why the title? The hymn 'Hallelujah, Anyhow' is reflective of the attitude I have attempted to carry through life, or at least my adult life. It speaks in a real way to the ups and downs, the peaks and valleys, and the sure knowledge that whatever happens along life's rugged pathway, 'it is well with my soul.'"[22] Through all the struggles, setbacks, and unexpected challenges of her life, she learned to pray and praise as she declared "hallelujah, anyhow." Singing hymns, then, was an act of worship in the storms of life. Thus, it makes sense that she regularly included hymns in her homiletical practice—something people came to admire and expect in her preaching. This emerged from her personal habit of attending to God in prayer through solitary worship. "I enter my prayer closet each day with a hymn on my heart and often

---

[18] Harris with Douglas, *Hallelujah, Anyhow*, 26–30, 35, 39–48, 65–69, 78–83.
[19] Harris with Douglas, *Hallelujah, Anyhow*, xv.
[20] I have been unable to locate the original source for this saying. It is also sometimes attributed to Martin Luther.
[21] Harris with Douglas, *Hallelujah, Anyhow*.
[22] Harris with Douglas, *Hallelujah, Anyhow*, xv.

on my lips," she wrote.[23] "My night prayer ends with a hymn."[24] In short, singing hymns was a formative practice that helped her cultivate a disposition that was attuned to God and God's world.

As a priest and eventually as a bishop, Barbara Harris would come to encourage others to understand the importance of cultivating a habitus of prayer, especially through her mentorship and support of African American women in ministry. This is seen perhaps most clearly in the words she offered to Gayle Elizabeth Harris on her consecration as bishop suffragan of the same Episcopal diocese that she previously served. Harris challenged Gayle Harris to realize that her new life as a bishop would not consist principally in the symbols of a ring, staff, and miter, which she would receive as a consecrated bishop. On the contrary, her real life, that is her most significant life, would be based in prayer. Harris' words are worth quoting at length: "Remember this: it is *prayer* that is your life and *prayer* that is your lifeline. Your mentor and mine, the late John Thomas Walker exhorted Allen Bartlett at his consecration some seventeen years ago, 'Pray often, sing when you can, weep daily over the city, and wash the feet of the weak and the lowly, the black and the white, the poor and the rich, the sick and the healthy, the believer and the unbeliever.'"[25] Let me draw attention to a couple of things in Harris' insightful words. For one, Harris understands the essence of a minister of the gospel's life to be a life of prayer. As she put it, prayer should be the preacher's life and lifeline. In this sense, she believes that "prayer is the heart of Christian speech."[26] The preaching life, then, must be a praying life nestled deep within the beautiful and brutal realities of human existence. She contends that it is only through attentiveness to God and God's world that we can learn how to speak faithfully. Second, like Martin Luther King Jr., Harris believes that prayer cannot be a substitute for engaging in the work of God's justice in the world. On the contrary, echoing her mentor, she speaks of prayer as a kind of

---

[23] Harris with Douglas, *Hallelujah, Anyhow*, xvi.

[24] Harris with Douglas, *Hallelujah, Anyhow*, xvi.

[25] Barbara C. Harris, *Parting Words: A Farewell Discourse* (Cambridge, Mass.: Cowley, 2003), 100, author's italics.

[26] Stanley Hauerwas, *Working with Words: On Learning to Speak Christian* (Eugene, Ore.: Cascade, 2011), 93.

posture that frames and fuels the work of loving and caring for God's world and all of God's people in it. Or, as she once put it elsewhere, "Prayer can change the way we see other people. Prayer can change the way we see ourselves, especially in relationship to and with other people. Prayer can change the way we view the world."[27]

As one nurtured by Christian communities of wisdom throughout her life, Barbara Harris lived her words. "I think that preaching should reflect your deepest beliefs and your practices," she once said in an interview, "not just your views . . . and I hope that my preaching reflects my deepest beliefs and practices of life, not just intellectual views."[28] This conviction was certainly true in relation to her disposition of prayer. Besides her mother and grandmother, she was encouraged in her spiritual life as a preacher by Henri Nouwen.[29] She read many of his writings and was honored by him on one occasion for her spiritual leadership. Additionally, her life of prayer as a preacher was shaped by her mentor, Van Samuel Bird, a Black Episcopal priest and longtime professor of sociology. Indeed, she stated that almost all her sermons began with a prayer she learned from Bird.[30] It reads, "O God, the light of the minds which know you, the joy of the hearts which love you, the strength of the wills which try to serve you: Grant us to know you, so as to love you, to love you so as to serve you, in whose service is perfect freedom. And since you called all of us to your service, make us worthy of that calling and empower us for that service, through Jesus Christ our Lord."[31] Harris engages in this prayer to maintain a disposition of openness and vulnerability before God as a preacher. In the words of theologian Rowan Williams, she recognized that faithful preaching "is only preserved in any integrity by seriousness about prayer."[32] Acknowledging God as the one who enables minds, hearts, and wills, her prayer guards against preaching being reduced to a technique. Moreover, she pleads for a deeper knowledge of God that leads to love

---

[27] Barbara Harris, "A Circle of Concern," in Simmons and Thomas, *Preaching with Sacred Fire*, 698.
[28] Harris, personal interview, February 26, 2019.
[29] Thompsett, *In Conversation*, 97–98.
[30] Barbara Harris, personal interview with the author, December 9, 2019.
[31] Harris with Douglas, *Hallelujah, Anyhow*, 71.
[32] Rowan Williams, *On Christian Theology* (Oxford: Blackwell, 2000), 13.

manifest in service. Her prayer echoes the Book of Common Prayer, as it speaks of such service as "perfect freedom."[33] As an affirmation of the priesthood of all believers, the prayer ends by acknowledging that all baptized members of God's church are called to service and must be empowered by God to faithfully complete that service. In short, the prayer reflects Harris' pursuit of prayer as the foundation from which her holistic preaching would flow.

Hagar, Harris, and Hermeneutics

The second distinctive of Black contemplative preaching seen in Harris is the mystical hermeneutic. One of the early influences on her in this sense was her immersion in the Episcopal tradition. As one who grew up attending Episcopal church services, Harris was regularly exposed to lectionary readings, which typically included readings from the Psalms, the Old and New Testaments, and the Gospels. The sermons she heard were usually preached from the Gospels, a pattern she followed in her proclamation. Like Thurman, King, and other contemplative preachers, Harris deeply cherished the Gospels. However, while Harris shared Thurman's emphasis on embracing the ethics of Jesus, her Christology differed from his in some ways. For her, Jesus was not simply an unparalleled moral exemplar or teacher to follow because of his unique religious experience. On the contrary, as seen in a sermon entitled "Looking for a Savior," she preached that "Jesus Christ" is not only "the one who was" and "the one who will come again" but is "the one who is—our Savior in our today."[34] Moreover, influenced by womanist scholars such as Renita Weems, she often offered intriguing exegetical forays into Jesus' interaction with women in the Gospels. For example, in a sermon honoring Li Tim-Oi, the first woman to be ordained in the Anglican communion, Harris quoted from Weems' *Just a Sister Away: A Womanist Vision of Women's Relationships in*

---

[33] This reference is from a collect for peace during morning prayer. The sentence from which it comes reads, "O God, the author of peace and lover of concord, to know you is eternal life and to serve you is perfect freedom." See *The Book of Common Prayer: And Administration of the Sacraments and Other Rites and Ceremonies of the Church* (New York: Oxford University Press, 2006), 99.

[34] Harris, *Parting Words*, 63.

the Bible as she exegeted the story of Mary Magdalene in the Gospel of John.³⁵

Harris seemed particularly moved by the emancipatory encounters that people had with God inside and outside the Gospels. For example, along with the story of the Samaritan woman's transformative encounter with Jesus, one of her favorite texts was the Hebrew Bible story of Hagar encountering God in the wilderness. Like the womanist scholar Delores Williams, Harris highlighted the biblical figure of Hagar as a premier example of an African woman who named God and found strategies for survival and enhancement of life in the midst of the wilderness.³⁶ For her, "the faith and the trust" Hagar maintained while living isolated "in the wilderness and believing the whole time" was a testimony to how God can provide in the midst of oppression and injustice.³⁷ Moreover, the fact that Hagar was "a sistah," as she put it, was particularly important in a world that denies and dismisses the value and dignity of Black women.³⁸ In other words, the story of Hagar witnesses to a lifegiving and liberating encounter with God by a marginalized woman. Finally, along with the story of Hagar, Harris was prone to draw on the Hebrew prophets. Though she does not seem to have done so as frequently as King, she saw her ministry within this lineage and would often refer to the words of the prophets Amos, Isaiah, Micah, Jeremiah, Habakkuk, and others.³⁹

Harris' ability to engage the biblical text in an imaginative and devotional manner was nurtured through the exposure she had to Black preachers in a range of contexts growing up. This included predominantly Black Episcopal churches, along with some Baptist contexts. Many of these preachers modeled using historical and critical

---

³⁵ Renita Weems, *Just a Sister Away: A Womanist Vision of Women's Relationships in the Bible* (San Diego: LuraMedia, 1988); Barbara Harris, untitled sermon, Anglican Church of Canada, Toronto, May 6, 2007, https://www.anglican.ca/faith/worship/resources/li-tim-oi/harris/.

³⁶ Delores Williams, *Sisters in the Wilderness: The Challenge of Womanist God-Talk*, anniv. ed. (Maryknoll, N.Y.: Orbis, 2013).

³⁷ Thompsett, *In Conversation*, 75.

³⁸ Harris, personal interview, December 9, 2019.

³⁹ See, for example, Barbara Harris, "The Heart of Prophetic Preaching," address delivered at West Virginia Clergy Conference, n.d.; Harris, *Parting Words*, 54, 58.

tools alongside a finely tuned imagination. Harris' own ability to do this was further enriched through her studies. For instance, while she did not have the traditional seminary training of an ordained priest, in addition to studying at the Urban Theology Unit in Sheffield, England, she studied the Old Testament and New Testament at Villanova University and took various courses at the Episcopal Divinity School.[40] She also received over a dozen honorary doctorates from notable colleges, universities, and theological schools, including Yale University.[41] Perhaps even more than Thurman and King, her sermons evidence a keen ability to engage the historical and cultural context of Scripture passages while making insightful connections that nurture the interior life of listeners and energize public social engagement.

However, as in the case of other contemplative preachers, Harris' mystical hermeneutic relied on various sources alongside Scripture to enrich the inner life of her listeners. For example, she drew on ancestral wisdom, personal anecdotes, and especially hymns as sacred texts that speak to the soul. Many of her sermons include European and European American hymns, as well as African American spirituals. Additionally, Harris' sermons often provided insightful social and political insights that spoke to the concrete challenges of the moment.

Indeed, along with Thurman, King, and Pauli Murray (the first African American woman ordained an Episcopal priest, a trailblazing lawyer, and an outspoken advocate for justice), Barbara Harris represented what Gary Dorrien and others have called the Black social gospel.[42] Just as he did for King and Murray, Thurman influenced Harris' inclusive proclamation that married social and spiritual concern. Of course, Thurman was not the only key influence on Harris' liberative preaching. For example, Paul Washington, a strong supporter of Black theology, civil rights activist, and noted Episcopal priest of the Church of the Advocate in Philadelphia, was deeply influential in Harris' life. Harris was mentored by Washington and served at the Church of the

---

[40] Harris, personal interview, December 9, 2019.
[41] Harris with Douglas, *Hallelujah, Anyhow*, 74.
[42] Gary Dorrien, *Breaking White Supremacy: Martin Luther King Jr. and the Black Social Gospel* (New Haven: Yale University Press, 2018).

Advocate for over twenty years.[43] Its commitment to being a church that "lives the gospel" deeply shaped her theological imagination and proclamation.[44] Still, she counted Thurman as one of her greatest preaching mentors.[45] She avidly read Thurman's works, listened to his preaching, and visited the interracial Church for the Fellowship of All Peoples, which he cofounded in San Francisco. Harris appreciated how Thurman embodied nonviolence, spoke the truth in love, and cultivated the interior lives of people engaged in social action.

One may also wonder if she inherited from Thurman an inclusive, holistic vision of community and creation that reflected her African ancestors. While rooted in the Black community, she ministered among European Americans and occasionally in the Latinx community. Harris also preached around the world, including in Canada, South Africa, South Korea, and Japan. Additionally, like Thurman, she demonstrated a mystical hermeneutic that showed concern for the more-than-human creation. In a 2010 sermon, she lamented the destruction of topsoil, overuse of electricity, and overdependence on oil. Rather than acting as "masters of creation," she said, "we are called to husband the earth's resources, not abuse them."[46] She concluded her sermon with a reference to the third stanza of James Weldon Johnson's famous "Lift Ev'ry Voice and Sing," known as the African American national anthem: "Lest our feet stray from the places our God where we met thee; Lest our hearts, drunk with the wine of the world we forget thee. Shadowed beneath thy hand, May we forever stand, True to our God, True to our native land."[47] Harris proclaimed, "While written for a particular people at a particular time, the words are applicable to all of us who call God's green earth our native land."[48] Here we see her insightful contemplative

---

[43] Barbara Harris, afterword to *Other Sheep I Have: The Autobiography of Father Paul M. Washington*, by Paul Washington with David McI. Gracie (Philadelphia: Temple University Press, 1994), 231–35.

[44] Harris and Douglas, *Hallelujah, Anyhow*, 25.

[45] Thompsett, *In Conversation*, 31.

[46] Barbara Harris, untitled sermon, "It Isn't Easy Being Green" Ecumenical Worship Service, Oak Bluffs, Mass., September 5, 2010.

[47] Harris, untitled sermon, "It Isn't Easy Being Green" service.

[48] Harris, untitled sermon, "It Isn't Easy Being Green" service.

theologizing, which brought Christian theology and African American hymnody to bear on the contemporary ecological crisis.

In her role as a senior leader of other ministers, Harris encouraged the development of preaching that addressed the totality of life—inner and outer, personal and social. As mentioned, like King, she sometimes included brief but penetrating social and ethical analysis in her preaching, especially when addressing a larger public.[49] Preaching a whole gospel necessitated engaging in matters of economics and policy. For example, when asked to write a chapter in honor of the African American homiletician Henry Mitchell, she submitted an essay offering an insightful treatment of preaching and justice in the inner city that evidenced astute social analysis.[50] For Harris, this was not about being politically correct. It was an effort to be faithful to the fullness of the gospel. At the West Virginia Clergy Conference on the topic "The Heart of Prophetic Preaching," following the revered African American preacher and civil rights leader Samuel DeWitt Proctor's Lyman Beecher Lectures at Yale Divinity School, she presented the four themes of the gospel as consisting of (1) "God's presence and participation in human affairs;" (2) "spiritual renewal that restores and redeems human nature and that is available to all;" (3) "the achieving of genuine community through God's enduring love for humanity;" and (4) "the experiencing of eternity in the here and the now."[51] For her, this all-encompassing gospel should be the focus and foundation of preaching. In her unique way, she was committed to a mystical hermeneutic that centered on encountering God's transforming presence, such that one is moved to pursue the flourishing of African American women and of all creation here and now.

---

[49] See, for example, Harris, "Circle of Concern," 696–700; Barbara Harris, "What a Time," sermon, Sunshine Cathedral, Fort Lauderdale, Fl., April 25, 2010; and Barbara Harris, untitled sermon, "It Isn't Easy Being Green" service.

[50] Barbara Harris, "Can the City Be Saved? (Or Why Is There a Church on Every City Corner?)," in *Preaching on the Brink: The Future of Homiletics: In Honor of Henry H. Mitchell*, ed. Martha J. Simmons (Nashville: Abingdon, 1996), 124–32.

[51] Harris, "Heart of Prophetic Preaching." See also Samuel D. Proctor, *"How Shall They Hear?": Effective Preaching for Vital Faith* (Valley Forge, Penn.: Judson, 1992).

Mixed Preaching

The last distinctive of Black contemplative preaching to consider in Harris' life and practice of preaching is her meditative homiletical style, formed through various African American and Episcopal influences. As noted, Harris was deeply shaped by Black preaching traditions. She had family members who were part of the AME church.[52] Growing up, she periodically attended various Black Baptist churches, including Wayland Temple Baptist Church, which her grandfather's brother, Smith Price, help found.[53] She also occasionally visited Grace Baptist Church, where Jeremiah Wright Sr. served as pastor.[54] Moreover, while she worked in public relations in Philadelphia, her office was next to the AME preachers' meeting room, in which she said she "heard some very interesting preaching."[55] Finally, she had close relationships with Black preachers in the Episcopal Church, such as Paul Washington, who shaped her proclamation. As a result of this exposure to Black preaching, Harris reflected some of the common characteristics of African American preaching traditions described by Martha Simmons and Frank Thomas: a focus on the Bible, experiential expression, existential exegesis, dependence on the Holy Spirit, and a celebratory and uplifting close.[56] Indeed, she was recognized as one who embodied the Black preaching tradition at its best, as seen by her inclusion in the leading African American preaching journal the *African American Pulpit*, the anthology *Preaching with Sacred Fire*, and the esteemed Brentwood Baptist Church Elder's preaching series.[57]

However, it is important to acknowledge that Harris did not engage in the kind of ecstatic preaching often thought of as characteristic of Black proclamation. In other words, Harris was shaped by various

---

[52] Thompsett, *In Conversation*, 11.
[53] Thompsett, *In Conversation*, 12. Harris, personal interview, December 9, 2019.
[54] Harris, personal interview, December 9, 2019.
[55] Harris in Thompsett, *In Conversation*, 29.
[56] Simmons and Thomas, *Preaching with Sacred Fire*, 7–8.
[57] Barbara Harris, "A Circle of Concern," *African American Pulpit* 7, no. 2 (Spring 2004): 31–33; Simmons and Thomas, *Preaching with Sacred Fire*, 695–700; and Barbara Harris, "Elder's Series 1 6 10 7 pm Rev Barbara Harris," Brentwood Baptist Church, May 23, 2015, YouTube video, 1:25:51, https://www.youtube.com/watch?v=uTBAf4KPbZE&t=2528s.

influences that led her to *not* preach in a loud, extroverted manner. Along with her personality and natural disposition, one of these influences was the preaching of the Episcopal Church. Of course, in a sense, there is no such thing as "Episcopal preaching" because of the diversity of backgrounds, styles, and personalities that shape preachers in the Episcopal Church. Preaching in the Episcopal Church is not monolithic. Nevertheless, it is hard to deny that much, though by no means all, Episcopal preaching tends to be rather contemplative, pensive, and reflective. Harris was shaped by this homiletical ethos. To be clear, Harris did not intentionally seek for her preaching to be formed by the Episcopal Church. Indeed, quite the opposite. For instance, she refused to take a course in homiletics from the Episcopal Church as she was preparing for ordination. When her bishop asked why she would not study homiletics, Harris responded, "Because the gift of preaching has been given to me. I'm not going to let the Episcopal Church mess it up."[58] Harris learned how to preach through the natural gifting of the Spirit and informal apprenticeship that is often characteristic of Black church contexts.[59] Even so, no one escapes being shaped by the tradition in which they are immersed. As presiding bishop of the Episcopal Church Michael Curry noted about Harris' preaching, it is "clearly out of the black preaching tradition, but it's very Anglican."[60]

The Episcopal Church's preaching is far from uniform, but at least two factors influenced Harris' meditative homiletical style. For one, Harris understood preaching to be a part of the larger liturgy of the church. For the Episcopal Church, "preaching interprets the gospel tradition in light of faith and in the context of the liturgical and pastoral occasion of the service."[61] This means that preaching is not divorced from the larger rituals of prayer, song, Scripture, and, most importantly, the Eucharist.[62] In other words, preaching is not

---

[58] Harris in Thompsett, *In Conversation*, 29.
[59] Henry H. Mitchell, *Black Preaching: The Recovery of a Powerful Art* (Nashville: Abingdon, 1990), 39.
[60] Thompsett, *In Conversation*, 84.
[61] Don S. Armentrout and Robert Boak Slocum, eds., *An Episcopal Dictionary of the Church: A User-Friendly Reference for Episcopalians* (New York: Church, 2000).
[62] Gerard S. Sloyan, "Liturgical Preaching," in *Concise Dictionary of Preaching*, ed. Will Willimon and Richard Lischer (Louisville: Westminster John Knox, 1995), 311–13.

simply about preaching. It is a part of the larger ecology of worship. Harris often preceded her sermons with liturgical prayers and ended them the same way, before leading the congregation to partake in the proclamation of Christ in the Eucharist.

Second, the Episcopal preaching tradition shaped Harris by introducing her to preaching that was generally more reflective, intellectual, and meditative than ecstatic or celebratory. To be sure, Harris' preaching is not a subdued, slow meditative performance. She rejected being described in this way.[63] She once journaled, "Lord, don't let me fall into intellectualism in the pulpit. That's not me!"[64] She preferred a "heart sermon" over "a head sermon."[65] This was by no means an anti-intellectual tendency, but it does seem to reflect Harris' desire to maintain "the fire" or embodied pathos characteristic of much of Black preaching.[66] Nevertheless, Harris was not a very demonstrative or ecstatic preacher. She most certainly agreed that she was no "whooper."[67] On the spectrum between ecstatic and meditative, Harris would be closer to the latter. Her homiletical style might be described as reflecting a controlled passion, that is, she embodied a mode of preaching that is expressive but not overly extroverted. Throughout her life, she maintained a mixed heritage of preaching influenced both by expressive African American preaching traditions and the Episcopal Church.

It is important to offer a word on Harris' meditative style in light of the criticisms sometimes leveled against Black people in the Episcopal Church. As Harold T. Lewis, a noted African American historian of the church, states, due to the denomination's reputation as one of the most elite Christian bodies in the United States, African American members of the Episcopal Church are sometimes criticized for allegedly assimilating into the norms of White respectability.[68] However, despite the

---

[63] Harris, personal interview, February 26, 2019.
[64] Harris with Douglas, *Hallelujah, Anyhow*, 88.
[65] Harris with Douglas, *Hallelujah, Anyhow*, 88.
[66] Thompsett, *In Conversation*, 84.
[67] Harris, personal interview, December 9, 2019.
[68] Harold T. Lewis, *Yet With a Steady Beat: The African American Struggle for Recognition in the Episcopal Church* (Valley Forge, Penn.: Trinity, 1996), 3.

traces of racism still to be found in the Episcopal Church,[69] there is a rich history of African American Episcopalians who have celebrated African American identity and culture and fought for racial justice in that church. Some of these remarkable leaders include Absalom Jones, James Holly, Tollie LeRoy Caution, and Deborah Harmon Hines, among many others. Harris was part of this lineage. For instance, she was part of the Philadelphia chapter of the Episcopal Society for Cultural and Racial Unity (ESCRU) and the Union of Black Clergy and Laity (UBCL).[70] As such, Harris was connected with Black Episcopalians whose membership in a predominantly White denomination did not equate to an assimilation into Eurocentric culture or rejection of their own heritage. While Harris' preaching tended to be more meditative than ecstatic, she was a critic of respectability and intellectualism in her predominantly White, upper-class, and well-educated denomination. Moreover, she was a lifelong advocate for women in ministry in ways that went far beyond Thurman and King in their times. Though Harris had some privilege, as a divorced Black woman without a traditional seminary education she experienced significant racism, sexism, and opposition, especially as she was being considered for the position of the first female bishop in the Anglican communion. Skillfully, she subverted the powers that sought to demean and dehumanize her. In her Black female "preaching body," she interpreted and preached the gospel of Jesus with a meditative homiletical style that maintained a sharp social critique and crossed boundaries.[71]

The direct critique that Harris offered of unjust systems was more in line with King's practice of contemplative preaching than Thurman's. In the tradition of the biblical prophets, she aimed to challenge people without chastising them. Reflecting on her proclamation, she

---

[69] David Paulsen, "Episcopal Church Releases Racial Audit of Leadership Citing Nine Patterns of Racism in Church Culture," Episcopal News Service (blog), April 19, 2021, https://www.episcopalnewsservice.org/2021/04/19/episcopal-church-releases-racial-audit-of-leadership-citing-nine-patterns-of-racism-in-church-culture/. Of course, the Episcopal Church is one of many denominational bodies struggling with entrenched racism in its structures. The denomination is to be commended for seeking to take additional steps to address the issue.

[70] Harris with Douglas, *Hallelujah, Anyhow*, 52, 59.

[71] Amy P. McCullough, *Her Preaching Body: Conversations about Identity, Agency, and Embodiment among Contemporary Female Preachers* (Eugene, Ore.: Cascade, 2018).

stated, "Speaking the truth in love has always been my goal, and the underlying premise of most of my preaching has been justice."[72] She proclaimed justice without shouting. Neither did she preach in King's grand, elevated style. Rather, she often employed wit, sarcasm, and colloquial language in her sermons while maintaining something of a conversational tone. Still, as Episcopal historian Fredrica Thompsett notes, Harris' sermons were often "inspiring and provocative."[73] This is seen perhaps nowhere clearer than in her sermon during the Integrity Eucharist at the 2009 General Convention for the Episcopal Church. Amid the controversy over whether or not lesbian, gay, bisexual, or transgendered (LGBT) clergy should be elected as bishops in the Episcopal Church, she proclaimed:

> God has no favorites. Anybody who fears God and believes what is right is acceptable to God. If indeed God, who doeth all things well, is the creator of all things, how can some things be more acceptable to God than others? How can some people be more acceptable to God than others? If you don't want LGBT priests as bishop, don't ordain them to the transitional diaconate. Better yet, be honest and don't bestow on them the sacrament of baptism to begin with! How can you initiate someone and then treat them like they're half-assed baptized?[74]

Here we see Harris' pointed prophetic challenge to the church. However, the meditative nature of her pronouncement can be overlooked, if by "meditative" we mean the slow, pensive speech on philosophical ideas. Whether or not one agrees with Harris' theological reasoning, we see how she raises thought-provoking rhetorical questions three times in a short time frame to encourage the audience to contemplate what she sees as the utter foolishness of the Episcopal policies of the time. She is adamant about affirming the full dignity of all peoples. However, as a recording of the sermon evidences, she does not raise her voice or shout.[75] Instead, she engages in inspiring, provocative meditative preaching that challenges the norm.

---

[72] Harris, personal interview, December 9, 2019.
[73] Thompsett, *In Conversation*, 34.
[74] Thompsett, *In Conversation*, 25.
[75] Barbara Harris, "Bishop Barbara Harris: Integrity Eucharist 2009," February 11, 2021, YouTube video, 2:35, https://www.youtube.com/watch?v=QA1MW7Vrxdc.

Still, Harris could occasionally offer more pensive prophetic meditative sermons, depending on her mood and the context. She delivered one such sermon, "Peace! Be Still," at an annual Episcopal Diocese convention near Boston on November 2, 2001—just a few months after the tragic events of September 11. In the sermon, she turns to the story of Jesus calming the sea in Mark 4:35–41 as a means of addressing over five hundred clergy and parish leaders struggling with responding to the realities of loss, pain, and fear.[76] Indirectly alluding to the possible U.S. invasion of Iraq, Harris called for a communal consciousness reflecting Ubuntu and for all those present "to center down, be still, and know that God is God and that God does all things well."[77] In so doing, she used a meditative homiletical style to address personal and social realities for the sake of communal flourishing.

"A Thirst for the Kingdom": A Close Reading

A close reading of one of Barbara Harris' sermons will help to further highlight the theo-rhetorical distinctives of Black contemplative preaching. The sermon we will explore is entitled "A Thirst for the Kingdom." While the sermon appears in Ella Mitchell's *Women: To Preach or Not to Preach*, I analyze it as it is found in Harris' collection of sermons entitled *Parting Words*.[78] Unfortunately, I have been unable to obtain details on the setting of the sermon, even after speaking with Harris about the context of the message. However, there are some basic details that can be deduced. Like the other sermons in *Parting Words*, "A Thirst for the Kingdom" was preached around the year 2001, preceding Harris' retirement as suffragan bishop.[79] Additionally, the sermon was preached to a congregation in the Episcopal Diocese of Massachusetts. Based on my conversation with Harris, the

---

[76] Robert J. Barcellos, "Episcopal Diocese Begins Convention at UMASS Today," *South Coast Today*, November 2, 2001, https://www.southcoasttoday.com/article/20011102/News/311029990.

[77] Harris, *Parting Words*, 19.

[78] See Barbara Harris, "A Thirst for the Kingdom," in *Women: To Preach or Not to Preach: 21 Outstanding Black Preachers Say Yes!* ed. Ella Pearson Mitchell (Valley Forge, Penn.: Judson, 1991), 55–60; and Harris, *Parting Words*, 33–45.

[79] Clane, "Parting Words—Not Last Words," 10.

congregation likely comprised at least some African Americans and European Americans.

The primary focus "A Thirst for the Kingdom" is to invite the audience to encounter God and cultivate a thirst for God's renewal, justice, and liberation. Here, Harris claims that one's personal inner encounter with God can lead to outer spiritual and social flourishing. Throughout the sermon, she evidences a habitus of prayer (ethos), a mystical hermeneutic (logos), and a meditative homiletical style (pathos) as she leads the audience to experience holistic transformation.

To begin, it is important to recall that Barbara Harris preached this sermon in the final year of her role as bishop in the Episcopal Diocese of Massachusetts. As such, her habitus of prayer is easily established. She is ending her tenure as the first female bishop in the entire Anglican communion. Her love for God and people is recognized. She has endured intense criticism and opposition with humility, courage, and grace. Like her maternal grandmother, she has cultivated a deep spiritual attentiveness to God and others in the midst of the hardships of her life. The four movements of the sermon are strengthened by her spiritual credibility.

In the first movement, Harris draws on a mystical hermeneutic through grounding the sermon in the story of Jesus and the woman at the well in John 4:5–26. Like other Black contemplative preachers, she highlights a text that witnesses to an emancipatory encounter with the divine. The woman at the well is described as "seeking something more than water."[80] Harris defines this seeking as a "thirst for God," which she equates with having a "thirst for the Kingdom of God."[81] This is the central focus of the sermon—cultivating a "thirst" (a word that appears over a dozen times) for God and God's reign.

To encourage her audience to cultivate this thirst, Harris' mystical hermeneutic reflects her womanist roots and specifically centers the Samaritan woman in the Gospel of John. While some feminist and womanist scholars challenge negative portrayals of the woman as a

---

[80] Harris, *Parting Words*, 33.
[81] Harris, *Parting Words*, 34.

sexually loose sinner,[82] Harris proposes that in fact "in this text we learn from the imperfect, the broken, the outcast, from the woman of questionable character."[83] At the same time, for her, the Samaritan woman is the embodiment of subversive wisdom. In other words, rather than focusing on learning from someone with an "unblemished reputation," she compels us to contemplate the wisdom of a social outcast who is seeking to survive in a world that was not made for her.[84]

However, before unpacking what we can learn from the Samaritan woman's search for something more than water, in the second movement of the sermon Harris highlights how God searches for the Samaritan woman. Or, to echo the fourteenth-century mystic Julian of Norwich, we might say Harris shows God's thirst for the woman.[85] To do so, she provides some detailed historical background on the passage that further grounds her mystical hermeneutic in Scripture. For example, alluding to Ezra and Nehemiah, she notes the shocking fact that Jesus chooses to spend time in the Samaritan village despite the "antagonism" that historically existed between Jews and Samaritans.[86] Indeed, she argues that it is common for God to reveal God's self in a shocking way. For her, the story of John 4 has intertextual connections with the parable of the Good Samaritan and the story of the newly cleansed Samaritan leper who returned to Jesus to express gratitude. In each of these stories, a Samaritan is highlighted as an exemplar to teach others. In other words, God has a pattern of coming to odd places and encountering people in transformative ways. Reflecting a meditative homiletical style, Harris raises the question, "Does [Jesus] not still stop in the odd places of our lives today?"[87] Her listeners are invited to consider how God might be showing up in unlikely ways in their own lives.

---

[82] See, for example, Love Lazarus Sechrest, *Race and Rhyme: Rereading the New Testament* (Grand Rapids: Eerdmans, 2022), 130–38.
[83] Harris, *Parting Words*, 34.
[84] Harris, *Parting Words*, 34.
[85] For an insightful treatment of Julian's meditations on God's thirst for humanity, see Wendy Farley, *The Thirst of God: Contemplating God's Love with Three Women Mystics* (Louisville: Westminster John Knox, 2015), especially 121, 129, 133, 141, 143–44.
[86] Harris, *Parting Words*, 34.
[87] Harris, *Parting Words*, 34.

As Harris describes Jesus' encounter with the Samaritan woman, she further explores the revelation of his character. For example, she notes that, in the Gospel of John, it is before the Samaritan woman that Jesus reveals "in no uncertain terms that he is Messiah," that is, the anointed one to rescue Israel.[88] However, Harris emphasizes that Jesus also reveals the woman's identity—things she would rather keep hidden. In the process, the woman realizes that she has encountered "someone different from anyone she has ever met or known."[89] As the conversation shifts, Harris shows how Jesus tells the woman that he offers water that can satisfy the deepest thirsts of her life. It is water greater than the well can ever provide. "Everyone who drinks of this water," Jesus says, "will be thirsty again, but those who drink of the water that I will give will never be thirsty."[90] Harris demonstrates how the encounter with Jesus transforms the Samaritan woman's life. Indeed, showing her habitus of prayer, she includes herself as one who, along with others, is "different because God has touched" her life.[91] In other words, she is not speaking about encountering God solely in a theoretical way. She identifies with the Samaritan woman's story. She has had an emancipatory encounter with Jesus, and she invites the audience into the same.

In the third movement, Harris turns to reflect on three "clear messages" we can glean from the Samaritan woman's encounter with Jesus.[92] In so doing, she shows the inclusive dimensions of her mystical hermeneutic. She states, "We can learn from all God's people even from such folk as the Samaritan woman—a street woman, if you will."[93] Even as Harris contemplates Jesus as the one who initiates a transforming encounter with the Samaritan woman, she also contemplates the agency and wisdom of the woman as a guide for our lives today. The first lesson she suggests is to make ourselves available to meet God at the well, that is, the place where we encounter God. Drawing on biblical scholarship alongside her devotional perspective, Harris suggests that the woman went to encounter God

---

[88] Harris, *Parting Words*, 37.
[89] Harris, *Parting Words*, 39.
[90] Harris, *Parting Words*, 39; John 4:13–14.
[91] Harris, *Parting Words*, 40.
[92] Harris, *Parting Words*, 39.
[93] Harris, *Parting Words*, 40.

in the burning heat of the day while "everybody else was looking for shade."[94] However, unfortunately, many do not come to the well. Showing a meditative homiletical style, she uses anaphora to offer a series of reasons of why people are "absent from the well."[95] Some feel scorned because of their "unconventional lives."[96] Some resist being near those they find "undesirable."[97] Some are self-absorbed in their own "small box of self-pity."[98] Some are immersed in the "pastimes and pleasures of this world."[99] Some are so arrogant that "they think they don't even need a drink" from the well.[100] However, for Harris, none of these excuses are valid. She contrasts these short-lived pleasures with the possibilities that come from going to the well. Using anaphora for another series, she argues that people who fail to come to the well do not recognize that Jesus offers "new hearts, new minds, new songs to sing, new ways of looking at life, new ways of loving other people—even the unlovable—if they have a thirst for the kingdom."[101] Rather than merely offering a cultural critique of the excuses people offer for absenting themselves from the liberating and lifegiving water of God, she offers a compelling vision of possibility for those who come to the well. The rhythm established by the repetition of the word "new" in the series facilitates an emotional appeal. Those at the well are invited into a new way of being and doing in the world through thirsting for God and God's reign.

Drawing upon her life experience to nurture interiority as part of her mystical hermeneutic, a second lesson that Harris states we can learn from the Samaritan woman is that we must bring a vessel to encounter God at the well. Speaking to those in the audience who "have not grown up in the country or visited a rural area where folks rely on wells," she notes that drawing water is not like using modern conveniences such as water faucets or pressing the button on a water fountain.[102] Rather, she

---

[94] Harris, *Parting Words*, 40.
[95] Harris, *Parting Words*, 41.
[96] Harris, *Parting Words*, 41.
[97] Harris, *Parting Words*, 41.
[98] Harris, *Parting Words*, 41.
[99] Harris, *Parting Words*, 42.
[100] Harris, *Parting Words*, 41.
[101] Harris, *Parting Words*, 41.
[102] Harris, *Parting Words*, 41.

says that "to make use of a well, you must bring something with which to draw water," as the Samaritan woman did.[103] We cannot come "to the well empty-handed" to receive God's grace.[104] At first glance, it may seem as if Harris is saying grace must be earned. However, ultimately, she calls for us to bring to God "open, trusting hearts and souls" in order to receive God's living water.[105] In other words, we need only bring our need for God and our trust that God's lavish grace can fill us.

The third and final lesson that Harris offers is that the inward transformation we experience with God should lead to outer engagement with others. She notes that the woman did not only receive the blessing of encountering Jesus as the living water— she went to share with others the news of her emancipatory encounter reflecting a kind of "mystical activism."[106] "The woman at the well," Harris says, "became a well woman, a *healed* woman, and she shared her wholeness with others."[107] She suggests that our healing is never just for ourselves; rather, those who encounter God are meant to be agents of God's healing to others. Unfortunately, we often "do not share what has been given to us."[108] Drawing on a saying common in the African American church to evoke reflection, she says, "When was the last time you told someone that Jesus has brought you 'a mighty long way'?"[109] Harris charges the audience to join the Samaritan woman in sharing the liberating work of God.

After articulating three lessons that we can learn from the Samaritan woman's transformative encounter with God, Harris transitions to the final movement of the sermon by returning to the question she raised at the beginning: "Do we have a thirst for the kingdom?"[110] She notes that this is not a question she is offering to the audience; rather, it is Jesus' question to the audience. It is Jesus who asks if we will turn to his living water or "settle for the temporary thirst quenchers of

---

[103] Harris, *Parting Words*, 43.
[104] Harris, *Parting Words*, 43.
[105] Harris, *Parting Words*, 43.
[106] Bostic, *African American Female Mysticism*, 129.
[107] Harris, *Parting Words*, 43, author's italics.
[108] Harris, *Parting Words*, 44.
[109] Harris, *Parting Words*, 44.
[110] Harris, *Parting Words*, 44.

life."¹¹¹ These include the material values of contemporary society, popularity, and good credentials. Exhorting her audience to cease turning to what "will never salve the thirst of our parched, dry souls," she calls for a thirst for God's reign.¹¹² She makes clear that to thirst for God is to "thirst for righteousness, for peace, for justice for the liberation of all God's people."¹¹³ In other words, she is calling for personal and social transformation, inner and outer renewal.

Reflecting her habitus of prayer, she alludes to two songs to deepen her audience's thirst for God. The first is an excerpt from Psalm 42:1. "If we gave our testimony today," she asks, "would we sing with the psalmist, 'As the deer longs for the water brooks, so longs my soul for you, O God?'"¹¹⁴ Like the psalmist, she hungers along with God's creatures for God. This gives a window into her desperation for the divine that fuels her journey for justice. The second song she cites is Horatius Bonar's "I Heard the Voice of Jesus Say." Harris quotes the song directly: "I heard the voice of Jesus say, 'Behold, I freely give the living water; thirsty one, stoop down, and drink and live!' I came to Jesus, and I drank of that life-giving stream; my thirst was quenched, my soul revived, and now I live in him."¹¹⁵ The hymn, like the psalm, is an aperture into Harris' life of attentiveness to God and an invitation for her audience to experience the holistic transformation at the core of God's kingdom.

In the conclusion, Harris does not lead the congregation into ecstatic celebration. Instead, showing her meditative homiletical style, she raises rhetorical questions again: "Do we have a thirst for the living water with which God truly enriches our lives? Do we have a thirst for the kingdom? Do we have a thirst to emerge as truly faithful Christians, to be more than we are? Do we have a thirst for God's kingdom?"¹¹⁶ The audience is moved not to shout but to consider their responses to these questions. This is evidenced by the final words

---

¹¹¹ Harris, *Parting Words*, 44.
¹¹² Harris, *Parting Words*, 44.
¹¹³ Harris, *Parting Words*, 44.
¹¹⁴ Harris, *Parting Words*, 45.
¹¹⁵ Harris, *Parting Words*, 45. See Horatius Bonar, "I Heard the Voice of Jesus Say." The representative text of the hymn can be found at Hymnary.org, accessed October 26, 2023, https://hymnary.org/text/i_heard_the_voice_of_jesus_say_come_unto.
¹¹⁶ Harris, *Parting Words*, 45.

of the sermon: "Each of us must respond for herself or himself. Jesus is patiently waiting for our answer."[117] The open-ended nature of the sermon's conclusion moves the congregation to think, reflect, and hopefully to act in ways that reflect a thirst for Jesus and his kingdom.

Conclusion

Since Bishop Harris' passing in 2020, mere weeks before the rapid spread of the COVID-19 pandemic in the United States, I have often thought back on the conversations that I was privileged to have with her. I didn't know her well, nor did I know her for a long time. Yet, I was deeply impacted by the brief time I was able to spend with her. Her stories, humor, and deep insights have remained with me. Of the many words she offered in our conversations, perhaps more than anything else, I have returned again and again to her words on the importance of integrity in the preaching life. "I hope that my preaching reflects my deepest beliefs and practices of life," she said, "not just intellectual views."[118] This is something she shared with me on more than one occasion. She didn't simply preach about the prophetic; she sought to live the prophetic. She didn't simply talk about prayer; she sought to live prayer. In so doing, she integrated contemplation and action in profound ways that serve as a model for contemporary ministers seeking to cultivate a deep spirituality that can undergird their engagement with the crises of our world.

Clearly, Barbara Harris was an important twentieth-century practitioner of Black contemplative preaching. This is not to say that the label of contemplative preacher is the best or only description that characterizes her ministry, but she clearly reflects the distinctives of Black contemplative preaching in at least some of her life and ministry. The legacy of prophetic contemplative proclamation that she, along with Thurman, King, and others, represented continues today in a diversity of expressions. It is this legacy that we explore in the next chapter as we see how Black contemplative preaching is a diverse enduring tradition that remains profoundly relevant in the midst of contemporary spiritual and social challenges.

---

[117] Harris, *Parting Words*, 45.
[118] Harris, personal interview, February 26, 2019.

5
The Endurance of Black Contemplative Preaching

> It can only make our journey toward justice more robust, more beautiful, when we offer a diversity of paths, a more expansive vision of action.
>
> Cole Arthur Riley, *This Here Flesh*[1]

Introduction

Let us return to the scene that opened this book. The occasion is the inauguration of President Joe Biden and Vice President Kamala Harris on January 20, 2021. The nation is divided, economic hardship abounds, and the country is in the throes of a deadly pandemic. Amanda Gorman, a 22-year-old African American woman and the first National Youth Poet Laureate, has been invited to deliver a poem. Within the context of intense political polarization, ongoing racialized violence, and the recent insurrection at the U.S. Capitol, the young Black Catholic's poem calls the nation toward a new way of seeing and being. The poem is captivating, rhythmic, and inspiring. While Gorman does not claim to be a preacher, it is hard to deny that the poem is "a sort of melodic sermon."[2] She stood before the nation as a poet, preacher, and mystic. Indeed, Gorman seemed to embody the kind of quotidian mysticism that Catholic theologian Andrew Prevot suggests is characteristic of everyday Black women

---

[1] Cole Arthur Riley, *This Here Flesh: Spirituality, Liberation, and the Stories That Make Us* (New York: Convergent, 2022), 127.

[2] Danté Stewart, "Amanda Gorman, My Grandma, and the Black Tears we Cried," *Religion News Service*, January 21, 2021, https://religionnews.com/2021/01/21/amanda-gorman-my-grandma-and-the-black-tears-we-cried-yesterday/.

seeking to live a life committed to love, embodied freedom, and joy.[3] With grace and courage, she demonstrated the power and potential of the spoken word to, in her words, "communicate a spirit that is larger than ourselves."[4] If we revisit the moment of her proclamation, I believe we can catch glimpses of a kind of contemplative sermonizing outside the traditional pulpit.

For one, along with alluding to the notion of a "city on a hill" based on the Sermon on the Mount, the title of the poem, "The Hill We Climb," echoes an important theme in mystical literature: ascent.[5] Though it has "Hellenistic origination" that stretches back to Pythagoras, Plato, and Plotinus, the image of ascent has been explored by mystics for centuries in various ways to consider the nature of the soul's journey toward union or oneness with God.[6] However, for Gorman, reflecting a holistic Africana spirituality, the mystical journey of ascent is a collective undertaking toward becoming a better nation. In this sense, the poem is a prayer for the nation's ongoing journey of becoming. However, the journey does not assume that perfection is the telos. Similar to Cindy Lee, Gorman evinces a "cyclical orientation" to formation given her belief that as a nation we may once again experience defeat and devastation.[7] Second, in her poem, Gorman repeatedly resists binary thinking and promotes an inclusive vision of belonging for all. For example, drawing on Scripture, she engenders a healed and whole imagination in which triumph is found not in brutal violence but in building bridges. In so doing, she reflects the kind of "mystical seeing" that popular Catholic writer Richard Rohr claims

---

[3] See, for example, Andrew Prevot, *The Mysticism of Ordinary Life: Theology, Philosophy, and Feminism* (New York: Oxford University Press, 2023), 222–66.

[4] Amanda Gorman quoted in Michelle Obama, "'Unity with Purpose': Amanda Gorman and Michelle Obama Discuss Art, Identity, and Optimism," *Time*, February 4, 2021, https://time.com/5933596/amanda-gorman-michelle-obama-interview/.

[5] Amanda Gorman, "WATCH: Amanda Gorman Reads Inauguration Poem 'The Hill We Climb,'" *PBS NewsHour*, January 20, 2021, YouTube video, 5:52, https://www.youtube.com/watch?v=LZ055ilIiN4.

[6] Julie Canlis, "Stages of Spiritual Ascent," in *Dictionary of Christian Spirituality*, ed. Glen G. Scorgie (Grand Rapids: Zondervan, 2011), 274.

[7] Cindy S. Lee, *Our Unforming: De-Westernizing Spiritual Formation* (Minneapolis: Fortress, 2022), 20.

is crucial for "spiritual and political leaders."[8] Rather than getting trapped in either/or thinking, hers is a vision of transcending divides. This does not mean avoiding naming historic and present injustices, but it does resist dehumanization of the other. And, most obviously, the poem itself is meditative, reflective, and (mostly) slow in its delivery. As she gracefully moved her hands in sync with the rhythm of her words, Gorman invited the nation to imagine a different future for the country. There is much more to Gorman's poem that could be explored. However, since I have examined it in greater detail elsewhere, here I simply highlight her as an example of the endurance and relevance of contemplative proclamation in the twenty-first century.[9]

Indeed, in the midst of the many crises of our times—political, environmental, economic—the Black contemplative preaching stream continues to flow in a diversity of ways and places. Its wisdom is found not solely in the past but also in the present. Thus, having considered Howard Thurman, Martin Luther King Jr., and Barbara Harris as notable twentieth-century exemplars of Black contemplative preaching in previous chapters, in this final chapter we encounter various contemporary models of contemplative proclamation. While numerous individuals could be considered, I have limited my focus to four contemporary Black preachers who I contend reflect Black contemplative preaching in at least some of their preaching ministry: Ineda Pearl Adesanya, Veronica R. Goines, Luke A. Powery, and Frank A. Thomas. To be clear, while each of these individuals exhibits a contemplative dimension in part of their life, ministry, and/or preaching, they do not necessarily describe themselves as contemplative preachers with the terms that I utilize in this book. A preacher's homiletical life and approach to sermons are shaped by a constellation

---

[8] Richard Rohr, *The Naked Now: Learning to See as the Mystics See* (New York: Crossroad, 2009), 29.

[9] For a more extensive examination of Gorman as a contemplative preacher, see E. Trey Clark, "Spirit, Spoken Word, and the Search for Common Ground: Amanda Gorman as Contemplative Preacher" (paper presented at Homiletical Theology Project Consultation on "Spirituality, Preaching, and Bridging Racial Divides: Exploring Black Contemplative Preaching" at Boston University, Boston, October 17, 2023). A version of this paper along with others from the consultation will be published in a special issue of *Homiletic* in late 2024.

of factors, including their personality, ecclesial background, education, mentors, ministry context, and more. Some may resist being labeled a contemplative preacher entirely because the moniker seems too parochial to describe their varied ministry. Furthermore, I do not offer a select examination of the distinctives of Black contemplative preaching in the life, thought, and practice of preaching of these contemporary exemplars as I did with Thurman, King, and Harris in previous chapters. Neither do I seek to offer a robust close reading of their sermons. Instead, I simply provide brief biographical information about each preacher discussed here, highlight a few contemplative aspects of their preaching, and offer a *glimpse* into how the traits of Black contemplative preaching are evident in their sermons. In so doing, I accentuate the multiple ways in which Black contemplative preaching is a source of theological wisdom that can help us address the political, ecological, and spiritual challenges of our times.

One more thing: with one exception, I have chosen to focus on sermons preached in the midst of COVID-19 and the increased visibility of White supremacy to stress how Black contemplative preaching speaks poignantly to contemporary social realities. Future work should offer a fuller examination of contemporary Black contemplative preachers in a range of contexts and periods. What follows is preliminary but, hopefully, compelling evidence that Black contemplative preaching has not ended but endures.

Preaching as Spiritual Direction: Ineda Pearl Adesanya

An ordained American Baptist minister, the Rev. Ineda Pearl Adesanya is a noted leader in spiritual direction and pastoral counseling in ecumenical and interfaith contexts.[10] Currently, she serves as university chaplain and director of spiritual and religious life for Willamette University in Salem, Oregon. Previously, she served as the associate minister of spiritual life at the historic Allen Temple Baptist Church in Oakland, California. An emerging scholar of Christian spirituality, Adesanya is completing her PhD in historical and cultural

---

[10] Some of the following information about Adesanya comes from her faculty page on Willamette University's website, accessed October 26, 2023, https://willamette.edu/offices/chaplain/staff/adesanya/index.html.

studies of religion, spirituality, and history at the Graduate Theological Union in Berkeley. She is the editor of *Kaleidoscope: Broadening the Palette in the Art of Spiritual Direction*, a pioneering "people of color-centered spiritual-direction curriculum."[11]

As a chaplain, spiritual director, and pastoral counselor, Adesanya finds herself engaged in contemplative proclamation both inside and outside of traditional liturgical contexts. In this light, she often reflects what Donyelle McCray has called a "mystical homiletic" as she cultivates spaces and places to help foster "divine consciousness."[12] Sometimes this takes place in local churches, at others, in a university setting as a chaplain.

Adesanya's contemplative approach to preaching is also fitting given she is a teacher and student of contemplative spirituality. While some operate with a narrow view of contemplation that would seem to be antithetical to preaching, Adesanya does not. Building on the work of Barbara Holmes, she states, "A contemplative act is an act of deliberate consideration with the intent of seeing or experiencing God. Whatever act, gesture, thought, song, or word that reflects or brings us into the tangible presence of the Holy Spirit is an act of contemplation."[13] Reflecting on how others perceive her preaching, she shares that she has been told that "her style of preaching presents as a contemplative act."[14] This resonates with her, since her aim is that "each time I stand before a congregation, through the words that I speak, both preacher and congregation, together, will see and experience God."[15] In other words, for Adesanya, preaching is a contemplative practice inasmuch as it invites listeners to attune themselves to the presence of the divine in the world.

Indeed, in this sense, we could also say that her contemplative proclamation is a form of spiritual direction. As Kay Northcutt notes

---

[11] Ineda Pearl Adesanya, *Kaleidoscope: Broadening the Palette in the Art of Spiritual Direction* (New York: Church, 2019), xi.
[12] Donyelle C. McCray, *The Censored Pulpit: Julian of Norwich as Preacher* (Minneapolis: Fortress Academic, 2019), 101.
[13] Ineda P. Adesanya, "Prayer and Social Justice," in *Ain't Gonna Let Nobody Turn Me Around: Stories of Contemplation and Justice*, ed. Therese Taylor-Stinson (New York: Church, 2017), 6.
[14] Adesanya, "Prayer and Social Justice," 7.
[15] Adesanya, "Prayer and Social Justice," 7.

in *Kindling Desire for God: Preaching as Spiritual Direction*, such preaching "wakes us up and alerts us to the presence of God stirring in our midst."[16] As a spiritual director, Adesanya preaches to help people experience such awakening to the divine through the movements of the Spirit in the sermonic moment.

I would like to briefly draw attention to a contemplative sermon that Ineda Pearl Adesanya preached on July 18, 2021, at Allen Temple Baptist Church, where the Rev. Dr. Jacqueline Thompson serves as senior pastor. The occasion of the sermon was the conclusion of Adesanya's tenure at Allen Temple as associate minister of spiritual life before she relocated to Oregon to serve as university chaplain and director of spiritual and religious life at Willamette University. Adesanya's sermon was entitled "What Now?" based on the Scripture text Isaiah 43:16–21.[17] Essentially, Adesanya's sermon is an invitation to discern and respond to the work of God amid loss, pain, and suffering during the COVID-19 pandemic. She begins by leading the congregation in a meditative reading of the Scripture passage, drawing from the Message Bible translation completed by Eugene Peterson. Her reading of the passage reflects a kind of abbreviated form of *lectio divina*, an ancient meditative approach to engaging Scripture to encounter the divine. She tells the listeners that she will "read [the passage] really slowly," and she invites them to "do what you have to do to really receive the word" and "discern what God is saying."[18] This contemplative engagement with the Scripture passage sets the tone for the entire sermon. She seeks to help the audience to be open and receptive to the possibility of encountering the living God. Following the reading of the Scripture, Adesanya explores the intersection of the context of the Scripture and that of her listeners. She begins by noting how the Scripture comes from a time in which the people of Israel were exiles in Babylon experiencing "great suffering physically, economically, emotionally, culturally,

---

[16] Kay L. Northcutt, *Kindling Desire for God: Preaching as Spiritual Direction* (Minneapolis: Fortress, 2009), 8.

[17] "Sunday, July 18, 2021 Worship—Reverend Ineda Adesanya," Allen Temple Baptist Church, July 18, 2021, YouTube video, 1:42:19, https://www.youtube.com/watch?v=FO8jhkIJjts. Adesanya's sermon begins at the 1:02:18 mark. The alternative title of the message that she mentions is "Now What?"

[18] "Sunday, July 18, 2021 Worship."

[and] religiously."¹⁹ She parallels this with the suffering that many have experienced during the pandemic as people have faced tremendous loss due to "the passing on of our loved ones," "loss of jobs," "strained family relationships," and more.²⁰ As a pastoral counselor, she engages in a version of "lament-based hospitality," building on the biblical text to create a safe space to name the anger, fear, and anxiety that has emerged for many in her historically Black congregation.²¹

In the second movement of the sermon, having surveyed the pain of the text and world, she raises and repeats the rhetorical question "What now? What now?"²² Here she begins to invite the congregation to recognize God's presence in the midst of the suffering. Along with Kay Northcutt, as a spiritual director, Adesanya assumes both that God is always present and that we need to "cultivate attentiveness" to the divine presence.²³ For her, just as God was inviting the people of Israel to attend to the new thing God was up to amid exile, so God is present in the suffering. She contends we must discern how to respond to God's work in our lives collectively and individually. She gives a personal example of her own journey of discernment in the midst of the pandemic, but she also encourages the listeners to realize that "God speaks to us all and into each of us very differently."²⁴ She asks, "How has God been speaking to you?"²⁵

The third movement focuses on how the congregation might respond to God. Adesanya notes how God called the people of Israel to praise God as God "provided rivers through the sun-baked desert," and so she calls the listeners to the same.²⁶ Drawing on the vernacular of her grandmother, she says praising God is the only thing "we got to do."²⁷ To illustrate the nature of praise, she shares how she praised her daughter for her perseverance during her final year of high school

---

[19] "Sunday, July 18, 2021 Worship."
[20] "Sunday, July 18, 2021 Worship."
[21] Eliana Ah-Rum Ku, "A Call for Practicing Hospitality Based on Lament in Preaching for a Wounded Community," *Homiletic* 47, no. 2 (2022): 15.
[22] "Sunday, July 18, 2021 Worship."
[23] Northcutt, *Kindling Desire for God*, 3.
[24] "Sunday, July 18, 2021 Worship."
[25] "Sunday, July 18, 2021 Worship."
[26] "Sunday, July 18, 2021 Worship."
[27] "Sunday, July 18, 2021 Worship."

and freshman year at Howard University amid the pandemic. She also mentions the praise that all should have offered "at least once by now" to politician Stacey Abrams.[28] However, she notes that praise directed toward God is different. It celebrates "what God has done."[29] Thus, for Adesanya, "praise is another form of prayer because prayer is simply communicating and connecting and nurturing relationship with God."[30]

The sermon ends exemplifying what homiletician Catherine Williams calls "the homiletical dyad of sermon and song," as Adesanya leads the congregation in singing "Every Praise" by Hezekiah Walker in order to communally embody prayerful connection with the divine.[31] She tells them she hopes they "remember the song in your heart."[32] With doxological fervor, she sings of how every praise is rightly due to God.

Ineda Adesanya's moving sermon clearly shows that Black contemplative preaching continues today. She reveals a habitus of prayer as she speaks of her own journey of seeking discernment with mentors and her pastor. In other words, she has a habit of opening herself up to God in community and individually, and she invites her listeners into the same. Also, near the end of the sermon, we catch a glimpse of her own life of prayer as she leads the congregation in singing a song by heart. Her enthusiasm for a life of prayerful praise cannot be contained. The mystical hermeneutic of Black contemplative preaching is seen as she chooses to focus on a passage that speaks to God's nearness and action in a time of suffering. Drawing on the Message paraphrase, she seeks to help her listeners encounter God through the text by preparing themselves to "really receive the word."[33] Moreover, she draws on the ancestral wisdom of her grandmother as she speaks of the imperative of responding to God's call. The embodied wisdom and example of Black women has a prominent place in the sermon: recall that she also references her daughter's perseverance and the political leadership of

---

[28] "Sunday, July 18, 2021 Worship."
[29] "Sunday, July 18, 2021 Worship."
[30] "Sunday, July 18, 2021 Worship."
[31] Catherine E. Williams, "Sermon and Song: A Musically Integrative Homiletic," *Yale Journal of Music and Religion* 7, no. 2 (2021): 94.
[32] "Sunday, July 18, 2021 Worship."
[33] "Sunday, July 18, 2021 Worship."

Stacey Abrams. In this sense, the womanist impulse of Black contemplative preaching comes to light to deepen the spiritual formation of the listeners. Third, unlike some of the sermons at Allen Temple, the sermon is not ecstatic. It involves no whooping. Adesanya's pace is at times meditative, especially as she invites listeners into a kind of *lectio divina* on the passage. She utilizes various rhetorical questions to open up space for prayerful consideration. The sermon does end on a more celebratory note as she sings "Every Praise." However, echoing the work of Cleophus LaRue, the transition into song might best be understood as a move toward "doxological praise" that invites listeners to contemplate and gaze upon God in and through the celebration.[34] In short, Adesanya's timely contemplative sermon demonstrates a concern for helping listeners see and experience God on their spiritual journey. As such, she is a prominent example of the endurance of Black contemplative preaching in the present.

Multicultural Contemplative Preaching: Veronica R. Goines

An ordained Presbyterian (USA) minister, Rev. Dr. Veronica R. Goines most recently served as the co-pastor of Forest Hill Presbyterian Church in Cleveland Heights, Ohio.[35] Previously, she served as the lead pastor of the historic, multicultural St. Andrews Presbyterian Church in Marin City, California. Additionally, she has been a chaplain to incarcerated youth and adults, hospital chaplain, and affiliate faculty member at San Francisco Theological Seminary and held leadership positions in the local, regional, and national bodies of the Presbyterian Church (USA). Recognized for her powerful ministry of preaching, she contributed to Cleophus LaRue's edited volume *More Power in the Pulpit: How America's Most Effective Black Preachers Prepare Their Sermons*.[36]

---

[34] Cleophus J. LaRue, *Rethinking Celebration: From Rhetoric to Praise in African American Preaching* (Louisville: Westminster John Knox, 2016), 53.

[35] Much of the following information about Goines comes from her biography on Forest Hill Presbyterian Church's website, accessed December 10, 2020, https://www.fhcpresb.org/staff/.

[36] See Veronica R. Goines, "Listening for God" and "Sermon: Neckbone Faith," in *More Power in the Pulpit: How America's Most Effective Black Preachers Prepare Their Sermons*, ed. Cleophus J. LaRue (Louisville: Westminster John Knox, 2009), 41–58.

For Goines, preaching is a deeply spiritual matter nurtured by the Black church tradition in which she was raised. And this tradition has left a contemplative imprint on her approach to preaching as a pastor in multicultural contexts. For instance, she embraces sermon preparation as a "spiritual practice of listening, waiting, and discerning."[37] As such, sermon preparation is a process oriented toward God. Or, in the words of William Turner, it requires an "openness for God to infuse" the entire undertaking.[38]

Prayer is crucial to cultivate this openness. According to Goines, "Prayer is the essential prerequisite for sermon preparation. It places me in the path of God and attunes my ear to the voice of God. Communion with God enables the excavation of the Scriptures and the discovery of the will of God for the people of God."[39] She admits that at times it is difficult to "find and hold my center" amid distractions.[40] However, like Henri Nouwen, she believes that a "word with power is a word that comes out of silence" and maintains space for quiet and concentration as part of sermon preparation.[41]

The sermon is not simply prepared in isolation, however. For Goines, though the sermon might begin to emerge out of "dialogue between the preacher and God," the message is ultimately shaped through rhythms of pastoral care and attention and the congregation's response during the sermon event itself. For example, recognizing the diversity of the congregation, she states the people of God "participate in and assist the birthing of the sermon," whether through "demonstrative shouts of joy" or "quiet contemplation."[42] In this sense, with Evans Crawford, she recognizes that "participant proclamation" might take the form of ecstatic celebration or silent meditation.[43]

---

[37] Goines, "Listening for God," 41.

[38] William Clair Turner Jr., *Preaching That Makes the Word Plain: Doing Theology in the Crucible of Life* (Eugene, Ore.: Cascade, 2008), 21.

[39] Turner Jr., *Preaching That Makes the Word Plain*, 21.

[40] Turner Jr., *Preaching That Makes the Word Plain*, 21.

[41] Henri J. M. Nouwen, *The Way of the Heart: Desert Spirituality and Contemporary Ministry* (San Francisco: HarperSanFrancisco, 1981), 56; Goines, "Listening for God," 41.

[42] Goines, "Listening for God," 45.

[43] Evans Crawford with Thomas Troeger, *The Hum: Call and Response in African American Preaching* (Nashville: Abingdon, 1995), 25–35.

The sermon that I offer as an example of contemporary Black contemplative preaching was delivered by Goines on February 14, 2021, at Forest Hill Presbyterian Church, a community that aspires to be intentionally diverse and inclusive.[44] While the sermon happened to fall on Valentine's Day, even more importantly it was preached during Black History Month and on Transfiguration Sunday. Fittingly, Goines chose to preach from the Gospel lectionary reading, Mark 9:2–9, the story of Jesus' transfiguration. The sermon was entitled "Mount of Transfiguration."[45] Building on the theme of the Gospel story, the sermon introduces a group gathered on a "very high mount in Brookhaven, Mississippi."[46] Mountains are often holy sites.[47] And this is true in Goines' sermon as she speaks of mountains literally and figuratively as places of renewal. She tells the story of a group of "fearful yet faithful Black women and men" (notice the foregrounding of women) who in 1955 during the civil rights movement regularly ascended the mountain in Brookhaven for prayer and discernment before descending to engage the world around them.[48] Amid the anger, hatred, bigotry, and threats of death from "resistant white Southerners," the group ascended a mountain to prayerfully choose one among them to "go before them to the courthouse to register to vote," one who unfortunately would soon be killed.[49] For

---

[44] "Forest Hill Presbyterian Worship," Forest Hill Presbyterian Church, February 14, 2021, YouTube video, 1:17:44, https://www.youtube.com/watch?v=mef5DRZ7mQg&t=3431s. Goines's sermon begins at the 35:00 mark. Given the sermon was preached during one of the peak points of the COVID-19 pandemic, the sermon was streamed online for congregants.

[45] "Forest Hill Presbyterian Worship."

[46] "Forest Hill Presbyterian Worship."

[47] Mountains in Scripture, mystical literature, and in many contemporary contexts are seen as places of potential divine encounter. Just think of the experiences of Moses, Elijah, and Jesus in the biblical witness, the mountain symbolism of mystics such as Gregory of Nyssa, Hildegard of Bingen, and Thomas Merton, or the contemporary phenomenon of Korean prayer mountains. For an examination of the spiritually formative potential of nature, see Belden C. Lane, *The Solace of Fierce Landscapes: Exploring Desert and Mountain Spirituality* (New York: Oxford University Press, 2007).

[48] "Forest Hill Presbyterian Worship."

[49] "Forest Hill Presbyterian Worship." In prayerful consideration on the mountain, the group chose Lamar Smith, with his wife's consent, since the couple had no children. However, Goines notes that soon Lamar would be "shot between the eyes and killed" as he showed up to the courtroom to register to vote.

Goines, this story of prayer and the pursuit of social engagement by a group of Black folks is not unique. She notes that "Black history is replete with the stories of women and men and girls and boys who regularly ascended the mount to be encompassed by God's transformative cloud of glory to cast off fear in order to take on faith to pursue those seemingly impossible tasks of sacrifice in the interest of liberation."[50] In this sense, to echo the work of Andrew Prevot, Goines seems to be demonstrating a history of Black quotidian mystics, that is, people who open themselves to encounter God in the midst of everyday life as they struggle for justice.[51]

It is with this backdrop that in the second movement of the sermon Goines delves deeper into the story of Jesus and his disciples ascending the mountain in Mark's Gospel. Drawing attention to the validation Jesus receives on the mountain, she says "God affirms Jesus as God's own."[52] Likewise, she says that as Christians our core identity and mission is validated in "God's presence and glory."[53] This leads to a focus on the importance of gathering in community with the people of God. Reflecting an African understanding of Ubuntu mentioned in earlier chapters as well as scriptural wisdom, she challenges individualism in the church and asserts the importance of community: "We are a body. We are connected to one another. We need each other to be what God wants us to be."[54] However, this communal connection does not pertain simply to the present but also to the past. Referencing the Ghanaian Adinkra symbol of sankofa, which captures the need to return to recover what is forgotten, she speaks of how the story of Jesus on the mountain alongside Moses and Elijah is a reminder that "we must go backward every now and then in order to move forward" as a community.[55] The people of God that we are connected to extends beyond those we can see. "We are connected not only to those we know in the present," she says, "but we are connected to those in our past and we are connected to those

---

[50] "Forest Hill Presbyterian Worship."
[51] See Prevot, *Mysticism of Ordinary Life*, chapter 6.
[52] "Forest Hill Presbyterian Worship."
[53] "Forest Hill Presbyterian Worship."
[54] "Forest Hill Presbyterian Worship."
[55] "Forest Hill Presbyterian Worship."

who will be coming in the future."⁵⁶ The encounter with God in community on the mountain is where we are "guided and prepared for what awaits us down in the valley."⁵⁷ This calls for a willingness to not stay where we are. We cannot seek to hold on to these mountaintop experiences like Peter in the gospel story. Reflecting the long history of uniting contemplation and action in the Christian tradition (something that will be more pronounced in the sermon by the next exemplar), Goines says the call is to "gaze not just on the mountain" but rather to go "down the hill."⁵⁸

The final movement of the sermon challenges the congregation to figuratively ascend the mountain to persevere on the journey of faith. She names the difficult work her racially diverse congregation is facing in terms of making real changes in light of a race equity survey, and she mentions that some are hesitant to move forward. Offering a kind of lament, she speaks of how she thought society would have progressed more than it has after some of the gains in the 1950s and '60s. She even states that "if it wasn't for the love my parents instilled within me I would hate white people" given the hate, injustice, and systemic evils still being perpetuated today.⁵⁹ As Luke Powery notes, such homiletical lament adds depth to the sermon and creates space to attend to the Spirit's presence even in pain.⁶⁰ And, for Goines, lament is not in opposition to hope. Not unlike Amanda Gorman's proclamation to the nation, she concludes the sermon by calling the congregation to "climb" with her to experience the inner renewal that is essential to pursuing the arduous road toward social transformation.⁶¹ This is something she does herself. Indeed, reflecting a kind of monastic habit, "every weekend," she says, "I have to shut away for a bit."⁶² This enables her to remember her commitment before God and to find renewal to go yet again down into the valley where the work God

---

⁵⁶ "Forest Hill Presbyterian Worship."
⁵⁷ "Forest Hill Presbyterian Worship."
⁵⁸ "Forest Hill Presbyterian Worship."
⁵⁹ "Forest Hill Presbyterian Worship."
⁶⁰ Luke A. Powery, *Spirit Speech: Lament and Celebration in Preaching* (Nashville: Abingdon, 2009), 93.
⁶¹ "Forest Hill Presbyterian Worship."
⁶² "Forest Hill Presbyterian Worship."

has called her to is to be done. Aware that we cannot progress on the journey dependent on our own resources, Goines ends the sermon by describing how it is ultimately through Jesus' victory on the cross that we have strength and hope to climb toward justice.

Veronica Goines' sermon is a profound example of Black contemplative preaching. First, she shows a habitus of prayer through referencing her own habit of getting away to pray in the midst of the challenges and demands of ministry. This provides an honest and inspiring window into her spiritual life. Second, the sermon's mystical hermeneutic is clearly visible through Goines' selection of Mark 9:2–9, a story about divine encounter, as the primary text for the message. Alongside Scripture, she draws on history and African ancestral wisdom such as the notion of sankofa to guide the audience on their path toward justice. The sermon also includes references to nature that hint at an appreciation for God's creation typical of the inclusive hermeneutic of Black contemplative preaching. Third, a meditative homiletical style is evident in Goines' engaging yet controlled delivery as she continually explores the image of a mountain. The sermon is not loud or extroverted, but it is moving. In short, Goines draws on the distinctives of Black contemplative preaching in directing her diverse audience toward encountering the divine presence as they together pursue God's justice in community for African Americans and all creation.

A Humanizing Homiletic: Luke A. Powery

An ordained minister in the Progressive National Baptist Convention with Holiness-Pentecostal roots, Rev. Dr. Luke A. Powery is the dean of Duke University Chapel and professor of homiletics and African and African American Studies at Duke Divinity School in Durham, North Carolina.[63] He previously served as a professor at Princeton Theological Seminary as well as an associate minister and music minister in the United States and international contexts. Powery is the author of several works, including *Spirit Speech: Lament and Celebration in Preaching*, *Dem Dry Bones: Preaching, Death, and Hope*, *Ways of the Word: Learning to Preach for*

---

[63] Much of the following biographical information comes from Powery's faculty page at Duke Divinity School, accessed October 26, 2023, https://divinity.duke.edu/faculty/luke-powery.

Your Time and Place (with Sally A. Brown), and *Becoming Human: The Holy Spirit and the Rhetoric of Race*.[64]

While Powery should not be pigeonholed as a contemplative preacher, I do think there are suggestive reasons to describe at least some of his preaching ministry as contemplative. For one, he has been deeply influenced by the life, ministry, and writings of Howard Thurman. Powery describes Thurman as a mentor and teacher on his vocational journey, regularly quotes Thurman in books and lectures, and teaches a seminar on Thurman at Duke Divinity School entitled "Deep River: Howard Thurman, Spirituality, and the Prophetic Life."[65] Additionally, Powery often alludes to Thurman's contemplative wisdom in his sermons—as seen in the sermon on contemplation and action that I examine below.

Second, Powery employs a contemplative understanding of prayer in his profound reflections on the relationship between preaching and prayer. Like Thomas Merton, Henri Nouwen, David Benner, Cole Arthur Riley, and other modern contemplative writers, he understands prayer as a way of life that involves "paying attention to and being present to God."[66] With this contemplative understanding in mind, he offers illuminating descriptions of the integration of prayer and preaching. Let me give three brief examples. For one, echoing Augustine, Powery believes that "before you are a preacher, you are called to be a pray-er."[67] Thus, he calls for preachers to develop a life oriented toward God in all things as the context out of which preaching comes. Related to this, Powery insists on the union of "contemplative prayer and ministerial action, including preaching."[68] For him,

---

[64] See Powery's *Spirit Speech*; Powery, *Dem Dry Bones: Preaching, Death, and Hope* (Minneapolis: Fortress, 2012); Sally A. Brown and Luke A. Powery, *Ways of the Word: Learning to Preach for Your Time and Place* (Minneapolis: Fortress, 2016); and Powery, *Becoming Human: The Holy Spirit and the Rhetoric of Race* (Louisville: Westminster John Knox, 2022).

[65] See, for example, Luke Powery, "'The Growing Edge' of Life and Ministry," in *Anchored in the Current: Discovering Howard Thurman as Educator, Activist, Guide, and Prophet*, ed. Gregory C. Ellison II (Louisville: Westminster John Knox, 2020), and *Becoming Human*.

[66] Brown and Powery, *Ways of the Word*, 68.

[67] Brown and Powery, *Ways of the Word*, 56.

[68] Brown and Powery, *Ways of the Word*, 64.

the two should be understood as "existing in a mutually supportive relationship."[69] A life of contemplative listening enriches and informs a life of proclamation.

Furthermore, Powery has written on the relationship between speech and silence. Lamenting the lack of attention given to listening among busy pastors, he calls for a recovery of silence. Why? He suggests that we may "hear the voice of God as our own voice is silenced."[70] Or, to put it differently, silence can help create an "openness to the living word through which the Risen Christ, who breathes the Spirit into the church, speaks to the church."[71] In short, silence can be a doorway to speech. Additionally, building on the work of Evans Crawford, Powery has reflected on how silence in a sermon creates space for contemplative reflection and prayer.[72] He understands preaching as emerging from listening and silence: "Preaching includes the silence of pauses and these pauses can be viewed as whispers of prayer or 'prayer pockets.' Every breath, every pause, is an inhale of the life of God. . . . The pause leaves space for the voice of God."[73] Prayer permeates Powery's understanding of proclamation. In the language of Tom Troeger, he believes prayer is the beginning and end of preaching.[74] Though he does not explicitly describe himself as a contemplative preacher, it may be hard to find any contemporary Black preacher who has written more movingly on the contemplative nature of proclamation. And, as we'll see, he has not just written about it but practiced it as well.

The sermon that I have chosen to demonstrate Powery's practice of contemplative preaching is entitled "The Fullness of Following Jesus."[75] It was preached on Transfiguration Sunday on February 27,

---

[69] Brown and Powery, *Ways of the Word*, 64.
[70] Brown and Powery, *Ways of the Word*, 64.
[71] Turner, *Preaching That Makes the Word Plain*, 28.
[72] See, for example, Crawford with Thomas Troeger, *The Hum*, 25–35.
[73] Luke A. Powery, "Invocation Vocation: Preaching and Praying," in *What's Right with Preaching Today? The Enduring Influence of Fred B. Craddock*, ed. Mike Grave and André Resner (Eugene, Ore.: Cascade, 2021), 93.
[74] Thomas H. Troeger, *The End of Preaching* (Nashville: Abingdon, 2018), 72.
[75] Luke Powery's sermon entitled "The Fullness of Following Jesus" is located online at "Sunday Morning Worship Service—2/27/22—Dean Luke A. Powery," Duke Chapel, February 27, 2022, YouTube video, 1:11:39, https://www.youtube.com/watch?v=gnRdFHnF9qg&t=3379s. A sermon manuscript can also be accessed online at Duke University Chapel, accessed October 26, 2023, https://chapel.duke

2022, at Duke Chapel at Duke University. The sermon took place immediately after Russia's invasion into Ukraine. Amid the horror of an emerging war, Powery offered a timely reminder of how God is present in prayer and pain. And, in doing so, he called for a holistic discipleship that embraces contemplation and action—a theme that Charlotte Radler and others note has been central in literature on Christian spirituality.[76] Following the Revised Common Lectionary, the Scriptural basis of the sermon was Luke 9:28–43a.

The sermon begins with Powery introducing Jesus' habit of prayerful retreat as he gathers with Peter, James, and John on a mountain. Referencing Howard Thurman, Powery suggests Jesus in his humanity is taking time to "to center down, to sit quietly and see [him]self pass by."[77] For him, Jesus' experience of transfiguration on the mountain as recorded in the Gospel of Luke has all the signs of being a moment of contemplation: "prayer, visions, doxology, tabernacles, and silence."[78] While contemplation is not limited to these signs of ecstasy, as Dyan Elliot notes, some of them have been a part of the experiences of rapture for mystics in the past.[79] And, despite its differences from some of these experiences, it is hard not to see the transfiguration as such an event. The picture in the Gospel of Luke is that God is tangibly present in the encounter on the mountain. Powery suggests we often long for such space to find connection and renewal with God—even if in a different kind of context and intensity. Seeming to reflect on personal experience, he speaks of the relaxation that comes from spending time away at "the Carolina beach to hear

---

.edu/sites/default/files/02.27.22%20-%20Luke%20A.%20Powery%20-%20The%20Fullness%20of%20Following%20Jesus.pdf.

[76] See Charlotte Radler, "*Actio et Contemplatio*/Action and Contemplation," in *The Cambridge Companion to Christian Mysticism*, ed. Amy Hollywood and Patricia Z. Beckman (New York: Cambridge University Press, 2012), 211–22.

[77] Howard Thurman, *Meditations of the Heart* (Boston: Beacon, 1981), 28, quoted in "Sunday Morning Worship Service."

[78] "Sunday Morning Worship Service."

[79] Dyan Elliot, "*Raptus*/Rapture," in *The Cambridge Companion to Christian Mysticism*, ed. Amy Hollywood and Patricia Z. Beckman (New York: Cambridge University Press, 2012), 189–99.

the ocean waves and smell the salty water."[80] Such a moment invites us to "inhabit the sacrament of pause."[81]

In the second movement, Powery introduces some tension to complexify his portrayal of contemplation. Similar to Thurman, he becomes a picture of what Donyelle McCray calls "the preacher at play."[82] He does not flatten out the text. He is not in a rush to come to conclusions. He slowly and carefully invites listeners to attend to the nuance of Scripture. While "there is a place for contemplation in the spiritual life," he says, contemplation is not the totality of life with Christ.[83] Jesus does not remain on the mountain. Contemplation alone leads to an incomplete spiritual life. Like Goines, Powery observes how Jesus ascends for contemplation but descends the mountain for action. Blending the horizons of the text and the preaching context, he states that Jesus "leaves the solace of silence for the noise and shrieks of the crowd in Ukraine. The serenity of the mountain is replaced with the struggles of the global marketplace. God is in the contemplation but what Jesus reveals is that God is also present in the action."[84] It's important to note that while speaking in the context of an emerging war, Powery refuses to dehumanize the Ukraine's "power-hungry neighbor" Russia.[85] The nondual thinking he embodies is part of "a humanizing homiletic" that honors the dignity of all people and pursues a material manifestation of the unity of the Spirit.[86]

Powery goes on to raise several rhetorical questions to help his listeners consider whether they follow Jesus' example. "You may have visions of God in contemplation on a mountain retreat but to what end?"[87] It is in coming down the mountain, Powery says, that Jesus "encounters and engages others who are suffering like the son of that desperate man who shouts out for help" in the text.[88] He says, "Jesus

---

[80] Elliot, "*Raptus*/Rapture," 189–99.
[81] "Sunday Morning Worship Service."
[82] Donyelle McCray, "Playing in Church: Insights from the Boundaries of the Sermon Genre," *Liturgy* 36, no. 4 (2021): 16.
[83] "Sunday Morning Worship Service."
[84] "Sunday Morning Worship Service."
[85] "Sunday Morning Worship Service."
[86] Powery, *Becoming Human*, 99.
[87] "Sunday Morning Worship Service."
[88] "Sunday Morning Worship Service."

comes down to bring healing and wholeness to us through his action. Sometimes, you don't need to get away to a mountain to pray and do more spiritual exercises to connect to God. Sometimes, you just need to engage people who are in pain because that's where you'll find Jesus, too."[89] Here Powery's words are reminiscent of Thomas Merton: "If you regard contemplation principally as a means to escape from the miseries of human life, as a withdrawal from the anguish and the suffering of this struggle for reunion with other men in the charity of Christ, you do not know what contemplation is and you will never find God in your contemplation."[90] Genuine contemplation of the God of justice means that our prayer cannot be untethered from a world in pain.

The final movement begins with a story Powery tells of the noted author and activist Tony Campolo. The story recounts how Campolo once refused to pray for funds for a missionary doctor at a rally full of "materially prosperous" people until after they all gave to meet the need.[91] Why? He was convinced the audience had the funds to actually meet the need. And, as it turns out, the audience collected more than enough money to do so. For Powery, the story is a reminder that we need "contemplation, prayer, *and* action," because "Jesus modelled both."[92]

Powery concludes that as followers of Jesus we are called to this kind of integrated way of being. The fullness of discipleship encompasses both a life of contemplation and a life of action. Echoing Thurman again, Powery says this is a call to "live the outer life in the inward sanctuary" and "express the inward sanctuary through the outer life."[93] This is something Powery seeks for himself. Using first-person language and alliteration, he shares, "I seek to be whole and have my bifurcated life—one that normally separates contemplation and action—healed, so that I might have one full life in Christ in the cloud of calm holy mountains and in the convulsing spasms of human

---

[89] "Sunday Morning Worship Service."
[90] Thomas Merton, *New Seeds of Contemplation* (New York: New Directions, 1961), 78.
[91] "Sunday Morning Worship Service."
[92] "Sunday Morning Worship Service."
[93] "Sunday Morning Worship Service." See Thurman, *Meditations of the Heart*, 173.

chaos."[94] When we live such an integrated way of life, we engage in what Prevot calls "integral doxology," that is, a liberatory practice grounded in the telos of praising God.[95] For, as Powery concludes, we should not only be people who sing hymns to God: we are called to "become a hymn for God by being an agent of healing in the world."[96]

Luke Powery's sermon is an unusually poignant example of the distinctives of Black contemplative preaching. We glimpse Powery's habitus of prayer as he speaks of how refreshing it is to take time away from normal routines to engage in "the sacrament of pause."[97] In other words, he seems to create space for contemplation in his own life. Also, near the end of the sermon, his use of first-person language suggests that he personally seeks to merge contemplation with action in order to have a "whole" life rather than a "bifurcated life."[98] Second, the fact that the sermon is primarily focused on a mystical encounter, the transfiguration as recorded in Luke 9, reveals a mystical hermeneutic. The text reflects on one of the perennial themes of Christian mysticism: the relationship between contemplation and action. The mystical hermeneutic is also seen in how Powery draws on the wisdom of Howard Thurman along with Scripture to nurture interiority and action. The inclusive, holistic nature of the mystical hermeneutic is subtly shown in how Powery speaks of being in nature as part of contemplation and his refusal to engage in dehumanizing binary thinking as he speaks of the war between Russia and Ukraine. Third, the sermon is delivered in a meditative homiletical style. The pacing is slow. Pauses are used frequently. Rhetorical questions appear at times. And the ending involves no whooping; rather, Powery offers a meditative doxological reflection. In short, in this sermon and others, Powery shows that the homiletical theology of Black contemplative preaching continues to be embodied in ways that speak to the social and political realities of the present.

---

[94] "Sunday Morning Worship Service."
[95] Andrew Prevot, *Thinking Prayer: Theology and Spirituality amid the Crises of Modernity* (Notre Dame, Ind.: University of Notre Dame Press, 2015), 221.
[96] "Sunday Morning Worship Service."
[97] "Sunday Morning Worship Service."
[98] "Sunday Morning Worship Service."

Contemplation and Celebration: Frank A. Thomas

The contemporary Black contemplative preacher discussed in this section is Rev. Dr. Frank A. Thomas.[99] An ordained Christian Church (Disciples of Christ) minister, Thomas served as a senior pastor for thirty-one years at two noted African American churches, New Faith Baptist Church of Matteson, Illinois (eighteen years), and Mississippi Boulevard Christian Church in Memphis, Tennessee (thirteen years). He is also the founder of the PhD program in African American preaching and sacred rhetoric at Christian Theological Seminary (CTS) in Indianapolis, Indiana. Currently, he is the Director of the Compelling Preaching Initiative and Nettie Sweeney and Hugh Th. Miller Professor of Homiletics at CTS. Thomas' many books include *They Like to Never Quit Praisin' God: The Role of Celebration in Preaching*, *How to Preach a Dangerous Sermon*, *Surviving a Dangerous Sermon*, and, most recently, *God of the Dangerous Sermon*.[100]

As one recognized for pioneering contributions to the role of celebration in preaching, Frank Thomas is not often thought of as a contemplative in the field of homiletics. However, as Barbara Holmes notes in her seminal study of contemplative practices in the Black church, Thomas served as the senior pastor of a growing church that "was unusual in that it incorporated intentional contemplative practices into its worship services."[101] Holmes was a member of the church. In a 2022 interview with Thomas, reflecting on her experience, she told him "you were the first contemplative preacher that I ever heard."[102] She states Thomas' sermonizing did not include

---

[99] Much of the following biographical information on Frank Thomas comes from his faculty page at Christian Theological Seminary, accessed March 30, 2021, https://www.cts.edu/cts-faculty/frank-a-thomas/.

[100] See Frank A. Thomas's *They Like to Never Quit Praisin' God: The Role of Celebration in Preaching*, rev. and updated (Cleveland: Pilgrim, 2013), *How to Preach a Dangerous Sermon* (Nashville: Abingdon, 2018), *Surviving a Dangerous Sermon* (Nashville: Abingdon, 2020), and *God of the Dangerous Sermon* (Nashville: Abingdon, 2021).

[101] Barbara A. Holmes, *Joy Unspeakable: Contemplative Practices of the Black Church*, 2nd ed. (Minneapolis: Fortress, 2017), xx.

[102] Barbara Holmes and Donny Bryant, "Preaching from the Depths of Life with Dr. Frank Thomas," November 18, 2022, in *The Cosmic We*, produced by the Center for Action and Contemplation, podcast, 1:10:00, https://cac.org/podcasts/preaching-from-the-depths-of-life-with-dr-frank-a-thomas/.

"performance or [w]hooping."[103] However, there was a "centered quietness" orienting his sermons.[104]

Thomas resonates with this understanding of his preaching. Indeed, to my knowledge, he has become one of the first widely known Black homileticians and preachers to describe himself as a "contemplative preacher."[105] For him, this entails an appreciation for "depth" through engagement in biblical and theological reflection on ideas in sermons.[106] This may sound rather cerebral, but the depth that Thomas speaks of is not simply a matter of intellectual engagement. Rather, he believes that there is an emotive quality to ideas.[107] Hence, he speaks of how, like a jazz musician, he can hear the music of "deeply emotive ideas" in a sermon.[108]

A second quality of contemplative preaching for Thomas is that it is at times "quiet."[109] While he has an appreciation for ecstatic celebration, he recognizes that "sometimes the emotion is not in the rhythm and the cadence" of the preacher but in the more subdued engagement with emotive ideas.[110] In the words of Robert Smith Jr., we might say Thomas' preaching is "celebration, but it is also *cogitation*," that is, deep consideration of ideas.[111] Additionally, Thomas holds that contemplative preaching gives special attention to matters of "vocal tone" and "voice inflection" as part of its meditative style.[112]

Now, on the surface, it might seem as if Thomas' articulation of contemplative preaching only pertains to the mechanics of the

---

[103] Holmes and Bryant, "Preaching from the Depths of Life."

[104] Holmes and Bryant, "Preaching from the Depths of Life."

[105] See "A Conversation with Rev. Dr. Frank A. Thomas Hosted by Dr. Gina M. Stewart," December 4, 2019, YouTube video, 1:00:15, https://www.youtube.com/watch?v=CCYkICe-Ick&t=1692s. Thomas's discussion of his preaching style begins at the 9:15 mark.

[106] Thomas, "Conversation with Rev. Dr. Frank A. Thomas."

[107] Thomas, *They Like to Never Quit Praisin' God*, 26.

[108] Thomas, "Conversation with Rev. Dr. Frank A. Thomas."

[109] Thomas, "Conversation with Rev. Dr. Frank A. Thomas."

[110] Thomas, "Conversation with Rev. Dr. Frank A. Thomas."

[111] Robert Smith Jr., "Preaching as a Contemplative Theological Task," in *Our Sufficiency Is of God: Essays on Preaching in Honor of Gardner C. Taylor*, ed. Timothy George, James Earl Massey, and Robert Smith Jr. (Macon, Ga.: Mercer University Press, 2010), 152.

[112] Smith, "Preaching as a Contemplative Theological Task," 152.

sermon event itself. However, this would be an inaccurate conclusion. For him, ultimately, the sermon must be undergirded by a life of prayer and dependence on the Spirit from start to finish: "If the Holy Spirit is going to do transformative work in the lives of people, the Spirit must be involved at the point where we commence sermon preparation. Involving the Spirit from the very beginning through prayer allows us to get in contact with God's intention for the sermon."[113] In other words, sermon preparation is not a matter simply of technique but of dependence on the divine.

An example of Thomas' contemplative proclamation is a message entitled "A Grain of Sand."[114] While Thomas has preached versions of the sermon in different contexts, this particular version of the sermon was preached in 2019 for *A Sermon for Every Sunday*, a website that provides lectionary-based video sermons for congregational worship, Bible study, Sunday school class, or individual use.[115] The sermon originally aired on September 2, 2019. Though it was not preached during the COVID-19 pandemic like the other sermons by contemplative preachers I am examining in this chapter, I have included it because it is a poignant example of Thomas' contemplative preaching. Also, Thomas uploaded the sermon on his personal YouTube channel for viewing on May 9, 2022. As such, it is representative of the growing trend during COVID of prerecorded sermons being uploaded online for a global audience.

The sermon begins by introducing Psalm 139 as one of Howard Thurman's favorite portions of Scripture. Indeed, Thomas notes Thurman prayed the psalm every day of his life. Why would he do this? Thomas says Thurman "found within the boundaries of this text, the presence of God speaking illuminating revelation on a daily basis."[116] Like other mystics before him, Thurman sought "to penetrate to the living source of the biblical message, that is to the

---

[113] Thomas, *They Like to Never Quit Praisin' God*, 86.

[114] Frank Thomas, "Frank Thomas Preaches a Grain of Sand from Psalm 139:17–18," May 8, 2022, YouTube video, 17:32, https://www.youtube.com/watch?v=pfu0QaK9tNo.

[115] "About," A Sermon for Every Sunday, accessed October 26, 2023, https://asermonforeverysunday.com/about-us/.

[116] Thomas, "Frank Thomas Preaches a Grain of Sand."

Divine Word who speaks in and through human words and texts."[117] Thus, Scripture became a key context for encountering the living God. Specifically, Thomas claims the psalm reveals God as "the all-knowing God," whose thoughts outnumber the sand of the sea.[118] Drawing attention to this theme, he invites listeners to attend to the psalm as he recites the first eighteen verses of the passage. He ends his reading by asking, "How vast is the revelation of God? How vast are the thoughts of God?"[119]

This leads Thomas into the second movement of the sermon, an exploration of the first of three different yet related aspects of the thoughts of God that "outnumber the grains of sand" (Ps 139:18, NIV). Thomas' first "point" (his term) is that the vastness of the thoughts of God should help us to cultivate a disposition of humility.[120] As a professor and author, he says that no matter how deep or profound one of his sermons or books might be, "I have to humble myself and realize that I'm handling one grain of a limitless ocean of the thoughts of God."[121] Seeming to address ministry leaders and volunteers in the church, he encourages his listeners to do likewise. Individually, the most beautiful music, insightful Sunday school lesson, and exemplary sermon is still simply a single "grain of God's thought of an endless seashore of God's thoughts."[122] Or, as Augustine famously put it in his *Confessions*, before the majesty and wonder of God "even the most eloquent are mute."[123] We cannot fully articulate the infinite wisdom and splendor of God.

Building on his first point, Thomas states that the thoughts of God can never fully be grasped in a lifetime because "one grain of sand is a micro-cosmos constituted by millions of atoms and protons and neutrons."[124] To help listeners contemplate the vastness of a single grain

---

[117] Bernard McGinn, ed., *The Essential Writings of Christian Mysticism* (New York: Modern Library, 2006), 3.
[118] Thomas, "Frank Thomas Preaches a Grain of Sand."
[119] Thomas, "Frank Thomas Preaches a Grain of Sand."
[120] Thomas, "Frank Thomas Preaches a Grain of Sand."
[121] Thomas, "Frank Thomas Preaches a Grain of Sand."
[122] Thomas, "Frank Thomas Preaches a Grain of Sand."
[123] Augustine, *The Confessions of Saint Augustine*, trans. Edward B. Pusey (New Kensington, Penn.: Whitaker House, 1996), 14.
[124] Thomas, "Frank Thomas Preaches a Grain of Sand."

of sand, he offers as an example how long it would take to count the atoms in a grain of salt. Thomas posits, "Let's assume that we are able to count one billion atoms per second, despite our considerable speed, we would need over five hundred years to count the number of atoms inside a tiny grain of salt."[125] He relates this to meditating on a single verse of Scripture. Even if we spent "five hundred years at one billion insights per second" we could not plumb the endless depths of God's revelation.[126] Thus, like Thurman, we can pray and engage the same Scripture for the rest of our lives and never exhaust its insight.

As he nears the final movement of the sermon, Thomas states that he is "really excited" to share his last point. His genuine sense of enthusiasm is contagious. In the words of his mentor Henry Mitchell, he recognizes that a person's "depths cannot cry out a message or conviction never lodged in those sacred precincts in the first place."[127] It is obvious he is preaching from the overflow of deep meditation on the passage. The final point that Thomas makes is that there is vast salvific potential in a single thought of God in Scripture. For him, salvation is not limited to the individual, though it includes it. Rather, his understanding of salvation extends to embrace the personal and communal, the soul and structures, the spiritual and physical. Demonstrating his expansive view of salvation, Thomas even speaks of how "one grain [of Scripture] can feed the world and remove the deterioration of what [Pope Francis in his encyclical *Laudato Si*] calls 'our common home,'" that is, the earth itself.[128] In other words, like Thurman, Thomas believes Scripture has the potential to challenge and correct our destructive ways of relating to God's creation in order to promote its flourishing for future generations.

As Thomas continues, he employs anaphora to illustrate some of the many Scriptures that have the potential to bring hope, justice, and transformation to people and the world at large. Reflecting on the potency in a single Scripture, he proclaims, "One verse, 'They that

---

[125] Thomas, "Frank Thomas Preaches a Grain of Sand."
[126] Thomas, "Frank Thomas Preaches a Grain of Sand."
[127] Henry H. Mitchell, *The Recovery of Preaching* (New York: Harper & Row, 1977), 34.
[128] Thomas, "Frank Thomas Preaches a Grain of Sand."

wait upon the Lord, shall renew their strength. They shall mount up on wings like eagles, they shall run and not be weary, they shall walk and not faint.' One verse, 'The steadfast love of the Lord never ceases, God's mercies never come to an end. They are new every morning, great is thy faithfulness.'. . . . One verse, 'In this world, you will have tribulation, but be of good cheer, for I have overcome the world.'"[129] He concludes by returning to the words of Psalm 139.

In traditional Black folk preaching as described by William Pipes, Gerald Davis, and Jon Michael Spencer, Thomas' series of statements might be seen as the celebratory climax of the sermon.[130] However, as a contemplative preacher who values celebration, in the final movement of the sermon, Thomas brings the oration to a close in a way that creates space for lament alongside celebration. Returning again to the words of Howard Thurman, he says that Thurman "noticed in people who work for justice and improving social conditions, something very similar to a kind of despair."[131] In naming the despair that people experience in the midst of the persistence of injustice and evil, Thomas honors the complexity of human life. For him, the "selfishness in the human spirit" makes it difficult for people to be concerned for those outside of their social group.[132] And Thomas contends this shows up both in the political realm and inside the church. Engaging in a kind of lament himself, he suggests we know the despair of working for change yet seeing it resisted. "We know it. We know it. We know it. We know it," he says.[133] Still, Thomas does not end the sermon in despair or lament. Alongside these emotions, he speaks of hope.

---

[129] Thomas, "Frank Thomas Preaches a Grain of Sand."

[130] William H. Pipes, *Say Amen, Brother! Old-Time Negro Preaching: A Study in American Frustration* (Detroit: Wayne State University, [1951] 1991); Gerald L. Davis, *I Got the Word in Me and I Can Sing It, You Know: A Study of the Performed African-American Sermon* (Philadelphia: University of Pennsylvania Press, 1985); Jon Michael Spencer, *Sacred Symphony: The Chanted Sermon of the Black Preacher* (Santa Barbara: Greenwood, 1987). Of course, Thomas has written on folk preaching himself. See, for example, Frank Thomas, *Introduction to the Practice of African American Preaching* (Nashville: Abingdon, 2016), especially chaps. 1 and 2.

[131] Thomas, "Frank Thomas Preaches a Grain of Sand." I have not been able to locate the source that Thomas is referencing. However, Thurman does address despair in his meditation "Life Goes On," in *Meditations of the Heart*.

[132] Thomas, "Frank Thomas Preaches a Grain of Sand."

[133] Thomas, "Frank Thomas Preaches a Grain of Sand."

Drawing on Thurman, he describes hope as "an inlet that connects the lagoon of the ocean."[134] And he contends a single grain or verse of Scripture can be the inlet or canal that allows a person "limitless access to the ocean of the hope of God."[135] He makes clear that he is not endorsing proof-texting or the failure to engage the whole of Scripture; rather, he insists only a verse is needed. He asks, "So what is your one verse?"[136] After sharing some of his own verses, such as Psalm 46:1, he concludes by commending to listeners Psalm 139:17–18 for ongoing meditation: "How precious to me are your thoughts O God? How vast is the sum of them? If I were to number them, they would outnumber the grains of sand on the many seas. In Jesus' name, Amen."[137]

Frank Thomas' "A Grain of Sand" sermon is a vivid example of contemplative preaching. The sermon reveals his habitus of prayer in that he is clearly seeking to live the truth into which he invites his listeners. While speaking of the importance of meditating on a verse of Scripture, he shares Psalm 46:1 as one of his favorites. Moreover, given lament is a form of prayer, Thomas' disposition of prayer is seen in the naming of despair amid the selfishness that perpetuates injustice in the world. In so doing, he shows he has developed a life that is attentive both to the presence of hope and to the presence of pain in God's world. Second, a mystical hermeneutic is seen in the way that Thomas concentrates the sermon on Psalm 139, a kind of prayer that reveals God's character and universal presence. Moreover, Thomas draws heavily on the wisdom of Howard Thurman alongside various Scriptures to nurture interiority. The inclusive aspect of the mystical hermeneutic is glimpsed in how Thomas speaks on the intersection of faith and creation care when he references Pope Francis' encyclical on the earth as our common home. Finally, Thomas' sermon is more meditative than ecstatic. While his speech heightens at points in the

---

[134] Thomas, "Frank Thomas Preaches a Grain of Sand." See Howard Thurman, "Jesus and the Disinherited," part 1 (seminar discussion), side A (January 22–23, 1975), transcript from the Howard Thurman Digital Archive, Pitts Theology Library at Emory University, Atlanta, http://thurman.pitts.emory.edu/files/show/437.

[135] Thomas, "Frank Thomas Preaches a Grain of Sand."
[136] Thomas, "Frank Thomas Preaches a Grain of Sand."
[137] Thomas, "Frank Thomas Preaches a Grain of Sand."

sermon, he does not whoop. Instead, he evinces a contemplative yet celebratory tone. In a word, like Martin Luther King Jr. and others, Thomas shows that contemplative preaching is not necessarily opposed to celebratory preaching as he draws his listeners to contemplate the thoughts of God and to act in ways that promote the justice and love of God.

Conclusion

Blackness is not bounded. The overlooked tradition of contemplative preaching in the Black church witnesses to this fact. It is a diverse, boundary-crossing tradition of proclamation that unites head and heart, spirituality and social engagement as it draws people toward a transformative encounter with the living God and radical reconciliation with all of creation. For Black contemplative preachers, the world is a cloister through which prayerful reflection, proclamation, and engagement with God's world emerges. As such, they reflect a more expansive kind of activism than is often recognized in the Black church—a tradition that continues today as we have seen.

It is important to note there are many other voices that could have been considered in this chapter as part of this living tradition (see appendix B). However, if nothing else, I hope this brief survey of contemporary preachers has demonstrated that Black contemplative preaching is a diverse and enduring stream of homiletical theology. At times, these preachers focus more on the inward journey. At others, they focus more on the outward journey. Some are meditative and pensive. Others are more demonstrative. In short, there is no single type of Black contemplative sermon or preacher. Each of them in their own unique way leads people to a liberating and lifegiving encounter with God that energizes redemptive engagement in God's world and often directly challenges unjust structures. Theirs is a wisdom that we desperately need to learn from today.

Conclusion

The Black contemplative homiletic tradition is a historic and enduring source of wisdom for people of all backgrounds seeking to live and lead faithfully in times of fragmentation, fear, and unrelenting fatigue. In the midst of pervasive fragmentation, Black contemplative preaching invites us to recover an inclusive way of being and seeing that honors the sacred in ourselves, our neighbor, and all creation. Howard Thurman spoke of this spacious way of seeing as the search for common ground. Martin Luther King Jr. repeatedly spoke of the beloved community. Bishop Barbara Harris relentlessly proclaimed the gospel for the least, the last, and the left out. This is the kind of vision we need today. Indeed, as King exemplified, such an inclusive way of being and seeing can help mobilize people from different backgrounds, persuasions, and beliefs toward working for the common good of society.

Thankfully, Black contemplative preaching continues in the life and proclamation of contemporary preachers. Reflecting the wisdom of Scripture and an understanding of Ubuntu, Veronica Goines calls for a recognition of our interdependence as the Body of Christ in a racialized world of hatred and violence. While there is a need for more preachers to build on Thurman's contemplative ecological vision that affirms our integral relationship with the more-than-human world, such a vision is glimpsed in Frank Thomas' concern for what Pope Francis has called our "Our Common Home." And amid the horror of war, Luke Powery chooses to employ language that reminds us of the humanity of both the suffering and those who are inflicting suffering.

In short, Black contemplative preaching provides a holistic way of being and seeing that can help repair the brokenness of our world in the present even as we await its complete restoration in the world to come. It raises some critical questions for consideration: What prevents us from seeing the humanity of others? What steps might we take toward enacting the oneness that we have with all creation, starting in our particular context? And how might the examples of others encourage us in the journey toward common ground in times when we are discouraged? These are some of many questions to consider.

Along with speaking to the fragmentation of our contemporary moment, Black contemplative preaching also speaks to the fear that looms large for many. Specifically, in the midst of anxiety and uncertainty, Black contemplative preaching invites us to recenter our souls through being grounded in God. This is profoundly seen in Thurman, King, and Harris. Before his time, Thurman recognized that "the body keeps the score" when it comes to trauma, fear, and pain, and thus he called for the habit of silence as one way to attend to the body and calm our nervous systems.[1] King cried out to God at his kitchen table while surrounded by the dangers and never-ending demands of his fight for justice, and he proclaimed that God is able to sustain us when we come to the end of our own resources. Harris recentered in God repeatedly through embracing hymns as a form of prayer amid racism, sexism, and bigotry and taught people to say through it all "Hallelujah, Anyhow."[2] Each of these twentieth-century Black contemplative preachers reveals that being grounded in the divine will look different depending on people's personality, call, age, stage of life, and context.

Today, Black contemplative preachers continue to invite people to cultivate a rootedness in God. In the midst of tremendous loss and uncertainty, drawing on her skills as a pastoral counselor, Ineda Pearl Adesanya creates sermonic space for lament to help people name the reality of pain affecting their lives. Veronica Goines uses storytelling

---

[1] Bessel A. Van Der Kolk, *The Body Keeps the Score: Brain, Mind, and Body in the Healing of Trauma* (New York: Penguin, 2014).

[2] Barbara C. Harris with Kelly Brown Douglas. *Hallelujah, Anyhow! A Memoir* (New York: Church, 2018).

to help people recognize they are part of a larger history in which people have persevered in the midst of profound suffering and social upheaval. Frank Thomas draws listeners to meditate on the depth of Scripture and encourages them to consider how a particular verse might be a daily source of hope and strength amid despair and challenging times. These are just a few of the different ways that Black contemplative preaching can provide grounding in the challenging uncertainties of life.

Some questions to consider for reflection include: How does our community tend to respond in the midst of anxiety and uncertainty, and why? What would it be like for us as individuals or as a community to experiment with a practice such as meditation or singing that enables us to turn to God for grounding in the presence of fear? How might we learn from the history of lament in the Black church tradition in particular and in the Christian tradition more broadly in responding to unpredictable pain and suffering?

Along with profound fragmentation and fear, many today experience great fatigue. Of course, fatigue comes in many shapes and forms. Mary-Frances Winters contends there is a particular kind of "Black fatigue" that affects the bodies, minds, and souls of people of African descent given the historical realities of our racialized society—a fatigue that often lands most heavily on the lives of Black women.[3] In the fast-paced life of Western culture, there is also "the fatigue of failing to keep up" with others around us as we repeatedly seek to "create and curate" a personal or ministry identity that we think will be respected by others.[4] In the midst of these and other kinds of fatigue on the journey toward justice, Black contemplative preaching calls us to reunite contemplation and action in ways that honor our God-given identity, limits, and call. Thurman stressed developing inner resources through prayer, meditation, and corporate worship that can sustain the pursuit of creating a friendly world. King kept days of silence as he cast a vision for redeeming America's

---

[3] Mary-Frances Winters, *Black Fatigue: How Racism Erodes the Mind, Body, and Spirit* (Oakland, Calif.: Berrett-Koehler, 2020).

[4] Andrew Root, *The Congregation in a Secular Age* (Grand Rapids: Baker Academic, 2021), 9.

soul and repeatedly challenged unjust structures. While keeping her practice of communing with God in her prayer closet, Harris called for people to cultivate a thirst for the kingdom that replenished their souls even as they worked for the liberation of all God's people.

Contemporary Black contemplative preachers also unite contemplation and action in the midst of fatigue. Amid the fatigue of grief during tremendous loss due to COVID-19, Ineda Pearl Adesanya facilitates space for reflection to help people discern the particular next steps in life God might be inviting them to take. Facing the pressures and strains of congregational leadership and social injustice, Veronica Goines speaks of the need for retreat as a practice for renewal and perspective in order to sustainably engage the path of pursuing God's justice for all. And Luke Powery calls for a kind of contemplative activism as he insists that God is present amid our "fervent prayers and faithful protests."[5] In short, in different ways, Black contemplative preachers stress that the life of prayer and the life of public service cannot be fully separated without detrimental results.

A few questions for reflection related to this theme include: In our personal life, do we tend to gravitate more toward contemplation or action? What about our community? How might we create space to discern what it looks like to faithfully live within our God-given limits and call in this season? And what difference might it make for our life and vocation if we were to rest more deeply and consistently in God's unconditional love?

There are additional ways that Black contemplative preaching speaks to the contemporary moment beyond the issues of fragmentation, fear, and fatigue. However, these are three clear areas. Unfortunately, these are realities that tend to characterize almost every period of history in some shape or form. As such, it is likely that Black contemplative preaching will continue to offer much-needed wisdom far beyond the present moment.

---

[5] I draw the phrase "contemplative activism" phrase from Bruce Epperly, *Prophetic Healing: Howard Thurman's Vision of Contemplative Activism* (Richmond, Ind.: Friends United, 2020). See also "Sunday Morning Worship Service—2/27/22—Dean Luke A. Powery," Duke Chapel, February 27, 2022, YouTube video, 1:11:39, https://www.youtube.com/watch?v=gnRdFHnF9qg&t=3379s.

Appendix A: Definitions

To avoid unnecessary confusion, in this appendix I offer brief definitions of three important words used in this book: mysticism, contemplation, and contemplative preaching. Volumes could be (and, in the case of mysticism and contemplation, have been) written on each of these words. However, since this book is not strictly focused on mysticism or contemplation, I only provide a brief treatment of their meanings as they pertain to the focus of my work. One of the most influential contemporary definitions of mysticism in the Western Christian tradition comes from Bernard McGinn. "Mysticism is that part, or element, of Christian belief and practice," he argues, "that concerns the preparation for, the consciousness of, and the effect of what the mystics themselves have described as a direct and transformative [encounter with] the presence of God."[1] Simply put, mysticism refers to the quest for a deep transforming encounter with the presence of God. Of course, Christian mysticism has a long and varied history across a range of regions and traditions. Attending to this history reminds us of the contextual nature of mystical theological reflection and "the embodied realities of mystical

---

[1] Bernard McGinn, *Modern Mystics: An Introduction* (New York: Crossroad, 2023), 11. This particular definition originally appeared in McGinn, ed., *The Essential Writings of Christian Mysticism* (New York: Modern Library, 2006), xiv. See my brief delineation of the six elements of this heuristic definition in the notes to the introductory chapter. Andrew Prevot has criticized McGinn's definition for its overreliance on Bernard Lonergan's transcendental theory of cognition. Rather than a consciousness-based definition of mysticism, Prevot proposes "a grace-based" definition. Among other things, he believes conceiving of mysticism as the grace of divine union more easily encompasses mystical experiences of ordinary life that are not "dependent on distinctions between altered and normal states of consciousness." See Andrew Prevot, *The Mysticism of Ordinary Life: Theology, Philosophy, and Feminism* (New York: Oxford University Press, 2023), 14, nn. 6–7.

life."[2] Drawing on African American scholars of mystical thought such as Alton Pollard, Joy Bostic, and Andrew Prevot, I understand African American Christian mystical experience as divinely enabled embodied contact with the presence of God, whether in unique mystical encounters or in the quotidian experiences of daily life, that often has transformative effects.[3] The mystical experience of people of African descent in the United States is not understood as unique in essence but in light of their cultural history and embodied experience in North America.

Given the overlap between the words *mysticism* and *contemplation*, I will periodically use them interchangeably. Still, it is helpful to offer a definition of contemplation. While the contemplative ideal can be traced back to the writings of Plato, in various Christian traditions contemplation has often been understood as a mode of prayer that aims toward experiencing direct awareness of God.[4] For some, such as St. Teresa of Avila (1515–1582) and St. John of the Cross (1542–1591), contemplation is largely a passive act that is not reliant upon human faculties. For others, such as St. Ignatius of Loyola (1491–1556), contemplation has more of an active dimension that engages the imagination and senses. In the modern era, recovering the work of the anonymous fourteenth-century author of *The Cloud of Unknowing*, Thomas Keating (1923–2018) helped to popularize contemplative or centering prayer. In his influential book *Open Mind, Open*

---

[2] Mark A. McIntosh and Edward Howells, introduction to *The Oxford Handbook of Mystical Theology*, ed. Edward Howells and Mark A. McIntosh (New York: Oxford University Press, 2020), 2.

[3] Alton Pollard, "African American Mysticism," in *African American Religious Cultures*, vol. 1, *A–R*, ed. Anthony B. Pinn (Santa Barbara: ABC-CLIO, 2009), Joy R. Bostic, *African American Female Mysticism: Nineteenth-Century Religious Activism* (New York: Palgrave Macmillan, 2013), and Prevot, *The Mysticism of Ordinary Life*, chapter 6. For a brief discussion of how Pollard and Bostic shape my work, see E. Trey Clark, "Contemplation, Proclamation, and Social Transformation: Reclaiming the Homiletical Theology of Black Contemplative Preaching" (PhD diss., Fuller Theological Seminary, 2021), 14–15.

[4] For a helpful brief essay on the nature of Christian contemplation, see Keith J. Egan, "Contemplation" in *The New Westminster Dictionary of Christian Spirituality* ed. Phillip Sheldrake (Louisville: Westminster John Knox, 2005), 211–12. See also the classic text by Cuthbert Butler, *Western Mysticism: The Teaching of Saints Augustine, Gregory and Bernard on Contemplation and the Contemplative Life* (New York: Dutton, 1923).

Heart, Keating writes, "Contemplative prayer is a process of interior transformation, a conversation initiated by God and leading, if we consent, to divine union."[5] He goes on to say that contemplative or centering prayer "is a way of putting yourself at God's disposal; it is He who determines the consequences."[6] For Keating, contemplation is both a practice and a gift of awakening to the reality of God. Or, to quote another influential twentieth-century spiritual writer, Thomas Merton (1915–1968), contemplation is the gift of "awakening to the Real within all that is real."[7]

Barbara Holmes has offered the most robust description of contemplation in the Black church in her pioneering work, *Joy Unspeakable*. For Holmes, contemplation "can be silent or evocative, still or embodied in dance and shout."[8] She challenges the notion that contemplation is a privilege reserved for those who have the luxury of retreating to a monastery. For her, contemplation is learning to attend to God amid the complex and often challenging realities of everyday life. The thread interwoven throughout the diverse manifestations of contemplative practice is "attentiveness to the Spirit of God."[9] Drawing on Holmes' work, I propose that Black contemplation may be defined as a constellation of communal and personal embodied spiritual practices engaged in by people of African descent in order to attend to God and God's world for the sake of spiritual and social flourishing. In Black Christian traditions, such practices are a means of turning one's focus "to the presence of God that has been made available in Christ by the Spirit."[10] With this definition in mind, I will be drawing attention to the agency of individual practitioners of Black contemplative practice—specifically the practice of contemplative preaching. I now turn to define this vital term.

---

[5] Thomas Keating, *Open Mind, Open Heart: The Contemplative Dimension of the Gospel* (New York: Continuum, 1997), 4.

[6] Keating, *Open Mind, Open Heart*, 36.

[7] Thomas Merton, *New Seeds of Contemplation* (New York: New Directions, 1961), 3.

[8] Barbara A. Holmes, *Joy Unspeakable: Contemplative Practices of the Black Church*, 2nd ed. (Minneapolis: Fortress, 2017), 5.

[9] Holmes, *Joy Unspeakable*, 5.

[10] John H. Coe and Kyle C. Strobel, eds., *Embracing Contemplation: Reclaiming a Christian Spiritual Practice* (Downers Grove, Ill.: IVP Academic, 2019), 6–7.

One of the earliest definitions of contemplative preaching I am aware of is found in an article entitled "Preaching and Contemplation" by the late Dominican priest Albert Nolan.[11] Reflecting on Thomas Aquinas' contention that preaching is the fruits of one's contemplation, Nolan defines contemplative preaching as "the kind of preaching that arises spontaneously out of a life dedicated to contemplative prayer."[12] Other scholars have offered helpful reflections on contemplative preaching as well, such as James Keating and Brother David Vryhof.[13] I think that something akin to contemplative preaching is also seen in Korean American homiletician Eunjoo Mary Kim's articulation of what she calls "spiritual preaching."[14] For her, the goal of spiritual preaching is to "form an alternative community by invoking the Holy Spirit to guide the corporate spirituality of the community toward eschatological spirituality."[15] Some of the African American scholars who have contributed descriptions of contemplative preaching include James Earl Massey, Robert Smith Jr., and Martha Simmons and Frank Thomas.[16] In my understanding, the Black contemplative preacher is similar to what Kenyatta Gilbert calls the "mystical-spiritualist" persona of the Black preacher in that both are concerned with prioritizing divine encounter in proclamation and embracing preaching as a "form of prayer as well as its fruit."[17] Building on the work of these scholars as well as my study

---

[11] Albert Nolan, "Preaching and Contemplation," *Grace and Truth* 1 (2002): 1–7.

[12] Nolan, "Preaching and Contemplation," 4.

[13] James Keating, "Contemplative Homiletics: Being Carried into Reality," *Nova et Vetera* 17, no. 1 (2019): 1–13; "Contemplative Homiletics," *Seminary Journal* 16, no. 2 (Fall 2010): 63–69; and "Deep Calls to Deep—'The Contemplative Preacher: Heart Speaks to Heart' by David Vryhof," Virginia Theological Seminary, September 17, 2019, YouTube video, 1:08:10, https://www.youtube.com/watch?v=F1hjDuQJyzA.

[14] Eunjoo Mary Kim, *Preaching the Presence of God: A Homiletic from an Asian American Perspective* (Valley Forge, Penn.: Judson, 1999), 68–71.

[15] Kim, *Preaching the Presence of God*, 70.

[16] James Earl Massey, "Contemplative Preaching," unpublished manuscript; Robert Smith Jr., "Preaching as a Contemplative Theological Task," in *Our Sufficiency Is of God: Essays on Preaching in Honor of Gardner C. Taylor*, ed. Timothy George, James Earl Massey, and Robert Smith Jr. (Macon, Ga.: Mercer University Press, 2010), 151–70; and Martha Simmons and Frank Thomas, eds., *Preaching with Sacred Fire: An Anthology of African American Sermons, 1750 to the Present* (New York: W. W. Norton, 2010), 491–92.

[17] Kenyatta R. Gilbert, *The Journey and Promise of African American Preaching* (Minneapolis: Fortress, 2011), 138.

of historical and contemporary figures, I offer the following working definition of Black contemplative preaching: *Black contemplative preaching is proclamation that (1) emerges from a habitus or disposition of prayer, (2) employs a mystical hermeneutical lens, and (3) embodies a meditative homiletical style in order to lead listeners into a divine encounter that contributes to the flourishing of African Americans and all creation.* While there are other potential features of Black contemplative proclamation depending on a host of factors related to the speaker and context of proclamation, this definition highlights three distinctives: a habitus of prayer, mystical hermeneutic, and meditative homiletical style. I elaborate on this definition near the end of chapter 1 of this book.

Appendix B: Twenty Contemplative Preachers in the Twenty-First Century

The following preachers reflect at least some aspects of Black contemplative preaching as described in this book. I am not suggesting that all these preachers identify as contemplative preachers or that all their sermons are contemplative. There may be other descriptors that better capture their preaching ministry (e.g., womanist, narrative, expository), or they may reject being limited by a label completely. The list simply reflects personal judgments that I have made. Further study is needed to confirm or challenge my claims.

Rev. La Ronda Barnes
Rev. Jasmine N. Bellamy
Rev. Brenda Bertrand
Rev. Dr. Kelly Brown Douglas
Rev. Dr. John R. Faison Sr.
Rev. Dr. James A. Forbes
Rev. Dr. Teresa L. Fry Brown
Rev. Moya Harris
Rev. Dr. J. Lee Hill Jr.
Rev. Drew Jackson

Rev. Dr. Willie James Jennings
Rev. Dr. Kirk Byron Jones
Rev. William H. Lamar IV
Rev. Mia M. McClain
Rev. Dr. Donyelle C. McCray
Rev. Dr. Otis Moss Jr.
Rev. Dr. Barbara L. Peacock
Rev. Dr. Shively T. J. Smith
Rev. Dr. Jay Williams
Rev. Eric Wilson

Bibliography

Adesanya, Ineda Pearl. *Kaleidoscope: Broadening the Palette in the Art of Spiritual Direction*. New York: Church, 2019.

———. "Prayer and Social Justice." In *Ain't Gonna Let Nobody Turn Me Around: Stories of Contemplation and Justice*, edited by Therese Taylor-Stinson, 1–10. New York: Church, 2017.

Ah-Rum Ku, Eliana. "A Call for Practicing Hospitality Based on Lament in Preaching for a Wounded Community." *Homiletic* 47, no. 2 (2022): 15–26.

Allen, Richard. *The Life, Experience, and Gospel Labors of the Rt. Rev. Richard Allen*. Philadelpha: F. Ford & M.A. Riply, 1880.

Alter, Alexandra. "Amanda Gorman Captures the Moment, in Verse." *New York Times*, March 26, 2021. https://www.nytimes.com/2021/01/19/books/amanda-gorman-inauguration-hill-we-climb.html.

Andrews, William L., ed. *Sisters of the Spirit: Three Black Women's Autobiographies of the Nineteenth Century*. Bloomington: Indiana University Press, 1986.

Aquinas, Thomas. *The Summa Theologiae*. Translated by the Fathers of the English Dominican Province. New York: Benziger Bros, 1947. Full text available at Christian Classics Ethereal Library. https://www.ccel.org/a/aquinas/summa/SS/SS188.html#SSQ188A6THEP1.

Aristotle. *Aristotle's Nicomachean Ethics*. Translated by Robert C. Bartlett and Susan D. Collins. Chicago: University of Chicago Press, 2011.

———. *On Rhetoric: A Theory of Civic Discourse*. Translated and edited by George A. Kennedy. New York: Oxford University Press, 1991.

Armentrout, Don S., and Robert Boak Slocum, eds. *An Episcopal Dictionary of the Church: A User-Friendly Reference for Episcopalians*. New York: Church, 2000.

Armstrong, Regis J., and Ignatius C. Brady, eds. and trans. *The Writings of St. Francis and Clare: The Complete Works*. New York: Paulist Press, 1982.

Augustine. *The Confessions of Saint Augustine*. Translated by Edward B. Pusey. New Kensington, Penn.: Whitaker House, 1996.

———. *Teaching Christianity (De Doctrina Christiana)*. In *The Works of Augustine: A Translation for the Twenty-First Century*, edited by Edmund Hill, translated by John E. Rotelle. Hyde Park, N.Y.: New City Press, 1996.

Baldwin, Lewis V. "The Attuning of the Spirit: Martin Luther King Jr. and the Circle of Prayer." In Baldwin and Anderson, *Revives My Soul Again*, 135–67. Minneapolis: Fortress, 2018.

———. *Never to Leave Us Alone: The Prayer Life of Martin Luther King Jr.* Minneapolis: Fortress, 2010.

———. *There Is a Balm in Gilead: The Cultural Roots of Martin Luther King, Jr.* Minneapolis: Fortress, 1991.

Baldwin, Lewis V., and Victor Anderson, eds. *Revives My Soul Again: The Spirituality of Martin Luther King Jr.* Minneapolis: Fortress, 2018.

Barcellos, Robert J. "Episcopal Diocese Begins Convention at UMASS Today." *South Coast Today*, November 2, 2001. https://www.southcoasttoday.com/article/20011102/News/311029990.

Battle, Michael. *Reconciliation: The Ubuntu Theology of Desmond Tutu*. Cleveland: Pilgrim, 1999.

Bennett, Robert A. "Howard Thurman and the Bible." In Young, *God and Human Freedom*, 122–41.

Best, Wallace D. *Passionately Human, No Less Divine: Religion and Culture in Black Chicago, 1915–1952*. Princeton: Princeton University Press, 2005.

Black, Edwin. "The Second Persona." In *Contemporary Rhetorical Theory: A Reader*, 2nd ed., edited by Mark J. Porrovecchio and Celeste Michelle Condit, 295–302. New York: Guilford Press, 2016.

Bolling, Landrum. "Landrum Bolling Interviews Howard Thurman." January 17, 2013. YouTube video, 2:02:08. https://www.youtube.com/watch?v=CGX4-Wv9UD0&t=6259s.

The Book of Common Prayer: And Administration of the Sacraments and Other Rites and Ceremonies of the Church. New York: Oxford University Press, 2006.

Bostic, Joy R. *African American Female Mysticism: Nineteenth-Century Religious Activism*. New York: Palgrave Macmillan, 2013.

Bourgeault, Cynthia. *The Heart of Centering Prayer: Nondual Christianity in Theory and Practice*. Boulder: Shambhala, 2016.

Brooks, Gennifer Benjamin. "The Missionary Connection: White Preaching in the British Colonies of the Caribbean." In *Unmasking

White Preaching: Racial Hegemony, Resistance, and Possibilities in Preaching, edited by Lis Valle-Ruiz and Andrew Wymer, 19–28. Lanham, Md.: Lexington, 2022.

Brown, Sally A., and Luke A. Powery, *Ways of the Word: Learning to Preach for Your Time and Place*. Minneapolis: Fortress, 2016.

Brueggemann, Walter. *The Practice of Prophetic Imagination: Preaching an Emancipating Word*. Minneapolis: Fortress, 2012.

Burke, Kenneth. *A Rhetoric of Motives*. Berkeley: University of California Press, 1969.

Butler, Cuthbert. *Western Mysticism: The Teaching of Saints Augustine, Gregory and Bernard on Contemplation and the Contemplative Life*. New York: Dutton, 1923.

Buttrick, George, ed. *The Interpreter's Bible*. Volume 6. Nashville: Abingdon, 1956.

Canlis, Julie. "Stages of Spiritual Ascent." In *Dictionary of Christian Spirituality*, edited by Glen G. Scorgie, 274–76. Grand Rapids: Zondervan, 2011.

Carson, Clayborne. "Editorial Note." In Carson, *Papers of Martin Luther King, Jr.*, vol. 6, 457.

———, ed. *The Papers of Martin Luther King, Jr.*, vol. 6, *Advocate of the Social Gospel, September 1948–March 1963*. Berkeley: University of California Press, 2007.

Carson, Clayborne, and Peter Holloran, eds. *A Knock at Midnight: Inspiration from the Great Sermons of Reverend Martin Luther King, Jr.* New York: Warner, 1998.

Christie, Douglas. *The Blue Sapphire of the Mind: Notes for a Contemplative Ecology*. New York: Oxford University Press, 2013.

Clane, John B. "Parting Words—Not Last Words." Foreword to Harris, *Parting Words*, 9–11.

Clark, E. Trey. "Contemplation, Proclamation, and Social Transformation: Reclaiming the Homiletical Theology of Black Contemplative Preaching." PhD diss., Fuller Theological Seminary, 2021.

———. "Hidden in Plain Sight: Reclaiming the Witness and Wisdom of Black Contemplative Preachers." *Homiletic* 47, no. 2 (2022): 3–14.

———. "Spirit, Spoken Word, and the Search for Common Ground: Amanda Gorman as Contemplative Preacher." Paper presented at Homiletical Theology Project Consultation on "Spirituality, Preaching, and Bridging Racial Divides: Exploring Black Contemplative Preaching" at Boston University, Boston, October 17, 2023.

Clayborn, Patrick. "A Homiletic of Spirituality: An Analysis of Howard Thurman's Theory and Praxis of Preaching." PhD diss., Drew University, 2009.

———. "Preaching as an Act of Spirit: The Homiletical Theory of Howard Thurman." *Homiletic* 35, no. 1 (2010): 3–16.

Coe, John H., and Kyle C. Strobel, eds. *Embracing Contemplation: Reclaiming a Christian Spiritual Practice*. Downers Grove, Ill.: IVP Academic, 2019.

Collier-Thomas, Bettye. *Daughters of Thunder: Black Women Preachers and their Sermons, 1850–1979*. San Francisco: Jossey-Bass, 1998.

Cone, James H. *Martin and Malcolm and America: A Dream or a Nightmare*. 20th anniv. ed. Maryknoll, N.Y.: Orbis, 2012.

———. "The Theology of Martin Luther King, Jr." *Union Seminary Quarterly Review* 40, no. 4 (January 1986): 21–39.

Crawford, Evans, with Thomas Troeger. *The Hum: Call and Response in African American Preaching*. Nashville: Abingdon, 1995.

Crawley, Ashon T. *Blackpentecostal Breath: The Aesthetics of Possibility*. New York: Fordham University Press, 2017.

Cressman, Lisa. *Backstory Preaching: Integrating Life, Spirituality, and Craft*. Collegeville, Minn.: Liturgical, 2018.

Cuniberti, Betty. "The Bishop of Controversy: Barbara Harris, Whose New Role Shatters Tradition, Tries a Touch of Diplomacy on Her Divided Church." *Los Angeles Times*, February 15, 1989.

Davis, Gerald L. *I Got the Word in Me and I Can Sing It, You Know: A Study of the Performed African-American Sermon*. Philadelphia: University of Pennsylvania Press, 1985.

"Deep Calls to Deep—'The Contemplative Preacher: Heart Speaks to Heart' by David Vryhof." Virginia Theological Seminary. September 17, 2019. YouTube video, 1:08:10. https://www.youtube.com/watch?v=F1hjDuQJyzA.

Doblemeier, Martin, dir. *Backs against the Wall: The Howard Thurman Story*. American Public Television, 2019. https://www.pbs.org/video/backs-against-the-wall-the-howard-thurman-story-cgv9gi/.

Dorrien, Gary. *Breaking White Supremacy: Martin Luther King Jr. and the Black Social Gospel*. New Haven: Yale University Press, 2018.

———. *The New Abolition: W. E. B. and the Black Social Gospel*. New Haven: Yale University Press, 2016.

DuBois, W. E. B. *The Souls of Black Folk*. In *W. E. B. DuBois: Writings: The Suppression of the African Slave Trade/The Souls of Black Folk/Dusk of Dawn/Essays*, edited by Nathan Huggins, 357–547. New York: Library of America, 1987.

Duckett, Alfred. "New Negro in the South: The Martin Luther King Story." *Sepia*, March 22, 1957.

"The Early Dominican Constitutions." In *Early Dominicans: Selected Writings*, edited by Simon Tugwell, 455–70. New York: Paulist Press, 1982.

Eckhart, Meister. "Selected Sermons." In *Meister Eckhart: The Essential Sermons, Commentaries, Treatises, and Defense*, translated by Edmund Colledge and Bernard McGinn, 177–208. New York: Paulist Press, 1981.

Edman, Irwin. *Richard Kane Looks at Life: A Philosophy Book for Youth*. Boston: Houghton Mifflin, 1926.

Edwards, Erica R. *Charisma and the Fictions of Black Leadership*. Minneapolis: University of Minnesota Press, 2012.

Edwards, O. C. *A History of Preaching*. Nashville: Abingdon, 2004.

Egan, Keith J. "Contemplation." In *The New Westminster Dictionary of Christian Spirituality*, edited by Phillip Sheldrake, 211–12. Louisville: Westminster John Knox, 2005.

Eisenstadt, Peter. *Against the Hounds of Hell: A Life of Howard Thurman*. Charlottesville: University of Virginia Press, 2021.

Elliot, Dyan. "*Raptus*/Rapture." In Hollywood and Beckman, *Cambridge Companion to Christian Mysticism*, 189–99.

Epperly, Bruce. *Prophetic Healing: Howard Thurman's Vision of Contemplative Activism*. Richmond, Ind.: Friends United, 2020.

Fairclough, Adam. *To Redeem the Soul of America: The Southern Christian Leadership Conference and Martin Luther King, Jr.* Rev. ed. Athens: University of Georgia Press, 2001.

Farley, Wendy. *The Thirst of God: Contemplating God's Love with Three Women Mystics*. Louisville: Westminster John Knox, 2015.

Floyd-Thomas, Stacey, ed. *Deeper Shades of Purple: Womanism in Religion and Society*. New York: New York University Press, 2006.

Floyd-Thomas, Stacey, Juan Floyd-Thomas, Carol B. Duncan, Stephen G. Ray Jr., and Nancy Lynne Westfield. *Black Church Studies: An Introduction*. Nashville: Abingdon, 2007.

Fluker, Walter E. *They Looked for a City: A Comparative Analysis of the Ideal of Community in the Thought of Howard Thurman and Martin Luther King, Jr.* Lanham, Md.: University Press of America, 1989.

"Forest Hill Presbyterian Worship." Forest Hill Presbyterian Church, February 14, 2021. YouTube video, 1:17:44. https://www.youtube.com/watch?v=mef5DRZ7mQg&t=3431s.

"Forest Hills Staff." Forest Hill Presbyterian Church. March 30, 2021. https://www.fhcpresb.org/staff/.

Fox, George. *The Journal of George Fox*. Edited by Rufus Jones. Richmond, Ind.: Friends United, 1976.

"Frank A. Thomas." Christian Theological Seminary. Accessed March 30, 2021. https://www.cts.edu/cts-faculty/frank-a-thomas/.

Frazier, E. Franklin, and C. Eric Lincoln. *The Negro Church in America/The Black Church since Frazier*. New York: Schocken, 1974.

Fry Brown, Teresa. *God Don't Like Ugly: African American Women Handing on Spiritual Values*. Nashville: Abingdon, 2000.

Galilea, Segundo. "Liberation as an Encounter with Politics and Contemplation." In *The Mystical and Political Dimension of the Christian Faith*, edited by Claude Geffré and Gustavo Gutiérrez, translated by J. P. Donnelly, 19–33. New York: Herder and Herder, 1974.

Garrow, David J. "The Intellectual Development of Martin Luther King, Jr.: Influences and Commentaries." *Union Seminary Quarterly Review* 40, no. 4 (January 1986): 5–20.

———. "King's Plagiarism: Imitation, Insecurity, and Transformation." *Journal of American History* 78, no. 1 (June 1991): 86–92.

Gates, Henry Louis, Jr. *The Black Church: This Is Our Story, This Is Our Song*. New York: Penguin, 2021.

Gilbert, Kenyatta R. *The Journey and Promise of African American Preaching*. Minneapolis: Fortress, 2011.

———. *A Pursued Justice: Black Preaching from the Great Migration to Civil Rights*. Waco: Baylor University Press, 2016.

Goines, Veronica. "Listening for God" and "Sermon: Neckbone Faith." In *More Power in the Pulpit: How America's Most Effective Black Preachers Prepare Their Sermons*, edited by Cleophus J. LaRue, 41–58. Louisville: Westminster John Knox, 2009.

Goodwin, Mary E. "Racial Roots and Religion: An Interview with Howard Thurman." *Christian Century* 90, no. 19, May 9, 1973.

Gorman, Amanda. "WATCH: Amanda Gorman Reads Inauguration Poem 'The Hill We Climb.'" *PBS NewsHour*, January 20,

2021. YouTube video, 5:52. https://www.youtube.com/watch?v=LZ055illiN4.

Graves, Michael P. *Preaching the Inward Light: Early Quaker Rhetoric*. Waco: Baylor University Press, 2009.

Grundy, Saida. *Respectable: Politics and Paradox in Making the Morehouse Man*. Oakland: University of California Press, 2022.

Haldeman, Scott. *Towards Liturgies That Reconcile: Race and Ritual among African-American and European-American Protestants*. New York: Routledge, 2007.

Hall, Francis B. *Practical Spirituality: Selected Writings of Francis B. Hall*, edited by Howard Alexander, Wilmer Cooper, and James Newby. Dublin, Ind.: Prinit, 1984.

Hanch, Kate. *Storied Witness: The Theology of Black Women Preachers in 19th-Century America*. Minneapolis: Fortress, 2022.

Harding, Rachel E. *A Refuge in Thunder: Candomblé and Alternative Spaces of Blackness*. Bloomington: Indiana University Press, 2003.

Harding, Rosemarie Freeney with Rachel Elizabeth Harding. *Remnants: A Memoir of Spirit, Activism, and Mothering*. Durham: Duke University Press, 2015.

Harding, Vincent. Foreword to Thurman, *Jesus and the Disinherited*.

Harris, Barbara. Afterword to *Other Sheep I Have: The Autobiography of Father Paul M. Washington*, by Paul Washington with David McI. Gracie, 231–35. Philadelphia: Temple University Press, 1994.

———. "Bishop Barbara Harris: Integrity Eucharist 2009." February 11, 2021. YouTube video, 2:35. https://www.youtube.com/watch?v=QA1MW7Vrxdc.

———. "Can the City Be Saved? (Or Why Is There a Church on Every City Corner?)." In *Preaching on the Brink: The Future of Homiletics*, edited by Martha J. Simmons, 124–32. Nashville: Abingdon, 1996.

———. "A Circle of Concern." *African American Pulpit* 7, no. 2 (Spring 2004): 31–33.

———. "A Circle of Concern." In Simmons and Thomas, *Preaching with Sacred Fire*, 695–700.

———. "Elder's Series 1 6 10 7 pm Rev Barbara Harris." Brentwood Baptist Church, May 23, 2015. YouTube video, 1:25:51. https://www.youtube.com/watch?v=uTBAf4KPbZE&t=2528s.

———. "The Heart of Prophetic Preaching." Address delivered at West Virginia Clergy Conference. N.d.

———. *Parting Words: A Farewell Discourse.* Cambridge, Mass.: Cowley, 2003.

———. Personal interview by E. Trey Clark, December 9, 2019.

———. Personal interview by E. Trey Clark, February 26, 2019.

———. "A Thirst for the Kingdom." In *Women: To Preach or Not to Preach: 21 Outstanding Black Preachers Say Yes!* edited by Ella Pearson Mitchell, 55–60. Valley Forge, Penn.: Judson, 1991.

———. Untitled sermon. Anglican Church of Canada, Toronto, May 6, 2007. https://www.anglican.ca/faith/worship/resources/li-tim-oi/harris/.

———. Untitled sermon. "It Isn't Easy Being Green" Ecumenical Worship Service, Oak Bluffs, Mass., September 5, 2010.

———. "What a Time." Sermon. Sunshine Cathedral, Fort Lauderdale, Fl., April 25, 2010.

Harris, Barbara C., with Kelly Brown Douglas. *Hallelujah, Anyhow! A Memoir.* New York: Church, 2018.

Hauerwas, Stanley. *Dispatches from the Front: Theological Engagements with the Secular.* Durham: Duke University Press, 1994.

———. *Working with Words: On Learning to Speak Christian.* Eugene, Ore.: Cascade, 2011.

Hayes, Diana L. *Forged in the Fiery Furnace: African American Spirituality.* Maryknoll, N.Y.: Orbis, 2012.

———. "A Great Cloud of Witnesses: Martin Luther King Jr.'s Roots in the African American Religious and Spiritual Traditions." In Baldwin and Anderson, *Revives My Soul Again*, 39–59.

Haynes, Lemuel. "The Presence of the Lord." In *Black Preacher to White America: The Collected Writings of Lemuel Haynes, 1774–1833*, edited by Richard Newman, 143–47. Brooklyn: Carlson, 1990.

Haywood, Chanta M. *Prophesying Daughters: Black Women Preachers and the Word, 1823–1913.* Rev. ed. Columbia: University of Missouri, 2016.

Herskovits, Melville J. *The Myth of the Negro Past.* Boston: Beacon, 1990.

Higginbotham, Evelyn Brooks. *Righteous Discontent: The Women's Movement in the Black Baptist Church, 1880–1920.* Cambridge, Mass.: Harvard University Press, 1993.

Hill, Edmund. "Translator's Note." In Augustine, *Teaching Christianity (De Doctrina Christiana)*, 95–97.

Hill, Johnny Bernard. *The Theology of Martin Luther King, Jr. and Desmond Mpilo Tutu.* New York: Palgrave Macmillan, 2007.

Hollywood, Amy, and Patricia Z. Beckman, eds. *The Cambridge Companion to Christian Mysticism*. New York: Cambridge University Press, 2012.

Holmes, Barbara A. *Joy Unspeakable: Contemplative Practices of the Black Church*. 2nd ed. Minneapolis: Fortress, 2017.

Holmes, Barbara, and Donny Bryant. "Preaching from the Depths of Life with Dr. Frank Thomas." November 18, 2022, in *The Cosmic We*, produced by Center for Action and Contemplation. Podcast, 1:10:00. https://cac.org/podcasts/preaching-from-the-depths-of-life-with-dr-frank-a-thomas/.

Humez, Jean McMahon. Introduction to *Gifts of Power*, by Rebecca Cox Jackson, 1–50.

Hurston, Zora Neale. *Jonah's Gourd Vine: A Novel*. New York: Perennial Library, 1990.

Irvin, Dale T., and Scott W. Sunquist. *History of the World Christian Movement*. Vol. 2, *Modern Christianity from 1454–1800*. Maryknoll, N.Y.: Orbis, 2012.

Jacobsen, David Schnasa, ed. *Homiletical Theology: Preaching as Doing Theology*. Eugene, Ore.: Wipf & Stock, 2015.

Jackson, Rebecca Cox. *Gifts of Power: The Writings of Rebecca Jackson, Black Visionary, Shaker Eldress*. Edited by Jean McMahon Humez. Boston: University of Massachusetts Press, 1981.

Jenness, Mary. *Twelve Negro Americans*. New York: Friendship Press, 1936.

Johnson, Alonso. *Good News for the Disinherited: Howard Thurman on Jesus of Nazareth and Human Liberation*. Lanham, Md.: University Press of America, 1997.

Johnson, Andre E., and Anthony J. Stone Jr. "'The Most Dangerous Negro in America': Rhetoric, Race, and the Prophetic Pessimism of Martin Luther King Jr." *Journal of Communication and Religion* 21, no.1 (2018): 8–22.

Johnson, James Weldon. *God's Trombones: Seven Negro Sermons in Verse*. New York: Penguin Books, [1927] 2008.

Johnson, Kimberly P. *The Womanist Preacher: Proclaiming Womanist Rhetoric from the Pulpit*. Lanham, Md.: Lexington, 2017.

Johnson, Mordecai Wyatt. "Work, Business, and Religion." In Simmons and Thomas, *Preaching with Sacred Fire*, 418–23.

Jones, Clarence B., and Stuart Connelly. *Behind the Dream: The Making of a Speech that Transformed a Nation*. New York: St. Martin's, 2011.

Keating, James. "Contemplative Homiletics." *Seminary Journal* 16, no. 2 (Fall 2010): 63–69.

———. "Contemplative Homiletics: Being Carried into Reality." *Nova et Vetera* 17, no. 1 (2019):1–13.
Keating, Thomas. *Open Mind, Open Heart: The Contemplative Dimension of the Gospel*. New York: Continuum, 1997.
Kim, Eunjoo Mary. *Preaching the Presence of God: A Homiletic from an Asian American Perspective*. Valley Forge, Penn.: Judson, 1999.
———. *Women Preaching: Theology and Practice through the Ages*. Eugene, Ore.: Wipf & Stock, 2004.
King, Coretta Scott. *My Life with Martin Luther King, Jr*. New York: Avon, 1969.
King, Martin Luther, Jr. "An Autobiography of Religious Development." In *The Papers of Martin Luther King, Jr.*, vol. 1, *Called to Serve, January 1929–June 1951*, edited by Clayborne Carson, 359–79. Berkeley: University of California Press, 1992.
———. "Draft of Chapter XIII, 'Our God Is Able.'" In Carson, *Papers of Martin Luther King, Jr.*, vol. 6, 530–31.
———. "I See the Promised Land." In Washington, *A Testament of Hope*, 279–86.
———. "Man of the Year." *Time*, January 3, 1964.
———. "The Misuse of Prayer." In Carson, *Papers of Martin Luther King, Jr.*, vol. 6, 590–91.
———. "On Accepting the St. Francis Peace Medal." *Peace* 1 (March 1964): 11–15.
———. "'O That I Knew Where I Might Find Him.'" In Carson, *Papers of Martin Luther King, Jr.*, vol. 6, 591–97.
———. "Our God Is Able." In Carson, *Papers of Martin Luther King, Jr.*, vol. 6, 243–46.
———. "Preaching Ministry." In Carson, *Papers of Martin Luther King, Jr.*, vol. 6, 69–77.
———. *The Radical King*. Edited by Cornel West. Boston: Beacon, 2015.
———. "Remaining Awake through a Great Revolution." In Washington, *A Testament of Hope*, 268–78.
———. *Strength to Love*. Minneapolis: Fortress, 2010.
———. *Stride toward Freedom: The Montgomery Story*. Boston: Beacon, 2010.
———. "The Three Dimensions of a Complete Life." In Carson and Holloran, *A Knock at Midnight*, 121–49.
———. *"Thou, Dear God": Prayers That Open Hearts and Spirits*. Edited by Lewis V. Baldwin. Boston: Beacon, 2012.

———. "A Time to Break Silence." In Washington, *A Testament of Hope*, 231–45.
———. "The UnChristian Christian." *Ebony* 20, no. 10 (August 1965): 76–80.
———. "Unfulfilled Dreams." In Carson and Holloran, *A Knock at Midnight*, 187–200.
———. *Where Do We Go from Here: Chaos or Community*. Boston: Beacon, 2010.
Kolk, Bessel A. Van Der. *The Body Keeps the Score: Brain, Mind, and Body in the Healing of Trauma*. New York: Penguin, 2014.
Kourie, Celia. "Reading Scripture through a Mystical Lens." *Acta Theologica* 31, no. 15 (2011): 132–53.
Laird, Martin. *Into the Silent Land: A Guide to the Christian Practice of Contemplation*. New York: Oxford University Press, 2006.
Lane, Belden C. *The Solace of Fierce Landscapes: Exploring Desert and Mountain Spirituality*. New York: Oxford University Press, 2007.
Lanzetta, Beverly J. "The Heart of a World Citizen: Martin Luther King Jr. as Social Mystic." In Baldwin and Anderson, *Revives My Soul Again*, 239–69.
LaRue, Cleophus J. *Rethinking Celebration: From Rhetoric to Praise in African American Preaching*. Louisville: Westminster John Knox, 2016.
Lassiter, Valentino. *Martin Luther King in the African American Preaching Tradition*. Eugene, Ore.: Wipf & Stock, 2001.
Lee, Cindy S. *Our Unforming: De-Westernizing Spiritual Formation*. Minneapolis: Fortress, 2022.
Lee, Hak Joon. *We Will Get to the Promised Land: Martin Luther King, Jr.'s Communal-Political Spirituality*. Cleveland: Pilgrim, 2006.
Lee, Jarena. "The Life and Religious Experience of Jarena Lee." In Andrews, *Sisters of the Spirit*, 25–48.
Lewis, Harold T. *Yet With a Steady Beat: The African American Struggle for Recognition in the Episcopal Church*. Valley Forge, Penn.: Trinity, 1996.
Lincoln, C. Eric, and Lawrence H. Mamiya. *The Black Church in the African American Experience*. Durham: Duke University Press, 1990.
Lischer, Richard. *The Preacher King: Martin Luther King, Jr. and the Word That Moved America*. New York: Oxford University Press, 1995.
Long, Charles H. *Significations: Signs, Symbols, and Images in the Interpretation of Religion*. Aurora, Colo.: The Davies Group, 1995.

Massey, James Earl. "Contemplative Preaching." Unpublished manuscript. N.d.
——. "Thurman's Preaching: Substance and Style." In Young, *God and Human Freedom*.
Mbiti, John. *African Religions and Philosophy*. 2nd ed. Portsmouth, N.H.: Heinemann, 1990.
McCaughan, Pat. "Service Celebrates Barbara Harris, Champion of 'the Last, the Least, and the Left Out.'" Episcopal Diocese of Los Angeles (blog). March 17, 2021. https://diocesela.org/news/service-celebrates-barbara-harris/.
McCray, Donyelle C. *The Censored Pulpit: Julian of Norwich as Preacher*. Minneapolis: Fortress Academic, 2019.
——. "Playing in Church: Insights from the Boundaries of the Sermon Genre." *Liturgy* 36, no. 4 (2021): 11–17.
——. "Solomon's Son: The Wise Tenderness of Howard Thurman." In *Can I Get a Witness? Thirteen Peacemakers, Community Builders, and Agitators for Faith and Justice*, edited by Charles Marsh, Shea Tuttle, and Daniel P. Rhodes, 39–57. Grand Rapids: Eerdmans, 2019.
McCullough, Amy P. *Her Preaching Body: Conversations about Identity, Agency, and Embodiment among Contemporary Female Preachers*. Eugene, Ore.: Cascade, 2018.
McDonald, Nicole Danielle. "Black Queer Preaching: A Close Reading of Bishop Yvette A. Flunder's Sermon, 'Silent No More.'" *Homiletic* 48, no. 1 (2023): 32–47.
McGinn, Bernard. *The Foundations of Mysticism: Origins to the Fifth Century*. New York: Crossroad, 1991.
——. *Modern Mystics: An Introduction*. New York: Crossroad, 2023.
McGinn, Bernard, ed. *The Essential Writings of Christian Mysticism*. New York: Modern Library, 2006.
McIntosh, Mark A., and Edward Howells. Introduction to *The Oxford Handbook of Mystical Theology*, edited by Howells and McIntosh, 1–5. New York: Oxford University Press, 2020.
McKinnis, Leonard Cornell, II. *The Black Coptic Church: Race and Imagination in a New Religion*. New York: New York University Press, 2023.
McMickle, Marvin A. *Where Have All the Prophets Gone? Reclaiming Prophetic Preaching in America*. Cleveland: Pilgrim, 2006.
Menakem, Resmaa. *My Grandmother's Hands: Racialized Trauma and the Pathway to Mending Our Hearts and Bodies*. Las Vegas: Central Recovery, 2017.

Merton, Thomas. *New Seeds of Contemplation*. New York: New Directions, 1961.

Miller, Keith D. *Voice of Deliverance: The Language of Martin Luther King Jr. and Its Sources*. New York: Free Press, 1992.

Mitchell, Henry H. "African American Preaching." In *Concise Encyclopedia of Preaching*, edited by William H. Willimon and Richard Lischer, 2–9. Louisville: Westminster John Knox, 1995.

———. *Black Preaching: The Recovery of a Powerful Art*. Nashville: Abingdon, 1990.

———. *The Recovery of Preaching*. New York: Harper & Row, 1977.

Mitchell, Mozella G. *Spiritual Dynamics of Howard Thurman's Theology*. Bristol, Ind.: Wyndham Hall, 1985.

Myers, Jacob D. *Preaching Must Die! Troubling Homiletical Theology*. Minneapolis: Fortress, 2017.

Neal, Jerusha Matsen. *The Overshadowed Preacher: Mary, the Spirit, and the Labor of Proclamation*. Grand Rapids: Eerdmans, 2020.

The New Oxford Annotated Bible: New Revised Standard Version. New York: Oxford University Press, 2010.

Noel, James A. "Contemplation and Social Action in African-American Spirituality." *Church and Society* 83, no. 2 (November–December 1992): 55–67.

Nolan, Albert. "Preaching and Contemplation." *Grace and Truth* 1 (2002): 1–7.

Northcutt, Kay L. *Kindling Desire for God: Preaching as Spiritual Direction*. Minneapolis: Fortress, 2009.

Nouwen, Henri J. M. *The Way of the Heart: Desert Spirituality and Contemporary Ministry*. San Francisco: HarperSanFrancisco, 1981.

Obama, Michelle. "'Unity with Purpose': Amanda Gorman and Michelle Obama Discuss Art, Identity, and Optimism." *Time*. February 4, 2021, https://time.com/5933596/amanda-gorman-michelle-obama-interview/.

Origen. *On First Principles: A Reader's Edition*. Translated by John Behr. New York: Oxford University Press, 2020.

Otto, Rudolf. *The Idea of the Holy: An Inquiry into the Non-rational Factor in the Idea of the Divine and Its Relation to the Rational*. Translated by John W. Harvey. New York: Oxford University Press, 1950.

Panton, Thelma M. "Thy Rich Anointing: The Lives and Ministries of Pauli Murray and Barbara Clementine Harris." *Sewanee Theological Review* 51, no. 4 (2008): 387–404.

Paris, Peter. *The Spirituality of African Peoples: The Search for a Common Moral Discourse*. Minneapolis: Fortress, 1995.

Pasquarello, Michael, III. *Dietrich: Bonhoeffer and the Theology of a Preaching Life*. Waco: Baylor University Press, 2017.

———. *Sacred Rhetoric: Preaching as a Theological and Pastoral Practice of the Church*. Eugene, Ore.: Wipf & Stock, 2005.

Paulsen, David. "Episcopal Church Releases Racial Audit of Leadership Citing Nine Patterns of Racism in Church Culture." Episcopal News Service (blog). April 19, 2021. https://www.episcopalnewsservice.org/2021/04/19/episcopal-church-releases-racial-audit-of-leadership-citing-nine-patterns-of-racism-in-church-culture/.

Payne, Charles M. *I've Got the Light of Freedom: The Organizing Tradition and the Mississippi Freedom Struggle*. 2nd ed. Berkeley: University of California Press, 2007.

Pinn, Anthony B. *Varieties of African American Religious Experience: Toward a Comparative Black Theology*. 20th anniv. ed. Minneapolis: Fortress, 2017.

Pipes, William H. *Say Amen, Brother! Old-Time Negro Preaching: A Study in American Frustration*. Detroit: Wayne State University, [1951] 1991.

Pitts, Walter. "West African Poetics in the Black Preaching Style." *American Speech* 64, no. 2 (Summer 1989): 137–49.

Plotinus. *The Enneads*. Edited by Lloyd P. Gerson. Translated by George Boys-Stones et al. New York: Cambridge University Press, 2018.

Pollard, Alton. "African American Mysticism." In *African American Religious Cultures*, vol. 1, *A–R*, edited by Anthony B. Pinn, 3–8. Santa Barbara: ABC-CLIO, 2009.

———. *Mysticism and Social Change: The Social Witness of Howard Thurman*. New York: Peter Lang, 1992.

Powery, Luke A. *Becoming Human: The Holy Spirit and the Rhetoric of Race*. Louisville: Westminster John Knox, 2022.

———. *Dem Dry Bones: Preaching, Death, and Hope*. Minneapolis: Fortress, 2012.

———. "'The Growing Edge' of Life and Ministry." In *Anchored in the Current: Discovering Howard Thurman as Educator, Activist, Guide, and Prophet*, edited by Gregory C. Ellison II, 133–43. Louisville: Westminster John Knox, 2020.

———. "Invocation Vocation: Preaching and Praying." In *What's Right with Preaching Today? The Enduring Influence of Fred B. Craddock*, edited by Mike Grave and André Resner, 137–50. Eugene, Ore.: Cascade, 2021.

———. *Spirit Speech: Lament and Celebration in Preaching*. Nashville: Abingdon, 2009.

Prevot, Andrew. *The Mysticism of Ordinary Life: Theology, Philosophy, and Feminism*. New York: Oxford University Press, 2023.

———. *Thinking Prayer: Theology and Spirituality amid the Crises of Modernity*. Notre Dame, Ind.: University of Notre Dame Press, 2015.

Prichard, Robert W. *A History of the Episcopal Church: Complete through the 78th General Convention*. 3rd rev. ed. New York: Morehouse, 2014.

Proctor, Samuel D. *"How Shall They Hear?": Effective Preaching for Vital Faith*. Valley Forge, Penn: Judson, 1992.

Quashie, Kevin. *The Sovereignty of Quiet: Beyond Resistance in Black Culture*. New Brunswick, N.J.: Rutgers University Press, 2012.

Raboteau, Albert. *Slave Religion: The "Invisible Institution" in the Antebellum South*. Updated ed. New York: Oxford University Press, 2004.

Radler, Charlotte. "*Actio et Contemplatio*/Action and Contemplation." In Hollywood and Beckman, *Cambridge Companion to Christian Mysticism*, 211–22.

Riley, Cole Arthur. *This Here Flesh: Spirituality, Liberation, and the Stories That Make Us*. New York: Convergent, 2022.

Robinson, Timothy. "He Talked to Trees! 'Thinking Differently' about Nature with Howard Thurman." *Spiritus* 21, no. 1 (Spring 2021): 1–19.

———. "'Resisting Whatever Separates One from the Ground of Being': Howard Thurman's Prophetic Appropriation of the Christian Mystical Tradition." In *Mysticism and Contemporary Life: Essays in Honor of Bernard McGinn*, edited by John J. Markey and J. August Higgins, 127–44. New York: Herder & Herder, 2019.

Rohr, Richard. *The Naked Now: Learning to See as the Mystics See*. New York: Crossroad, 2009.

Root, Andrew. *The Congregation in a Secular Age*. Grand Rapids: Baker Academic, 2021.

Ruffing, Janet K. Introduction to *Mysticism and Social Transformation*, edited by Janet K. Ruffing, 1–25. Syracuse, N.Y.: Syracuse University Press, 2001.

Schade, Leah. *Creation-Crisis Preaching: Ecology, Theology, and the Pulpit*. St. Louis, Mo.: Chalice, 2015.

Schreiner, Olive. *A Track to the Water's Edge: The Olive Schreiner Reader*. Edited by Howard Thurman. New York: Harper & Row, 1973.

Sechrest, Love Lazarus. *Race and Rhyme: Rereading the New Testament*. Grand Rapids: Eerdmans, 2022.

Simmons, Martha. "Whooping: The Musicality of African American Preaching Past and Present." In Simmons and Thomas, *Preaching with Sacred Fire*, 864–84.

Simmons, Martha, and Frank Thomas, eds. *Preaching with Sacred Fire: An Anthology of African American Sermons, 1750 to the Present*. New York: W. W. Norton, 2010.

Sloyan, Gerard S. "Liturgical Preaching." In *Concise Dictionary of Preaching*, edited by Will Willimon and Richard Lischer, 311–13. Louisville: Westminster John Knox, 1995.

Smith, Luther. *Howard Thurman: The Mystic as Prophet*. 3rd ed. Richmond, Ind.: Friends United, 2007.

Smith, Robert, Jr. "Preaching as a Contemplative Theological Task." In *Our Sufficiency Is of God: Essays on Preaching in Honor of Gardner C. Taylor*, edited by Timothy George, James Earl Massey, and Robert Smith Jr., 151–70. Macon, Ga.: Mercer University Press, 2010.

Smith, Shively T. J. "'I Can See It. Now, How to Say It?' Hearing the Aesthetic Dimension of Howard Thurman, the Interpreter." In *The Unfinished Search for Common Ground: Reimagining Howard Thurman*, edited by Walter Earl Fluker, 30–39. Maryknoll, N.Y.: Orbis, 2023.

Spencer, Carole Dale. "Quaker Spirituality." In *Dictionary of Christian Spirituality*, edited by Glen G. Scorgie, 704–5. Grand Rapids: Zondervan, 2011.

Spencer, Jon Michael. *Sacred Symphony: The Chanted Sermon of the Black Preacher*. Santa Barbara: Greenwood, 1987.

Spillers, Hortense J. "Martin Luther King and the Style of the Black Sermon." *Black Scholar* 3, no. 1 (September 1971): 14–27.

Steele, Amy Elizabeth. "Howard Thurman and the Roots of a Black Mystical Aesthetic." *Spectrum: A Journal on Black Men* 9, nos. 1–2 (Autumn 2021): 183–210.

———. "The Mystical Aesthetic: Howard Thurman and the Art of Meaning." PhD diss., Vanderbilt University, 2012.

Stewart, Danté. "Amanda Gorman, My Grandma, and the Black Tears We Cried." *Religion News Service*, January 21, 2021. https://religionnews.com/2021/01/21/amanda-gorman-my-grandma-and-the-black-tears-we-cried-yesterday/.

"Sunday, July 18, 2021 Worship—Reverend Ineda Adesanya." Allen Temple Baptist Church. July 18, 2021. YouTube video, 1:42:19. https://www.youtube.com/watch?v=FO8jhkIJjts.

"Sunday Morning Worship Service—2/27/22—Dean Luke A. Powery." Duke Chapel, February 27, 2022. YouTube video, 1:11:39. https://www.youtube.com/watch?v=gnRdFHnF9qg&t=3379s.

Thomas, Frank A. "A Conversation with Rev. Dr. Frank A. Thomas Hosted by Dr. Gina M. Stewart." December 4, 2019. YouTube video, 1:00:15. https://www.youtube.com/watch?v=CCYkICe-Ick&t=1692s.

———. "Frank Thomas Preaches A Grain of Sand from Psalm 139:17–18." May 8, 2022. YouTube video, 17:32. https://www.youtube.com/watch?v=pfu0QaK9tNo.

———. *God of the Dangerous Sermon*. Nashville: Abingdon, 2021.

———. *How to Preach a Dangerous Sermon* (Nashville: Abingdon, 2018).

———. *Introduction to the Practice of African American Preaching*. Nashville: Abingdon, 2016.

———. *Surviving a Dangerous Sermon*. Nashville: Abingdon, 2020.

———. *They Like to Never Quit Praisin' God*. Rev. and updated. Cleveland: Pilgrim, 2013.

Thomas, Gerald Lamont. *African American Preaching: The Contribution of Dr. Gardner C. Taylor*. New York: Peter Lang, 2009.

Thompsett, Fredrica Harris, ed. *In Conversation: Michael Curry and Barbara Harris*. New York: Church, 2017.

Thompson, Lisa L. *Ingenuity: Preaching as an Outsider*. Nashville: Abingdon, 2018.

Thornton, John K. *The Kongolese Saint Anthony: Dona Beatriz Kimpa Vita and the Antonian Movement, 1684–1706*. New York: Cambridge University Press, 1998.

Thurman, Howard. "Building a Friendly World." *Growing Edge* (Winter 1950).

———. *The Centering Moment*. Richmond, Ind.: Friends United, 1969.

———. *The Creative Encounter: An Interpretation of Religion and the Social Witness*. Richmond, Ind.: Friends United, [1954] 1972.

———. "Dilemmas of the Religious Professional." Hester Lectures III, side A, Golden Gate Baptist Theological Seminary, Mill Valley, Calif., February 11, 1971. Transcript from the Howard Thurman Digital Archive, Pitts Theology Library at Emory University, Atlanta. https://thurman.pitts.emory.edu/items/show/258.

———. *Disciplines of the Spirit*. Richmond, Ind.: Friends United, 1963.

---. *The Growing Edge*. Richmond, Ind.: Friends United, 1956.

---. "Howard Thurman." Museum of the African Diaspora, November 27, 2018, YouTube video, 14:50. https://www.youtube.com/watch?v=xg2mlTu25qs&t=104s.

---. Interview by Roberta Byrd Barr, Seattle, Wash., January 1969.

---. *Jesus and the Disinherited*. Boston: Beacon, [1949] 1996.

---. "Jesus and the Disinherited." Part 1 (Seminar Discussion), side A, (January 22–23, 1975). Transcript from the Howard Thurman Digital Archive, Pitts Theology Library at Emory University, Atlanta. http://thurman.pitts.emory.edu/files/show/437.

---. *The Luminous Darkness: A Personal Interpretation of the Anatomy of Segregation and the Ground of Hope*. Richmond, Ind.: Friends United, 1965.

---. "Man and the World of Nature." In *The Papers of Howard Washington Thurman*, vol. 2, *Christian, Who Calls Me Christian? April 1936–August 1943*, edited by Walter Earl Fluker, 101–6. Columbia: University of South Carolina Press, 2012.

---. *Meditations of the Heart*. Boston: Beacon, 1981.

---. *Mysticism and Social Action: Lawrence Lecture and Discussions with Dr Howard Thurman*. International Association for Religious Freedom, 2015. Kindle.

---. *The Search for Common Ground: An Inquiry into the Basis of Man's Experience of Community*. Richmond, Ind.: Friends United, 1971.

---. *Sermons on the Parables*. Edited by David B. Gowler and Kipton E. Jensen. Maryknoll, N.Y.: Orbis, 2018.

---. "To Mordecai Wyatt Johnson, 18 June 1918." In *The Papers of Howard Washington Thurman*, vol. 1, *My People Need Me, June 1918–March 1936*, edited by Walter Earl Fluker, 1–3. Columbia: University of South Carolina Press, 2010.

---. *The Way of the Mystics*. Edited by Peter Eisenstadt and Walter Earl Fluker. Maryknoll, N.Y.: Orbis, 2021.

---. "What Shall I Do with My Life? The Natural Order." Howard Thurman Virtual Listening Room, Howard Gotlieb Archival Research Center, Boston University. Accessed July 15, 2020. http://archives.bu.edu/web/howard-thurman/virtual-listening-room/detail?id=358566.

---. *With Head and Heart: The Autobiography of Howard Thurman*. New York: Harcourt Brace, 1979.

---. "Worship and Word: A View of the Liberal Congregation and Its Sermons." In *The Papers of Howard Washington Thurman*, vol. 4, *The*

Soundless Passion of a Single Mind, June 1949–December 1962, edited by Walter Earl Fluker, 327–33. Columbia: University of South Carolina Press, 2017.

Townes, Emilie M. *In a Blaze of Glory: Womanist Spirituality as Social Witness*. Nashville: Abingdon, 1995.

Troeger, Thomas H. *The End of Preaching*. Nashville: Abingdon, 2018.

Tucker, Joseph L. *The Other Black Church: Alternative Christian Movements and the Struggle for Black Freedom*. Minneapolis: Fortress, 2020.

Turman, Eboni Marshall. *Toward a Womanist Ethic of Incarnation: Black Bodies, the Black Church, and the Council of Chalcedon*. New York: Palgrave Macmillan, 2013.

Turner, William Clair, Jr. *Preaching That Makes the Word Plain: Doing Theology in the Crucible of Life*. Eugene, Ore.: Cascade, 2008.

Ulanov, Ann, and Barry Ulanov. *Primary Speech: A Psychology of Prayer*. Atlanta: John Knox, 1983.

Varickasseril, Jose. "Contemplation and Proclamation: New Testament Perspectives." *Third Millennium* 21, no. 1 (2018): 5–26.

Vesely-Flad, Rima. *Black Buddhists and the Black Radical Tradition*. New York: New York University Press, 2022.

Wacquant, Loïc. "A Concise Genealogy and Anatomy of Habitus." In *The Oxford Handbook of Pierre Bourdieu*, edited by Thomas Medvetz and Jeffrey J. Sallaz, 528–36. New York: Oxford University Press, 2019.

Walker, Alice. *In Search of Our Mothers' Gardens: Womanist Prose*. Orlando: Harcourt, 1983.

Walker, Wyatt Tee. Foreword to Baldwin, *Never to Leave Us Alone*, vii–viii.

Wallace, Maurice O. *King's Vibrato: Modernism, Blackness, and the Sonic Life of Martin Luther King Jr.* Durham: Duke University Press, 2022.

Warren, Mervyn A. *King Came Preaching: The Pulpit Power of Dr. Martin Luther King Jr.* Downers Grove, Ill.: InterVarsity, 2001.

———. "To Tell the Truth: Martin Luther King Jr.'s Preaching and Spirituality." In Baldwin and Anderson, *Revives My Soul Again*, 169–84.

Washington, James, ed. *A Testament of Hope: The Essential Writings and Speeches of Martin Luther King, Jr.* New York: HarperSanFrancisco, 1991.

Weems, Renita. *Just a Sister Away: A Womanist Vision of Women's Relationships in the Bible*. San Diego: LuraMedia, 1988.

Willard, Dallas. *The Spirit of the Disciplines*. New York: HarperCollins, 1988.

Williams, Catherine E. "Sermon and Song: A Musically Integrative Homiletic." *Yale Journal of Music and Religion* 7, no. 2 (2021): 82–97.

Williams, Delores. *Sisters in the Wilderness: The Challenge of Womanist God-Talk*. Anniv. ed. Maryknoll, N.Y.: Orbis, 2013.

Williams, Rowan. *On Christian Theology*. Oxford: Blackwell, 2000.

Wilmore, Gayraud. *Black Religion and Black Radicalism: An Interpretation of the Religious History of African Americans*. 3rd ed. Maryknoll, N.Y.: Orbis, 1998.

Winters, Mary-Frances. *Black Fatigue: How Racism Erodes the Mind, Body, and Spirit*. Oakland, Calif.: Berrett-Koehler, 2020.

Yang, Sunggu. *King's Speech: Preaching Reconciliation in a World of Violence and Chasm*. Eugene, Ore.: Cascade, 2019.

Young, Henry J., ed. *God and Human Freedom: A Festschrift in Honor of Howard Thurman*. Richmond, Ind.: Friends United, 1983.

Index

Abel, 27
Abernathy, Ralph D., 81
Abrams, Stacey, 128–29
Adams, Charles G., 26
Adesanya, Ineda Pearl, 10, 123–29, 150, 152
Africa/African, 3n8, 4, 15–16, 16n10, 20, 22–23, 75, 75n32, 88, 105; spirituality, 15, 33–34, 40–41, 70, 75n32, 77, 105, 122
African Methodist Episcopal (AME) church, 28–31, 107
Allen, Richard, 27–30, 72
Allen Temple Baptist Church, 124, 126, 129
Ambrose, Nancy, 41–42, 45, 52
Amos, 75, 103
Anthony the Great (Anthony of Egypt), 21
Aquinas, Thomas, 1, 18, 34, 88, 156
Aristotle, 34, 36, 54n89, 56
Augustine, 13, 16–17, 29, 76, 99, 135, 144

Baldwin, Lewis V., 65n143, 70n12, 71–72, 75, 80, 81n60
Barbour, J. Pius, 79
Barnes, La Ronda, 159
Basil the Great, 16
Bartlett, Allen, 100
Bellamy, Jasmine N., 159

beloved community, 74–77, 92, 149
Benner, David, 135
Bernard of Clairvaux, 17
Bertrand, Brenda, 159
Bethune, Mary McLeod, 52
Bible: *see* mystical hermeneutic; Scripture
Biden, Joe, 1, 121
Bird, Van Samuel, 101
Black/African American preaching: see *preaching*
Black, Edwin, 34
Black fatigue, 151
body, the: Body of Christ, 132, 149; and preaching, 21, 74, 110; Spirit-filled, 33; and spiritual practices, 63, 74; and trauma, 43, 150; *see also* meditative homiletical style
Bonar, Horatius, 118
Book of Common Prayer, 102
Bostic, Joy R., 30, 154
Boston University, 38, 54, 64, 65n143, 74
Bourgeault, Cynthia, 35n75
Brooks, Gennifer Benjamin, 5
Brooks, Phillips, 77n41
Brother Carper, 25
Brown, Lerita Coleman, 43
Brudder Coteney, 25
Buddha (Siddhartha Gautama), 48

Burke, Kenneth, 62
busyness, 8, 61–63, 151

Campolo, Tony, 139
Canticle of Brother Sun, 18
capitalism, 67
Carner, Jennifer, 26
Carson, Clayborne, 84
Catherine of Siena, 19
Caution, Tollie LeRoy, 110
celebration, 3, 36, 63, 78–83, 129; *see also* frenzy
Chavis, John, 26
Christie, Douglas, 50
Christology, 47, 102
Chrysostom, John, 16
church: African American/Black church, 2, 4, 6, 10–11, 14, 23–24, 28–31, 64, 74, 117, 130, 148, 151, 155; Allen Temple Baptist Church, 124, 126; Barbara Harris upbringing in, 99, 102–3, 107; Black women and, 52; Brentwood Baptist Church, 107; Church of the Advocate, 104–5; Church for the Fellowship of All Peoples (Fellowship Church), 38–39, 54, 105; Church of God in Christ, 82; Colonial Church, 49; definition of Black church, 2n6; Dexter Avenue Baptist Church, 76; Forest Hill Presbyterian Church, 129, 131; Grace Baptist Church, 107; history of, 7; Holt Street Baptist Church, 73–74; Howard Thurman first pastorate, 62; Howard Thurman upbringing in, 41, 51; Martin Luther King Jr. upbringing in, 71, 74–75, 79–80; Mississippi Boulevard Christian Church, 141; New Faith Baptist Church, 141; unity of the, 132; Wayland Temple Baptist Church, 107; White church, 27; *see also* African Methodist Episcopal (AME) church; Episcopal Church; mystic preachers; preaching
Cicero, 17
civil rights movement, 21–22, 65, 68, 74, 80, 92, 131
Clayborn, Patrick, 40
colonialism, 22, 48, 84, 88–89
common ground, 48–50, 53–54, 149–150
Cone, James H., 70n12, 77, 79
contemplation, 1–4, 14, 18–19, 31, 41, 44, 48, 50, 53, 88, 125, 130, 137; Africana contemplation, 15; contemplation and action, 13–14, 29, 31, 70–74, 92, 119, 133, 135, 137–40, 151–52; contemplative activism, 152; contemplative ecology, 50; contemplative prayer, 154–55; contemplative theology, 28, 105–6; definition of, 3–4, 14, 154–55; doxological contemplation, 29; *see also* contemplative preaching
contemplative preaching: biblical precedents of, 13–15; contemporary examples of, 1–2, 9, 121–52, 159; definition of, 14–15, 33–36, 156–57; historical examples of, 6, 15–22, 27–33; *see also* Harris, Barbara; King, Martin Luther, Jr.; mystic preachers; Thurman, Howard
COVID-19, 1, 119, 121, 124, 126–28, 131n44, 143, 152
Crawford, Evans, 54, 130, 136
Crawley, Ashon T., 4–5
creation care, 8, 37–38, 49–50, 105–6, 145, 147, 149, 150; *see also* ecopreaching
Cressman, Lisa, 34

Cross, George, 46
Curry, Michael, 108

David (Son of Jesse), 87
Davis, Gerald, 146
De Doctrina Christiana (*Teaching Christianity*), 13, 16
discipleship, 57, 64, 90, 92, 137, 139; *see also* spiritual formation
division, 1, 8, 38, 121; *see also* fragmentation
Dominic of Guzman, 18
Dorrien, Gary, 49, 55n95, 65n146, 75, 77, 104
Douglas, Kelly Brown, 98, 159
DuBois, W. E. B., 25
Dunbar, Paul Laurence, 90

Easton, Hosea, 26
Eckhart, Meister, 6, 16, 19, 47–48, 72
ecopreaching, 18, 37–38, 49–50, 105–6, 145, 147, 149; *see also* creation care
education, 24–26, 30, 32, 71, 74, 78–79, 91, 104, 110, 124, 127–28
Edwards, Erica, 68
Edwards, Jonathan, 6
Edwards, O. C., 25
Eisenstadt, Peter, 47
Elaw, Zilpha, 6
Elliot, Dyan, 137
emancipatory encounter, 30, 35, 40, 97, 103, 113, 115, 117
Episcopal Church, 95, 99, 102–3, 107–12
Eucharist, 108–9, 111

Faison, John R., Sr., 159
fatigue, 8, 62, 91, 149–52; *see also* Black fatigue
fear, 91–92, 112, 127, 131–32, 149–52

Floyd-Thomas, Stacey, 2n6, 63n135, 97n9
Fluker, Walter Earl, 38, 65
Fox, George, 16, 19–20
Forbes, James A., 159
Forest Hill Presbyterian Church, 129, 131–33
fragmentation, 8, 53, 78, 149–52; *see also* division
Francis of Assisi, 16–18, 21, 41, 47–48, 76
Franklin, Aretha, 79
Franklin, C. L., 81
Frazier, E. Franklin, 15n10
frenzy, 25; *see also* celebration
Fry Brown, Teresa L., 28, 159

Gandhi, Mohandas Karamchand, 48, 76
Garrow, David J., 70
Gates, Henry Louis, Jr., 68
George, David, 23
Gerson, Lloyd, 61n128
Gilbert, Kenyatta R., 15n10, 22, 42, 69, 156
God: character of, 75, 85, 115, 147; glory of, 8, 26, 29, 82–83, 87, 98, 132; grace of, 3, 53, 117, 153n1; love of, 7, 13, 71, 106, 146, 148, 152; mystery of, 13, 19, 87; presence of, 4, 13, 27–28, 42, 44, 91, 125–26, 143, 153–55
Goines, Veronica R., 10, 123, 129–34, 138, 149–50, 152
Gorman, Amanda, 1–2, 121–23, 133
Graves, Michael P., 20
Gregory the Great, 6, 17
Gregory of Nyssa, 131
griot, 15, 35n74

Habakkuk, 103
habitus, 34

habitus of prayer, 33–36, 40–45, 56–57, 59, 70–74, 83, 85, 88, 91, 98–102, 113, 115, 118, 128, 134, 140, 147, 157
Hagar, 102–3
Hall, Francis B., 55
Hall, Prathia Laura Ann, 68
Harris, Barbara, 7, 10, 92–93, 95–119, 123, 124, 149–50, 152
Harris, Beatrice Price, 98
Harris, Gayle Elizabeth, 100
Harris, Kamala, 1, 121
Harris, Moya, 159
Hayes, Diana, 70
Haynes, Lemuel, 27–29, 40
Hegel, G. W. F., 76
Herskovits, Melville J., 15n10
Higginbotham, Evelyn, 24
Hildegard of Bingen, 6, 17, 131n47
Hill, J. Lee, Jr., 159
Hines, Deborah Harmon, 110
Holly, James, 110
Holmes, Barbara A., 1, 3, 35, 70n11, 83, 125, 141, 155
Holt Street Baptist Church, 73
Holy Spirit, 4, 7, 14, 17, 20, 30–32, 39–40, 42, 44–45, 52–56, 64, 72, 74, 80–81, 107–8, 125–26, 136, 138, 143, 155–56
homiletical theology, 6–7, 39, 56, 65, 70, 140, 148
hope, 2, 29, 83, 86, 89, 98–99, 133–34, 145–47
Hosier, Harry ("Black Harry"), 23
Hugo, Victor, 88
Humbert of Romans, 19
Humez, Jean McMahon, 31
Hurston, Zora Neale, 3
hymns, 18, 35, 98–100, 104, 106, 118, 140, 150; *see also* song

"I Have a Dream" speech, 67–68, 80
inauguration, 1, 121
Invisible Institution, 23–24
Isaiah, 13–14, 45, 103

Jackson, Drew, 159
Jackson, Jesse, 65n146
Jackson, Mahalia, 68, 79–80
Jackson, Rebecca Cox, 27, 31–32, 40
Jasper, John, 23
Jennings, Willie James, 159
Jeremiah, 103
Jesus, 7, 14, 20–21, 40, 45–47, 49, 55, 57, 60, 62, 75–76, 90, 98, 101–3, 112–19, 131–32, 134, 136–39
John of the Cross, 3n11, 154
Johnson, James Weldon, 105
Johnson, Mordecai, 27, 32–33, 51
Jones, Absalom, 26, 110
Jones, Clarence B., 68n7
Jones, Kirk Byron, 159
Jones, Rufus, 42, 47–48, 53, 61n128
Julian of Norwich, 114
justice, 1, 4, 7, 10, 13, 26, 65, 68–69, 75–78, 83–84, 89, 91–92, 95–100, 103–4, 106, 110–11, 113, 118, 121, 123, 132–34, 139, 145–48, 150–152; *see also* liberation

Keating, James, 156
Keating, Thomas, 43, 154–55
Keats, John, 86
Kim, Eunjoo Mary, 9, 30, 156
King, Alberta, 79
King, Coretta Scott, 79–81
King, Martin Luther, Jr., 7, 10, 64–65, 67–93, 97, 100, 102–4,

106, 110–11, 119, 123–24, 148–51
King, Martin Luther, Sr., 79

Laird, Martin, 54
Lamar, William H., IV, 159
lament, 86, 105, 127, 133, 136, 146–147, 150–151
Lanzetta, Beverly J., 69
LaRue, Cleophus J., 9, 36, 129
Lassiter, Valentino, 80
Laudato Si', 145, 147, 149
lectio divina, 126, 129
Lee, Cindy, 122
Lee, Hak Joon, 70, 75n32, 77
Lee, Jarena, 27, 29–32, 98
Lewis, Harold T., 109
Lewis, John, 65n146
Levison, Stanley, 67n2
liberation, 14, 113, 118, 132, 152; *see also* justice
Liele, George, 23
Lischer, Richard, 75, 77n41, 78
Lonergan, Bernard, 153n1
Long, Charles H., 16n10
Lowell, James Russell, 89
Luther, Martin, 99n20

Marshall, Daniel, 23
Mary, the mother of Jesus, 14, 21
Mary Magdalene, 103
Massey, James Earl, 32, 39–40, 51, 156
Mays, Benjamin, 79
McClain, Mia M., 159
McCray, Donyelle C., 31, 40, 125, 138, 159
McGinn, Bernard, 4, 16, 153
meditation, 3, 3n11, 34, 43–44, 53, 55, 61, 64, 72–73, 78, 130, 145, 147, 151
meditative homiletical style, 33, 35–36, 40, 50–58, 63, 78–83, 85–87, 107–14, 116, 118, 123, 129, 134, 140, 147–48, 157; *see also* body, the
Meek, Frederick, 84, 88
Merton, Thomas, 2, 131n47, 135, 139, 155
Micah, 103
Middle Passage (Maafa), 15, 22
Miller, Keith, 78
Mississippi Boulevard Christian Church, 141
Mitchell, Ella, 112
Mitchell, Henry H., 23, 106, 145
Mitchell, Mozella, 48
mixed-type sermon, 26
Morehouse College, 32, 38, 51–52, 74, 79
Moses, 13–14, 82, 131n47, 132
Moss, Otis, Jr., 159
Murray, Pauli, 6, 104
mysterium tremendum et fascinas, 13
mystic preachers, 15–22; *see also* contemplative preaching
mystical hermeneutic, 33, 35–36, 40, 45–50, 56–57, 60, 63, 74–78, 83, 85–89, 102–6, 113–16, 128, 134, 140, 147, 157; *see also* Scripture
mystical homiletic, 31, 125
mysticism: and activism, 10, 30, 117; and ascent, 122; definition of, 4, 4n13, 153–54; and experience, 10, 13, 30, 35, 153n1, 154; quotidian, 121, 132, 154; and union, 48, 122, 153n1, 155; and vision, 18, 49, 55, 69; *see also* contemplation

Nolan, Albert, 156
Nommo, 52, 81
nondualism, 35, 35n73, 69, 78, 122, 138
nonviolence, 48–49, 76, 85, 105

Northcutt, Kay L., 125, 127
Nouwen, Henri, 101, 130, 135

Origen of Alexander, 35n73

Pasquarello, Michael, III, 7n22
Peacock, Barbara L., 159
Peterson, Eugene, 126
phronesis (practical wisdom), 54, 54n89
Pipes, William, 146
Plato, 122, 154
Plotinus, 61, 122,
poetry, 1–2, 86, 89–90, 121–123
Pollard, Alton, 154
Pope Francis, 145, 147, 149
Powery, Luke, 10, 44, 123, 133–40, 147–48, 150–52, 154–57
prayer, 1, 8, 13, 17–18, 29–35, 40–45, 48, 54–64, 68, 70–74, 80, 85–86, 91, 98–102, 102n33, 108–9, 119, 122, 128–32, 134–37, 139–40, 143, 145, 147; *see also habitus* of prayer
preacher: character of, 34, 36, 54n89; identity of, 11, 38–39, 151; style of, 108–9, 111, 123–25; *see also habitus* of prayer; meditative homiletical style; preaching
preaching: Black/African American, 3–7, 9, 22–27, 34–36, 80, 107–9; celebration and, 3–5, 25, 36, 63, 69, 78–83, 107, 109, 118, 129–30, 141–48; folk, 4–5, 25–26, 69, 146; intellectual, 26, 28, 50, 78, 81, 96, 109, 142; and jazz, 142; prophetic, 6–7, 7n24, 106; queer, 6; as spiritual direction, 124–29; streams of, 5–6, 25–26; womanist, 6, 62–63, 95–119, 129, 159; *see also* contemplative preaching; mystic preachers; prophet/prophetic witness

Prevot, Andrew, 29, 121, 132, 140, 153n1, 154
Price, Mary Matile Sembley, 98
Proctor, Samuel DeWitt, 106
prophet/prophetic witness, 1–2, 6–7, 13, 21–22, 38–39, 47, 67, 69, 75, 77, 82, 95–97, 103, 106, 110–12, 119
Protten, Rebecca, 23
Pythagoras, 122

Quakers (or Society of Friends), 20, 28, 31, 42, 47, 53, 55
Quashie, Kevin, 5

racism, 24, 28, 39, 43, 48, 57, 69, 76–77, 98–99, 110, 110n69, 133, 150–51
Radler, Charlotte, 73, 137
Randolph, A. Philip, 67
Rauschenbusch, Walter, 76
reconciliation, 32, 69, 76–77, 148
respectability, 5, 51, 79, 109–10
rhetoric, 17, 20, 25, 34, 36, 56–64, 67–69, 80, 82–92, 111–19, 127, 129, 138, 140
Riley, Cole Arthur, 135
Robins, Henry B., 46
Robinson, Timothy, 41, 47
Rochester Theological Seminary, 32, 46
Rohr, Richard, 35n75, 122
Royce, Josiah, 76
Rustin, Bayard, 67

sankofa, 132, 134
Schreiner, Olive, 47
Schweitzer, Albert, 37
Scripture, 17, 20, 30, 35, 35n73, 35n74, 42, 45–46, 48, 50, 60–61, 74–76, 85, 88, 103–4, 107, 114,

122, 126, 130, 131n47, 134, 138, 140, 143–45, 147, 149, 151; *see also* mystical hermeneutics
Sembley, Ida Brauner, 98
sensus plenior, 35
sermon: *see* preaching
sexism, 98–99, 110, 150
Shakers, 31
Sharpe, Reginald, Jr., 26
Shigematsu, Ken, 9
silence, 3–5, 14, 43, 48, 50, 53–55, 72, 77, 80, 130, 136–38, 150–51
Simmons, Martha, 6, 26–27, 33, 38, 96, 107, 156
Singh, Sadhu Sundar, 6
slavery, 4, 13, 15n10, 16, 21–24, 26, 28, 32, 41–42, 45–46
Smith, Luther, Jr., 38
Smith, Robert, Jr., 28, 142, 156
Smith, Shively T. J., 54, 159
song, 80, 108, 118, 125, 128–29; *see also* hymns
Spencer, Jon Michael, 146
Spillers, Hortense, 78
spiritual direction, 124–29
spiritual formation, 70, 122, 129, 155; *see also* discipleship; prayer; spirituality
spirituality, 11, 19, 28, 35, 41, 63, 77, 137, 156; African American/Black, 3–4, 14, 15, 22, 33, 41–42, 70–71, 75n32, 77, 122; contemplative, 43, 125; preaching and, 35, 40, 49, 70, 96; and social justice, 10, 48, 70, 98, 148; womanist, 98; *see also* contemplation; mysticism
Stearns, Shubal, 23
Stewart, Gina S., 26
storytelling, 15, 35, 35n74, 42, 62–63, 80, 82, 96, 103, 112–19, 131–32, 139, 150–51

suffering, 24, 29, 87, 126–28, 138–39, 149, 151

Taylor, Barbara Brown, 9
Taylor, Gardner C., 6
Teresa of Avila, 3n11, 154
Thomas, Frank A., 6, 10, 25, 27, 33, 38, 96, 107, 123, 141–49, 151, 156
Thompsett, Frederica Harris, 111
Thompson, Jacqueline, 126
Thompson, Lisa L., 3
Thoreau, Henry David, 76
Thurman, Howard, 7, 10, 33, 36–65, 71, 75–76, 78–81, 93, 97, 102, 104–5, 110, 119, 123–24, 135, 137–40, 143, 145–47, 149–51
Thurman, Sue Bailey, 52
Till, Emmett, 49
Tillich, Paul, 76
Tim-Oi, Li, 102
Townes, Emilie, 98
trauma, 43, 63, 150
Troeger, Thomas, 136
Truth, Sojourner, 25, 72, 98
Turman, Eboni Marshall, 51–52, 79
Turner, William Clair, Jr., 130

Ubuntu, 58, 71, 112, 132, 149

Villodas, Rich, 9
Vita, Kimpa (Dona Beatriz), 16, 21, 22, 30
Vryhof, David, 156

Walker, Alice, 63n135, 97
Walker, Hezekiah, 128
Walker, John Thomas, 100
Walker, Wyatt Tee, 72
Wallace, Maurice O., 79

war, 21, 24, 38, 69, 77, 86, 89, 137–38, 140, 149
Warren, Mervyn A., 78, 80
Washington, Paul, 104, 107
Weems, Renita, 102
Whitefield, George, 23
whooping, 25–26, 35, 69, 81, 83, 129, 140
Williams, Catherine, 128
Williams, Delores, 62, 103
Williams, Jay, 159
Williams, Rowan, 101
Wilmore, Gayraud, 15n10, 24
Wilson, Eric, 159
Winters, Mary-Frances, 151
womanism, 6, 51, 62, 63n135, 95–119, 159
worship, 3–5, 20, 23–25, 31, 40, 53–55, 57, 62–63, 71, 80, 90, 99, 108–9, 141, 151
Wright, Jeremiah, Sr., 107

www.ingramcontent.com/pod-product-compliance
Lightning Source LLC
Chambersburg PA
CBHW020837020526
44114CB00040B/1239